D1238375

I FLEW WITH THE LAFAYETTE ESCADRILLE

The author at the Pau, France training area. Crash helmet is painted with skull and crossbones to ward off jinx. (Courtesy Soubiran Collection, Smithsonian Institution)

I FLEW WITH THE LAFAYETTE ESCADRILLE

by Edwin C. Parsons

E. C. SEALE & COMPANY, INC.
INDIANAPOLIS, INDIANA

LIBRARY OF CONGRESS CATALOG NUMBER 63-19991

PRINTED IN THE UNITED STATES OF AMERICA

FOREWORD

Early in 1916, a year before the United States entered World War I, a handful of valiant Americans banded together as the Lafayette Escadrille to forge their mark in history in the skies over France. Be it for fame, adventure or patriotism, they stepped forward to meet the common enemy long before their own nation realized the true extent of the threat to world freedom.

Once the United States had entered the war and had begun to send totally inexperienced pursuit units to the front, many of the Escadrille pilots who were still alive proved invaluable in passing along to their countrymen the lessons learned while flying under the French flag. Although it is not possible to measure accurately the contributions of any single unit, such as the Lafayette Escadrille, to the successful termination of World War I, it is safe to say that many U. S. Air Service pilots owe their lives to those who had already learned the new science of war in the air through those bleak and dismal months of 1916 and 1917. The Lafayette Escadrille was a guiding hand extended which was gratefully clasped by many.

During their days with the Escadrille, some of these men met death, while others lived out the war; but each, in his own way, earned immortality for himself and the Escadrille. As long as there remains a man with a love for flying in his heart, or one who has experienced the indescribable thrill of passing along through the tranquil solitude of the firmament, the memory of the Lafayette Escadrille and of those who served it so nobly will endure.

This is the chronicle of an elite group of men, written by one of their own who survived the holocaust. The vivid account of battles in the air, the flush of success over a fallen foe, the sorrow from the loss of a comrade—all of these carry the reader back across the decades to that exciting period of so long ago.

In essence, one does not read this book—he lives it.

Wright-Patterson Air Force Base
April, 1963

KIMBROUGH S. BROWN
Lt. Colonel, USAF
Director, USAF Museum

PREFACE TO THE NEW EDITION

Although this book was originally written and published over twenty-five years ago under the title of THE GREAT ADVENTURE, it has been nearly half a century since the experiences and events depicted in this book occurred. Naturally, there is no longer the romantic concept of knights of the air, fighting for mastery in individual combat. During the intervening years, only the clouds remain the same.

Those of us fortunate enough to have survived have witnessed tremendous strides made in military planes, armament and tactics; but inevitably, and doubtless necessarily with this progress, has come regimentation, and to a large extent, deprivation of individual initiative.

Unquestionably, however, there remains the same love of country, spirit of self-sacrifice and burning desire to conquer new worlds that actuated the thirty-eight young Americans who served in the Lafayette Escadrille.

In the two decades subsequent to World War I, thousands of words were written about the daring young eagles in French and American uniforms, who were almost always described as fighting victoriously in the skies over war-torn France. For the most part, these lurid accounts of fictitious air battles and men bore faint resemblance to the real thing. Due to the great publicity given the Lafayette Escadrille before the United States entered the war, the Escadrille and its pilots were given great prominence in these imaginative yarns, largely written by men who never heard a gun fired in anger.

We were, for the most part, enthusiastic young idealists with a dash of adventurous spirit, fighting in a new element for a country not our own, but fighting for what we thought was right. We flew crates then, but we thought they were all right, for we had no precedent to guide us. We fumbled our way through, learning by trial and often fatal error, setting our own pioneering precedents for those who would follow us in the years to come.

In the past few years, there has been a tremendous and amazing resurgence of interest in World War I aviation, not only on the side of the Allies, but on the side of our former enemies. Several aviation historical societies have been formed, with hundreds of dedicated younger men as members, deeply and sincerely interested in the facts of that historic period.

Fortunately, several books on World War I aviation have appeared in recent years, whose authors with one or two exceptions, have made exhaustive research for authentic material. However, it is virtually impossible to get the true flavor from bare facts unless an author were there, fighting with the Lafayette Escadrille and knowing its members intimately.

As this is written, there are six of us still alive. Because of our pride in the Lafayette Escadrille and its accomplishments, and with deep reverence for the memories of our comrades-in-arms, we feel that this is the time to retell the real story of the Escadrille, as written by one who flew with it.

Apologies are in order that space precludes more detailed coverage of many fine youngsters who fought so bravely; but we are proud of them all.

My special thanks are due the David-Stewart Publishing Company, the E. C. Seale and Company (publishers of this new edition) and Harry C. Block, Jr. of the Aviation Historical Society of Indianapolis, for their efforts in making the reprint of this book possible.

E. C. Parsons
Rear Admiral, USN (ret)

Osprey, Florida
April, 1963

PUBLISHER'S ACKNOWLEDGMENT

The publisher extends grateful appreciation to those whose enthusiasm and cooperation helped recreate Admiral Parsons' inspiring saga of American history: to Colonel Paul Rockwell, brother of Kiffin; to Colonel Carl Dolan; to Henry Sweet Jones; to Alex Imrie and to Colonel G. B. Jarrett for their photographs; to the National Air Museum of the Smithsonian Institution for the photographs from the Soubiran Collection; to Lt. Colonel Kim Brown, Director of the USAF Museum; to Len Morgan, many of whose suggestions have been incorporated; to George Cooke of CROSS & COCKADE Journal; to Major Gene Guerny and Captain Joseph Skiera of the USAF Book Program; and to Hugh Wynne, Ed Averkieff and Rick Burns for their excellent drawings.

It is with a great sense of privilege that we again make this—one of the outstanding accounts to come from World War I—available to the many enthusiasts of what were the most thrilling days of air combat. We hope that the many who have not yet found the fascination of that era will discover it in reading this volume.

Contents

List of Illustrations

CHAPTER I

Bottle of Death

THE MORNING STRAFE was finished in the semiquiet Vosges sector of the Western Front. The deep-throated rumble of the big cannon and the sharp, shrill chatter of machine guns had gradually died away as a smiling sun spread its warming rays over the mountainous countryside. Like the temporary respite of a storm-battered ship in the eye of a hurricane, a spurious atmosphere of peace hovered over war-torn Alsace.

On both sides of the barely separated lines, the tension of the night watches over, scratching, bearded, burrowing gnomes emerged from sheltering caverns and filled their lungs with the bracing spring air as they gobbled the morning "*soupe.*"

Bellies full, pipes alight, happy, despite their wretchedness, with merely being alive, they relaxed in the somnolent hush of midmorning.

Suddenly a faint humming drone as of a far-distant swarm of bees broke through the stillness. As if drawn by a magnetic force, heads twisted skyward and eyes searched eagerly. Gesticulating arms and excited fingers pointed out an infinitesimal flashing speck in the great void.

Silvered wings shimmering like gossamer in the sunlight, high over the little village of Thann, a tiny Nieuport pursuit plane soared through a cloud-flecked sky inside the German lines.

"Ah, but he is lucky, that one," sighed one of the poilus enviously, "away from all this crap. He flies and goes back to a soft bed, good food and plenty to drink, even trollops if he wants them. When the weather's bad, he doesn't even fly. No worries. He doesn't even know what war is."

"Hah, *mon vieux,*" another disputed, "that shows how little you know about it. You just try it once and you'd wish you were back here in these nice cozy trenches, crap and all. You think he hasn't any worries? What about just keeping those things in the air? That's trouble enough for anybody. He gets blasted from the ground and fired on from the air when he meets the Boches. His ship gets afire, or something breaks and he falls. Then *pouf!* They mop you up with sponges, if they can find you. It's a long way down, and when you hit you don't bounce."

"That's right," a third broke in. "They deserve all the soft living and the trollops they can get. They don't last long."

He pointed an accusing finger at the first man.

"You think you're a bloody hero because you've been over the top twice in a year and a half. They go over the top twice a day, maybe more, and think nothing of it. Every time they leave the ground, the chances are about two to one they won't come back. I wouldn't blame them for getting drunk and staying that way."

"Well, maybe they do have it tough a few hours a day," the first retorted, unconvinced, "but just the same I wish I was in his boots. At least, if I'm going to get it, I'd have a rare time before I got bumped and not have to live like an animal in a stinking hole in the ground."

"You can have it," the second remarked. "I'll take mine on the ground, stinks and all. If you get hit, you at least know you haven't got far to fall."

Hand lightly gripping the rubber-handled stick, unconscious of the comments and even of the presence of his earth-bound comrades crowding the trenches so far below him, the keen eyes of the blue-uniformed young man in the silver plane expectantly searched the vast reaches of the sky.

Taking time out to duck his head for an instant inside the cockpit for a quick look at his oil pulsator and revolution counter, he noted with a slight qualm of disquiet that he had less than half an hour's gas left in his tank. His expressive face wore a strangely mingled look of rapidly fading hope and frustrated ambition. His flight was nearing its end without definite accomplishment.

Suddenly above the roar of his motor there came a succession of crashing, deep-throated roars like the growls of an angry bulldog. The little ship trembled and bounced. Just under the tail, then above, below, on all sides, little balls of flame-centered black smoke blossomed with disconcerting abruptness, raveling out and hanging in the heavens like giant sooty blooms on a devil's cactus. An alert German battery had swung into action and, with shrieking shrapnel, was resenting this alien bird winging its placid way over their territory.

The lean weather-beaten face of the North Carolina Yank, Corporal Pilot Kiffin Rockwell, broke into a flashing smile as he hastily banked the tiny plane, dived a hundred meters and quickly changed course. He leaned over the side of the cockpit and derisively thumbed his nose in the general direction of the German lines.

"Come on, you blighters, shoot 'em up. Waste some more," he taunted. "You all sure need the practice."

He had to grin again, as he realized the absurdity of his action, for the words were torn from his mouth and hurled into space by the blast of the rushing slipstream.

As he straightened the little ship out, a slight frown erased the smile from his face, for his alert ear caught a distinct break in the even rhythm of the barking Le Rhone rotary motor, separated from his fur-booted feet by only a thin fire wall. One cylinder was missing completely and another intermittently. The rev. counter showed a wavering drop of almost two hundred turns. Shaking his head disappointedly, Kiffin reluctantly swung the nose of the tiny bus towards his own lines.

Then his whole body stiffened and his hand tensed on the stick. He peered long and intently at the sight of another plane slightly below him inside the French lines, diving abruptly in his direction. He nodded in satisfaction, and his eager fingers caressed the trip leading to the single Lewis machine gun mounted on the center section of the top plane above his head.

Sharply outlined in white on the upper wing of the other plane were the menacing black crosses of the Imperial German Air Force.

There was no hesitation on Rockwell's part. Faltering motor or fuel exhaustion meant nothing to him. The quarry, so long and so avidly hunted, was in full view. His nose went over, and he sliced down in a steeply banking dive.

At sight of him the German plane went into an almost

Kiffin Y. Rockwell (Courtesy Paul A. Rockwell)

Kiffin Rockwell adjusting his machine gun on the field at Behonne, near Bar-le-Duc, during the battle of Verdun. (Courtesy Paul A. Rockwell)

vertical plunge, while the machine gunner in the rear cockpit worked frantically to bring his swiveled guns to bear.

Wings bowed with the speed of his dive, wind shrieking a banshee wail through straining wires, Rockwell hurled his little pursuit ship down like a streak of lightning.

Panic-stricken, the German gunner opened fire as the silver thunderbolt drew steadily closer. Rockwell heard the whine of singing lead and felt the shock as one of the enemy slugs found its mark in a main spar of the vibrating, protesting ship.

Face frozen in a mask of grim determination, he set his teeth and held his fire till he was within twenty or thirty meters of the black-crossed enemy. Then, just a fraction of a second before he had to pull away to avoid a collision, Kiffin's tense fingers hurled over the trip and he opened fire.

Four times the Lewis barked, and then it jammed! The terrific wind blast had lifted the pan, and a cartridge was inextricably caught crosswise in the block.

Kiffin swore a mighty oath as he swung away and started to work frantically with fumbling fingers on the jammed breech. But there was no need for more. It was all over.

As the German observer collapsed and fell back stone dead on his pilot, the machine gun dropped from its position and pointed straight up in the air. His nerveless hand slipping from the stick, the pilot slumped down in his bucket seat, his wabbling head lolling over the side.

The clumsy German plane wavered erratically for a brief moment, slipped off on a wing, then dove vertically for the torn earth, smearing the clear background of the sky with a long sliver of black, greasy oil smoke.

Following his victim till the plane piled up in a blazing pylon of death, Rockwell swooped close to the ground and saw the wreckage burning fiercely in the first-line German trenches. He had turned the trick with but four bullets, and his ship had been hit only once.

Bug-eyed, the men in the trenches had watched the brief combat with bated breaths. According to their nationality, they were as elated or depressed over its outcome as if they had participated in the struggle.

Individual air combats had no actual far-reaching effect on the outcome of the war, but outside of his own very limited area of trenches they offered the only chance the front-line soldier had to see or know anything of the titanic struggle of which he was a part. He was a privileged spectator of a gigantic, spectacular jousting contest to the death between knights-errant of the air in a limitless arena.

It appealed to his imagination. No great wonder that the victorious, bemedaled aviator assumed heroic, almost godlike proportions to the man in the trenches. In truth, he was undoubtedly only a very frightened young man.

Rockwell's astonishing and magnificent victory was reported by front-line observers while his faltering motor was slowly carrying the jubilant pilot back to the field at Luxeuil-les-Bains. There a mighty welcome awaited him, for this was the first official victory of the newly formed American Escadrille. The date was May 18, 1916, less than a month after America, with the formation of the squadron, had fired her first shots as a unit in the World War.

The news caused a tremendous wave of excitement in Paris, and Kiffin's brother Paul, with whom he had served in the Foreign Legion and who had been invalided out on account of wounds, sent out a rare and precious bottle of very old Bourbon.

To palates surfeited with the sun-kissed but disappointingly innocuous wines of France, its amber contents held a glowing promise.

The always generous Kiffin immediately pulled the cork, expecting everyone to share in his prize and drink to his success. Before a drink had been poured, and while mouths were still watering in anticipation, good old Victor Chapman, who didn't drink much anyhow, popped up with a very potent suggestion.

"Hey, wait a second," he said in his deep-toned voice. "We can get plenty of liquor, but not like this. It's rare stuff. Let's save it for rare occasions."

"What could be rarer than this?" Elliot Cowdin protested, his dry throat rasping and a hurt look in his eyes.

"Fellows, let's make it a real Bottle of Death," Chapman urged, ignoring Cowdin's look of disappointment. "Naturally, Kiffin gets the first drink, and from now on every man who brings down a German is entitled to one good slug. It 'll be something worth working for."

The idea was enthusiastically hailed, and so, with appropriate ceremonies in champagne, the Bottle of Death was inaugurated.

When the ceremony was started, no one had any idea but that the bottle would outlive the Escadrille, but such was the startling success of that intrepid band that the contents were soon exhausted. It was never replaced, but the empty bottle was faithfully guarded by Billy Thaw, our American commanding officer, and only came to light again when he died recently.

CHAPTER II

Hell on Wings

WHAT A HOST of romantic memories are conjured up by the name of the Lafayette Escadrille!

Before America's entry into the war and for some months afterward, the effect that this tiny band of American volunteers flying in the uniforms and planes of France and fighting their spectacular battles in the sky had on public opinion, both at home and abroad, was tremendous. Only now are historians beginning to realize what a part they played in America's entry into the war and the molding of pro-Allied support.

But we boys knew nothing of this and more than likely shouldn't have cared much if we had known. We had other things on our minds.

It was that virulent disease known as "the unconquerable pioneering spirit of our hardy forefathers" that led most of us into sticking our noses into something where we had no real business. And I'll wager that just like us, if they could have only been brought to admit it, those "hardy pioneers" had plenty of moments when they wished they'd stayed where they were and minded their own affairs.

None of us had any real idea of what we were getting

into. We had hold of the bear's tail and no one to help us let go. With few exceptions, I believe most of us would have welcomed an opportunity to bow out gracefully.

In fact, some, after they'd awakened to what they'd let themselves in for, stole away on silent feet before they'd heard any guns fired in anger, perhaps not so gracefully or honorably, but most wisely. While there was some slight criticism at the time, it may well be they were the smart ones after all.

I wouldn't for the world cast any disparagement on either the motives or ideals of my comrades, and there was certainly no question of their courage in action. But no man can exist and fight shoulder to shoulder, facing almost certain death day after day, without being able to peer pretty closely into naked souls. Viewed down the mellowing vista of years, the Great Adventure had its romantic side, but at the time it was just plain unvarnished hell on wings.

Popular belief built us into legendary characters and credited us with being an heroic race of supermen without fear or reproach.

We were far from supermen or iron men or any other strange breed of cat. There was no thought of heroism in our minds, and our habits and morals left plenty of latitude for reproach, had anyone cared to make an issue of the matter.

We were merely very wild, but very frightened, youngsters, fighting with unfamiliar weapons in a new element, leaping to fame and being made heroes overnight by newspaper publicity. We certainly placed no credence in what overenthusiastic reporters and sob sisters wrote about us.

The slightest indication of swank or taking ourselves seriously was more than sufficient cause for a riding that would leave egos raw and bleeding.

Our sole claim to real heroism was in being half scared to death and doing our best in spite of it!

I presume, after all, that's what makes all heroes, and the lucky ones are those who get the breaks in spite of themselves. For any man in actual combatant service who claims that he knew no fear is either a damn fool or just plain liar, with the chances about 99 per cent in favor of the latter.

The Escadrille was a strange potpourri of types thrown into the great melting pot of the war. We came from all walks of life. Rich and poor, college men and boys whose only education had been in the school of hard knocks. A devil's brood of grousing, reckless, undisciplined, irresponsible wildcats, all a trifle screwy (for to be war aviators we had to be just a little nuts), but a loyal crew, ready to fly, drink or fight at the drop of a hat. Motives were as varied as the men themselves. Some sought adventure, others revenge, while a pitiful few actually sacrificed themselves in the spirit of purest idealism.

The adventurer fought and died side by side with the idealist. An "ace," hero of aerial encounters, could and would, when on the ground, revert to type and become a charlatan or a ruffian.

The Escadrille didn't spring full fledged into being, and although Norman Prince is generally credited with being its founder, it is almost impossible to credit any one person with its inception. Its formation as a unit was gradual and the result of long and arduous work on the part of many enthusiastic men, who refused, for over a year, despite official rebuffs and heartbreaking discouragements, to give up the idea.

Americans were by no means strangers, either in active combat forces of the French army or in auxiliary units, where they rendered distinguished service with the Medical Corps and as volunteer drivers for the American Ambulance.

When the war broke out, many of the heroic youngsters who were later to become famous pursuit pilots decided from various motives to fight for France and volunteered in the Foreign Legion, the only active unit in which foreigners were permitted to enlist.

Among them were Billy Thaw of Pittsburgh, the playboy of the Riviera, one of the earliest hydroplane pilots; Victor Chapman, a student at Beaux Arts; and Bert Hall, famous for his tall stories and penchant for marrying, who was driving a Paris taxi.

They were soon joined in the Second Regiment of March of the Legion by Jimmy Bach, Kiffin Rockwell, Bob Soubiran, Billy Dugan, Paul Pavelka and Edmond Genet.

After rigorous training, these youngsters rendered heroic service with the Legion in the bloodiest attacks of trench warfare for varying periods. Every one was wounded at least once, and that they survived at all in the terrific carnage was miraculous.

Daily their imaginations were stirred by the sight of the rackety old planes staggering over their heads. Fed up to their necks and preferring anything to the muck and gore and rigors of trench life, they felt a compelling urge to get into the war in the new element.

Diplomatically pulling wires, but with considerable difficulty over bitter official protests, first Thaw, Jimmy

Bach and Bert Hall, then Rockwell and Chapman got themselves transferred from the Legion to aviation. Already being a pilot, Thaw was sent out to the front early in 1915 to an active line squadron, the first American volunteer pilot of the war.

In the meantime, Didier Masson, the one-man aviation force of Obregon and Carranza, had become fed up with tin-pot revolutions. He came to France, where he had learned to fly in 1909, and found no difficulty in getting into the aviation on account of his previous experience.

Other young Americans, among them Elliot Cowdin, Jim McConnell, Dudley Hill, Robert Rockwell, Clyde Balsley, Chouteau Johnson and Larry Rumsey, had volunteered in the American Ambulance and, as 1915 wore on, managed by persistent efforts to soften up French resistance enough to gain admittance as student pilots in the French aviation schools.

Meanwhile the greatest of all American aces, that heroic, inscrutable and strangely mysterious figure, Raoul Lufbery, was learning to fly in order to avenge the death of his dearest friend, the French pilot, Marc Pourpe, brought down by the enemy in one of the first air battles of the war.

Two other young Americans, Norman Prince and Frazier Curtis, having learned to fly in an American civilian school, went to France early in 1915 with the idea of forming an all-American volunteer squadron. They were successful in enlisting the sympathetic aid of Dr Edmund Gros, a prominent American physician practising in Paris, Mr Robert W. Bliss and Mr Robert Chanler, long-time American residents of Paris, but they met stern rebuffs in nearly every quarter from French officials.

Eventually, through Mr Bliss, they were brought in

Ambulance driver James McConnell and Legionnaire Paul A. Rockwell. (Courtesy Paul A. Rockwell)

Kiffin Rockwell, William Thaw holding the lion cub, Whiskey, and Paul Pavelka, in Paris. (Courtesy Paul A. Rockwell)

William Thaw (Courtesy C. H. Dolan II)

Norman Prince (Courtesy Soubiran Collection)

contact with a gracious and farsighted Frenchman, M. Jarousse de Sillac. It was largely due to his wholehearted co-operation that French officialdom was led to see the light.

There were two reasons why the French were so strongly set at first against a squadron of volunteers. One was the need of ceaseless vigilance against spies. Unfortunately, one German had already gotten into French aviation by means of a forged American passport and, before he was unmasked and summarily executed, had caused untold damage.

In the second place there was really no place or need for volunteer aviators. Hundreds of young Frenchmen were clamoring for admittance to this new and romantic branch of the service, which, above all, offered surcease from the horrors of the trenches, to say nothing of the chance to wear fantastic uniforms and impress the pretty girls almost to the point of tears.

But the French are smart diplomats. They wanted American support desperately, and when they eventually saw the possibilities offered by the publicity attendant on the spectacular efforts of prominent young Americans flying as a unit in French uniform, they slowly began to relent. However, this change of heart took nearly a year, and meantime Prince and Curtis were accepted as aviation students.

So, during 1915, while French officialdom was being hounded from all quarters, Thaw, Hall, Cowdin, Masson, Prince, Lufbery and Bach were flying with various French squadrons at the front, while the others were either still in training schools or attached to the Paris Air Guard.

Before he had finished his training, Curtis had a bad

crash at Pau. He was forced to ask for his discharge on account of continued ill health, but worked tirelessly with Prince and Dr Gros in Paris toward the formation of the Escadrille, while Thaw was using his powerful influence through military channels toward the same end.

The greatest appreciation that could be offered Dr Gros for his unselfish, untiring interest and labor, not only in assisting to bring the Escadrille into being and his watchful care during its existence, but in preservation of its glorious memory, would fall far short of his just reward.

We didn't always see eye to eye with him during the war, and frequently a vague thought penetrated our thick skulls that possibly he was engineering considerable publicity for his own benefit. Only in the semisanity of post-war mental readjustment did we begin to realize what he meant to us. The Escadrille would no doubt have flown its way to fame and glory, but it couldn't have been the same without him.

Near the end of 1915, General Hirschauer, chief of French Military Aeronautics, finally yielded and gave a rather reluctant consent to the grouping of all American flyers in one squadron. It was the beginning of the actual realization of a great vision. However, what with the tons of paper work and the proverbial slowness of military channels, it was not until April of 1916 that the dream became a reality.

While they were impatiently waiting for the French to fulfill their promise, Thaw, Cowdin and Prince got into a jam which nearly put the Escadrille out of business before it was started.

The three boys got a military leave to return to America for a month. Overjoyed to see their families again, to gorge themselves on succulent American food without deprivations or restrictions and to live a normal life, it never occurred to them that they were jeopardizing their own futures and that of the squadron.

They couldn't realize what demigods they had become to the American public. Much against their wills, from the moment of their arrival they were lionized and kept constantly in the public eye. They made grand copy for a nation athirst for first-hand news of the war.

Everywhere they went, they were followed by German secret-service agents. A demand was made by the German ambassador on the American State Department to have them interned, charging that active combatants in the uniform of a warring power in a neutral country constituted a breach of neutrality.

While the harried American officials were trying to arrive at a solution, the three boys solved it for them, much to the relief of everyone concerned, except the disgruntled Germans.

Exchanging code mesages before their leave was up, the trio got together secretly and pulled a fast one with true Yankee ingenuity. By fast stepping in as wild a chase as has ever been seen in the greatest movie thriller, they shook off their annoyingly burr-like but totally bewildered shadows and, with the aid of sympathetic, helpful port authorities, slipped out of the country on a fast French liner before anyone knew they had gone.

It was an agonizingly narrow squeak, but they had created a tremendous enthusiasm and a real sympathy for France in their brief appearance.

CHAPTER III

Jimmy Bach, Unsung Hero

IN THE FIRST YEAR of the war, with the Escadrille still only an idle dream and but four intrepid Yanks—Thaw, Hall, Bach and Lufbery—covering themselves with glory flying in front-line squadrons, disaster overtook one of these hardy buzzards.

Jimmy Bach is one of the great unsung heroes of the war in the air, for he has the distinction (and in his opinion, a very doubtful one) of being the first American in any branch of the service to be taken prisoner.

That he is also credited with being the first American to bring down an enemy plane in the World War does little to alleviate the heartache he suffered in spending more than three years, despite his frantic efforts to escape, as a most unwilling and unappreciative guest of the Kaiser.

He never had the chance to fly the speedy little pursuit planes with synchronized guns, or the fast, stable observation ships that characterized the French air service in the later years of the war. Nor to fraternize, carouse and fight side by side with his countrymen in the air.

When Jimmy first went to the front, pilots did everything from bombing and reconnaissance to landing spies far in German territory. They did it cheerfully with ships that would have caused later aviators to scream in violent protest. The ships were generally conceded to be kept in the air only by the use of strong charms and fervent prayer.

Night flights without the use of any landing lights were common practice. Landings were made by the light of the moon or from memory, and woe betide the pilot whose memory played him false on a dark night.

These bold souls were the real pioneers, and every flight was an epic one. Occasionally they got away with it indefinitely, but most of the time calamity of one kind or another stole up and laid them low.

Poor old Jimmy had to swallow a bitter pill. He survived all the dangers of the air, but he came within a gnat's eyelash of perishing miserably at the hands of a German firing squad.

Bach was in Paris when the war broke out and enlisted in the Foreign Legion in August 1914. He served for four months in the hottest fighting of the Marne as a mud-stained, cootie-ridden poilu.

He was one of that famed band of Legionnaires who made the historic march, under full equipment, of fifty-six kilometers, from Verzenay to Fismes; the longest, most terribly grueling forced march made by any soldiers in the World War. From four in the morning till eleven at night, with only a cup of bitter black coffee to sustain them, they marched without food, practically without a halt, except for the ten-minute rest period each hour.

It was a killing test for men fresh from civilian life. The last few kilometers were so sodden in misery that the men staggered on automatically in a sort of a daze. When a halt was called, they threw themselves down and slept on rock piles or anything else at hand to keep them out of the mud.

Gradually becoming immune to such hardships, Jimmy went through all the stiffest engagements and hand-to-hand fighting with hardly a scratch and, in December, put in his application along with Thaw and Hall, his comrades in the platoon, for a transfer to aviation.

Thanks to the kindly help of a French officer pilot, Lieutenant Brocard, who was later to command the whole aviation force, Jimmy's application was the first to get favorable action. He was withdrawn from the trenches and ordered to an aviation school, which in the early days was an unheard-of feat for an alien.

In the early summer of 1915 he completed his crude training course and was sent to the Escadrille M.S.-38, one of the first organized squadrons in active service. They were equipped with the old Morane-Saulnier Parasol monoplanes, a two-place job powered with a sixty-horse-power Gnome rotary motor and looking, just as its name implies, like a gigantic, elongated umbrella.

The fuselage was suspended on a post far below the single set of fragile wings. With a top speed of less than eighty miles an hour and the certainty of losing the wings if it ever fell into a spin, the Morane at that time was the fastest and most reliable ship on the front.

Machine guns were just coming into general use on planes, although the idea of synchronization, so that they could be fired through the propeller, was only in the very crude experimental state. One gun was mounted on a swiveled support on the fragile wing far above the pilot's head, while the other was on a solid frame mounted on the turtle back of the fuselage. Great care had to be used so that neither gun would strike the propeller in the excitement of a hot fight.

Air duels were rare, but Jimmy was to strike the first blow for America. He was on a long-distance reconnaissance in the vicinity of Mézières. On the way back, he met a black-crossed Aviatik, homeward bound from a like mission in the French lines.

Frequently, enemy planes in similar situations might pass with a friendly wave. No one was really looking for trouble. It was generally conceded that it took sufficient skill just to keep the fragile, cranky old planes in the air without seeking additional hazards.

Unfortunately for his well-being, the misguided German observer got nasty and overconfidently picked the wrong man and the wrong moment to become decidedly aggressive. Instead of letting well enough alone and taking his information safely back home, he opened fire from short range on the peacefully inclined French ship. As he ripped a long burst into the Morane, slugs shook the frail plane from stem to stern. With sulphurous breath, a bullet tore through the loose folds of Jimmy's coveralls.

Bach's blood boiled at the buzzard's unexpected and uncalled-for attack. He banked and signaled his observer to get ready for action. Then he went after the Hun full motor.

The Morane was slightly faster than the Aviatik. The Boche observer had his guns trained on Bach, but his shots were going wild. Jimmy drew up closer on the German ship.

He reached up and trained the Lewis on his top wing to bear on the enemy plane. The Aviatik started to dive. Bach pushed hard on his stick and held the Parasol down with one hand, while he aimed his wing gun with the other. It was the ultimate in freehand shooting.

Seventy-five yards behind the fleeing German, he poured out a leaden fusillade. Ten or twelve rounds and the wind-blown drum on the Lewis jammed tight. There was no time to free the gun.

But Jimmy's aim had been good. A chance shot plugged the obstreperous German observer squarely between the eyes. He folded up in his cockpit like an empty grain sack.

Bach's gun was useless, but his observer, Lieutenant Giroux, tapped him on the shoulder and with a grim smile pointed significantly to his own Lewis.

Jimmy nodded acknowledgment and opened the throttle of the barking Gnome as far as it would go. The Morane hurtled downward in an almost vertical dive. The thin wing fluttered, trembled and bowed; the wires stretched out taut, moaning with the strain, but they held. The Parasol sliced under the tail of the Aviatik.

Pressed against his safety belt, Giroux crouched calmly behind his black barrel. The Morane was shaking so hard from the vibration that it was almost impossible to center on his target.

Suddenly, for a brief instant, he caught the Aviatik full in his sight, fifty yards above his head. Fire curled in a leaping tongue from the sweeping muzzle. The Aviatik bounced and staggered as slugs bit into the oil-stained belly. Torn bits of linen dripped from wings and fuselage.

All at once, as if crushed by a giant hand, a wing folded slowly back. As the black-crossed ship fell into a deadly spin, a shower of fire shot out from the gleaming, whirling cylinders of the Oberusel motor. Trailing a smudgy finger of oily smoke, the Aviatik dropped both wings less than five hundred meters below. The slim fuselage shot like an arrow to earth in the German lines.

Fearful of losing his own wings in the terrific dive, Jimmy retarded the Gnome and, carefully nursing the Parasol on to a level keel, banked to turn for the French lines. He pulled his throttle open. The Gnome flooded, coughed uneasily and wheezed to a dead stop!

The pursuit of the German had carried the French plane quite a distance back into the German lines. The prevailing wind was blowing toward Berlin. The brown, snakelike line of the trenches seemed an agonizingly long distance away. It was going to be desperately close.

Bach was determined not to be robbed of the fruits of his first victory. He stretched the Morane's glide till the wings wavered from loss of speed. Down he plunged till the heaped-up, chalky German trenches and the hideous desolation of no man's land flashed under his wings.

Then, just beyond the French first-line trenches, he squashed down in a wild welter of barbed wire and deep shell holes. The Parasol plowed on a few feet, turned over and broke up in a tangled mass of splintered struts and torn linen. Lieutenant Giroux was thrown clear and suffered a broken arm, but Bach escaped with only a few minor cuts and bruises. It was a thrilling but glorious climax to the first enemy plane brought down by an American.

It was most unfortunate that Bach couldn't stay to enhance a reputation so well commenced. He lost his liberty and nearly his life trying to save a comrade in distress.

Jimmy had made several successful night flights across

the lines to land spies. He had been most fortunate in not having motor failures or cracking up in strange fields, landing without the aid of lights or even flares.

Late in September he was called with Sergeant Mangeot, another of the Escadrille 38's pilots, to a conference with the captain and two French civilians.

"Tomorrow morning at dawn," the captain ordered, "you will take these two gentlemen from the intelligence service over to a field they have chosen near Rocroi and land them. They intend to blow up a section of the railroad between Mézières and Hirson. They will transport a quantity of high explosive with them, so you must be exceptionally careful on your landing. When they have finished their detail, they are going to gather information concerning enemy troops and will make their own way back to our lines, so your duty will have been completed when you land them safely."

Bach turned to look at Mangeot, and they nodded in unison. Words were unnecessary. Missions were getting tougher and tougher. Landing two spies in enemy territory in broad daylight with cargoes of high explosives would certainly have its moments.

"Let's hop over now and look for a landing field," Jimmy worriedly suggested to Mangeot.

One of the intelligence men spoke up.

"No need for that, gentlemen. We are from the vicinity and know the country well. We have decided on the field where you will land us. It will not be necessary to describe it. We will direct you from the air."

Unfortunately, these two well-meaning warriors were soldiers of the ground, and this was their first flight. The field they selected in their ignorance was a nightmare. It was fairly large, surrounded by dense woods on all sides, but terribly rough, covered with bushes, small trees and stumps hidden in the long grass.

Blissfully unaware of the terrors in store for them, Bach and Mangeot circled down for a landing in the early light of the dawn. They must have been directed by the hand of Providence, for they were successful in setting both ships down with their load of explosives without accident. In a few seconds the two civilians were on their way with their lethal burdens.

Jimmy socked on full throttle and, after a short, bumpy run in which he was nearly capsized by the tall grass, got off the ground. Banking sharply to avoid the high trees, he turned back toward the French lines.

Skimming the field, he saw Mangeot start to take off, hit something and somersault into a complete washout of his plane. Bach could have closed his eyes to the accident, pretended not to see it and saved himself without difficulty, but his was not the character to desert a comrade in distress.

Without hesitation he turned back and glided in for another hazardous landing. As his wheels touched and the Morane bumped to a stop, Jimmy saw Mangeot climb out of the tangled wreckage of his ship and race madly toward his rescuer.

Breathlessly, the grateful sergeant clambered into the rear cockpit and Jimmy gunned his motor for the second take-off.

The tail lifted as they gathered speed, and the Parasol was just about to leave the ground, when, with a jarring crash, the whirling blades of the propeller hit a hidden stump and shattered into a hundred pieces. The racing motor nearly tore itself from its bed and, carried by its own momentum, the Morane plunged at express-train speed into the trees at the end of the field, piling up in a gorgeous crash.

Jarred but unhurt, the two pilots climbed ruefully out of the tangled wreck and raced for the shelter of the forest. They were in a mighty tough spot, and well they knew it.

If all four men were unfortunate enough to be taken prisoners and it should be proved that the airmen had landed the two civilians, death at the guns of a firing squad was inevitable.

There were only two very slim rays of hope:

If the spies remained uncaptured, there was still a slight chance for the young pilots in case of their own capture. The only other hope was the exceedingly slim one of making their way through miles of enemy territory and slipping through to the French lines.

Spurred on by the excited shouts of enemy troops surrounding their wrecked planes, the two war birds hastily plunged deeper into the forest. It was a noisy flight, and they realized they were only prolonging the agony. They located a couple of small trees and climbed into the concealing branches.

Thirsty, hungry and scared, with the hot rays of the sun beating down on their unprotected heads, they clung to their precarious perches for the whole long day, while ominously cursing searching parties beat through the underbrush.

They waited till long after dark before, with cramped muscles shrieking protest, they climbed down and made their uncertain way through the woods in what they hopefully imagined was the general direction of safety. While brush tore at their clothes and faces, they fell into bogs and bumped their heads against unseen trees.

They were thoroughly exhausted when they finally emerged from the forest. Stumbling across a plowed field, they suddenly found themselves in the high-walled courtyard of a farm. There was a tiny fire in one corner, and the figure of a uniformed man bent over it. They turned to beat a hasty retreat, but a stick cracked under Mangeot's foot. A dark figure loomed up in the gloom, and a harsh, guttural voice called:

"Wer ist das?"

Mangeot started to run, tripped over some unseen obstacle and fell. He was pounced on by half a dozen shadowy forms who mysteriously materialized out of nowhere.

In the midst of flashing lights, excited shouts and barking rifles, Jimmy darted in the opposite direction and found a road. Encumbered by his heavy flying suit, Bach fled down it as fast as his trembling limbs and heaving lungs would let him. At the end of three or four hundred yards, he skidded to a stop when he ran smack into a whole squad of grinning Jerries.

Surrounded on every side by the gaping mouths of high-powered gun muzzles, Jimmy was quickly convinced that further flight was impossible. Much against his will, he was roughly hustled back to join the apprehensive Mangeot at the farmhouse.

"Nice try, Jim," Mangeot congratulated him. "I never had a chance. Eight of these monkeys all jumped on me at the same time."

"And I had to pick the particular road to run down where half the German army was marching," Jimmy mourned bitterly. "Brother, we're in a sweet mess now. If you've got any particular saints you especially favor, better start praying now they don't find those two bozos we brought over with us, or it's 'Caput' for us. May be anyhow, but if they don't find 'em, we've still got a chance."

"Don't be silly, old cabbage," Mangeot replied earnestly. "I started to pray the minute they got me."

Fortunately, both pilots were dressed in regulation uniform under their furred combinations and equipped with cards of identification. Mangeot was a sergeant and Bach only a corporal but, like most Americans, was sufficiently unmilitary not to wear any insignia of rank. Since it never occurred to the Germans that an American in the French army wouldn't be an officer, they were given the small courtesies extended to officers and made as comfortable as possible pending their removal to Corps Headquarters in the city of Laon.

While both pilots acknowledged that the wrecked ships were theirs, they otherwise maintained a discreet silence, refusing to divulge information of any sort, even under the lure of glittering promises. They anxiously sat tight and hoped for the best.

They were captured on the 23rd of September and taken to Laon the following day, but it was the 20th of October before they were brought to trial before a military court on charges of aiding espionage and sabotage, with the additional charge against Bach that he was an American *franc-tireur* or mercenary. It was to score heavily against him, for he was a supposedly neutral American, fighting in the uniform of the enemy. The penalty for the conviction of a *franc-tireur* was death!

Suspicion was justifiably strong against the two boys. The spies had evaded capture and succeeded in blowing up the railroad track the same night that Bach and Mangeot were captured. It was a natural conclusion on the part of the Germans that the two-place planes on the Rocroi field, with only the pilots in evidence, had a great deal to do with that piece of sabotage.

The prosecuting officer at the court-martial was very bitter in his denunciation and, backed up by strong circumstantial evidence, insisted that Bach and Mangeot be found guilty and shot immediately.

Jimmy got up and pleaded his own case so strongly, however, that no verdict was rendered at the first trial. Further evidence was demanded, and a second court was appointed for ten days later.

Realizing the seriousness of the situation, Jimmy felt that, unaided, he might not be so fortunate in the next trial in stalling off the wolves who clamored for his extinction. He was fortunately well equipped with funds and received permission to engage the services of one of Berlin's smartest lawyers.

The attorney came to Laon, but he was none too hopeful. The ten days which elapsed between the first and second trials were nerve racking, for the two spies might be captured at any moment. Jimmy felt as if he were sitting on top of a live volcano.

But when the court convened, there was no further incriminating evidence. The Berlin lawyer threw himself heart and soul into the defense of his clients. Thanks in a large measure to his brilliant and impassioned oratory, when the final tense moment arrived and the judge advocate rose to read the verdict in grave, sonorous tones, he said:

"By the unanimous verdict of this court, the French

aviators Bach and Mangeot, accused of espionage, are found not guilty. It is directed that they be held and confined as honorable prisoners of war."

Jimmy and Mangeot both vented their relief in whoops of unrestrained joy and were nearly penalized for contempt. It was a very narrow escape in both trials for Bach that he was not convicted and shot.

The United States government might have protested, but it would have been merely a gesture, for Jimmy was a regularly enlisted French soldier, as he was forced to prove. The diplomats, even had they been permitted to make the attempt, wouldn't have had a leg to stand on. And by the time they got around to it, had Jim been found guilty, the handsomely engraved protest wouldn't have done him much good. He would have long since been decorated with what the French so aptly call the "Croix de Bois," where one is not kissed on the cheek, but slapped in the face with a spade.

Laon was close enough to the lines to tempt Bach and Mangeot, once they had gotten over the jitters from the narrow escape from the death sentence, to try an escape from the prison. Unfortunately, on the day before they had set to make the attempt, Jimmy was separated from his companion and sent to a military prison in Bavaria.

Here he at once started making new plans for an escape. This fortress was in an old château, situated on a high rocky hill, with unscalable cliffs on three sides and the single entrance closely guarded. Jimmy found that it was by no means an impossible feat to get out of his quarters, but that discovery and recapture would be almost inevitable on the narrow mountain road that was the only exit.

He got himself a job driving a supply wagon and bided his time until his guard, lulled into security by the apparent docility of his prisoner, had relaxed his vigilance for a few seconds.

Then Jimmy leaped from the wagon one evening, just as they were leaving the town on the way back to the château, and amid a hail of bullets from the suddenly awakened guard disappeared into the gloom. Frightened by the firing, the horses started to run, and the guard's aim was so disturbed by the swaying wagon that Jimmy got away without injury.

He cautiously stole his way that night to a neighboring village and took refuge in the house of a woman, who he had been informed by his comrades in the prison was from Alsace-Lorraine and friendly to the French. It was one of the many underground channels established early in the war to aid in the safety of escaping prisoners.

But what his comrades didn't know was that the woman was suspected and her house held under constant surveillance.

Just before dawn the place was surrounded, and Jimmy was forced once again to submit to inglorious capture at the hands of a hard-boiled German sergeant and his squad.

Before he was led away, he was forced to witness the execution of the kindly woman who had befriended him. He could never forget that sight.

After spending considerable time in solitary confinement, Bach was eventually taken to the bastile at Nuremberg, from which, although he made several abortive attempts, there was no escape. There he remained the rest of the war, the dean of all American prisoners.

When he was captured, he had a head full of thick black

hair. As a result of his privations, when he returned to Paris after the Armistice, he was nearly bald, and what little hair remained was snow white.

Jimmy's only regret, however, is that he couldn't have served America as gallantly as he served France.

CHAPTER IV

Guts vs. Erudition

WHEN, by the usual latrine telegraph, the news filtered through that the French had consented to the formation of an all-American squadron of volunteers, a dozen other aspiring young eaglets hurried to transfer or enlist in the aviation.

From the Legion came Bobby Soubiran, with twenty months' service; Billy Dugan, Dennis Dowd and Edmond Genet, with almost as much.

From the ambulance service came the sweet-natured, gentlemanly Ronald Hoskier, Willis Haviland, Steve Bigelow, myself, Walter Lovell, Harold Willis, former Harvard crew man, and Kenneth (Siwash) Marr, the Alaskan sourdough, who had brought over a string of huskies for ambulance service in the snowy reaches of the Vosges Mountains.

Practically unknown to each other, one by one we volunteered in the Foreign Legion for the duration of the war and, after medical inspection and several days at Legion Headquarters at Dijon, were transferred immediately to the primary flying schools, without the necessity of trench service.

We were a heterogeneous crew, in all degrees of physical

condition, mentality and education. But the French neither asked nor apparently cared where or how much we'd gone to school and paid scant attention to physical handicaps. Their greatest and practically only requirement was that we should have that intangible something called guts.

It offered a sharp contrast to the requirements of the American military authorities for aviators when the United States entered the war. We felt at the time that their emphatic insistence on a college education and perfect health seemed a bit too severe for the type of service the boys would of necessity have to perform.

We knew from experience that a man had guts and a natural flying ability or he hadn't. All the book learning and physical examinations in the world couldn't give those two things to him or take them away if he had them.

However, there were, without doubt, excellent reasons on both sides for the apparent wide divergence in requirements. The French couldn't afford to be too severe. They had no particular thought of demanding a higher type of man for the air corps with a view of building toward the future. They knew that if they didn't win the war, there might not be any future.

In any event, Headquarters were only too well aware that the flying hours of a war aviator's life were pitifully few. Although I'm not certain of the authenticity of the figures, it was claimed at one time that the average was considerably less than fifteen hours over the lines.

Realizing the terrific hazards and the probability of such extremely short service, the French sought the fighter type who could learn to fly a plane well and shoot a machine gun accurately, whether or not they were men who could later develop any of the larger qualifications of warfare.

On the other hand, with such an abundance of fine material in the United States, eager to be thrown to the wolves of war, Headquarters doubtless felt the necessity of demanding certain qualifications, assuming that if a man was going to live and rise in the army, he would be a more useful soldier of the air if he had a brain which could function beyond the mere essentials of acrobatic flying and good machine gunning.

However, it seemed to us on the front, where only the fittest or the luckiest survived, that a natural-born flyer, a man capable of handling a ship well and shooting straight, even if he couldn't write his own name, was worth ten mediocre flyers with college degrees. Calculus and trigonometry were of pitifully little use against an enemy equipped with the lethal weapons of warfare. Opportunities were few to use ancient languages on a balky motor, nor was a complete mastery of the classics necessary to aim a machine gun truly.

Ability, courage and a cool head appeared to be the best qualifications. Ofttimes too much knowledge was filled with danger and defeated its own ends, for it led to too much imagination, the ruination of many an otherwise splendid young war bird.

In view of the problematical span of our existence, we felt, too, that the necessity for perfect health was a trifle too heavily stressed. We couldn't understand, as long as a man's chances of living through it were so slim, why flat feet, enlarged tonsils, missing teeth or inability to walk straight backwards along a crack unequivocally and unconditionally condemned him for the air service and a chance to knock down a few of the enemy before he, too, went west.

After serving at the front with the French aviation for a year or so, knocking off my share of the enemy among a few of my own countrymen and hundreds of Frenchmen, most of whom never saw the four walls of a college classroom, I was granted a month's leave to come back to America.

There I ran into dozens of my old pals, all in some earth-bound branch of the service, and almost without exception they told me the same sad tale. They had tried to enter aviation, but had been turned down, generally because of some very minor physical defect or because they had failed to come up to the mark in some very nonessential type of educational requirement.

Perhaps they were luckier than they knew, but after my years of service with anything but perfect types, bodily and mentally, who had proved such crack flyers and outstanding aces, I demanded further details. When they outlined the rigid qualifications necessary for acceptance, visions of hordes of superairmen, mechanical genii, hurling the deadly ammunition of compound Greek verbs at the bewildered Germans entered my mind, and I snickered silently as I recalled the terrific difficulties that had beset my own path when I volunteered for service with the French. It was a most enlightening experience which I know was shared by practically all my comrades.

In the first place, I was far from a perfect specimen of youthful manhood. In my prep-school days, due to an unfortunate accident with a ring, I had lost the first two joints of the little finger of my right hand. That in itself would have been enough, I gathered, to bar me from American aviation.

I was addicted to swollen tonsils, the lid of my left eye

drooped, and under the influence of too much bug juice one eye stared straight ahead, while the other wandered off into space. I could see all right, although others were slightly suspicious of my ability under such conditions.

Owing to the evils of early intemperance and too many cigarettes, violent exercise always brought on a well-defined case of what, in horses, is known as the heaves. These minor defects, I'm afraid, would have considerably lowered my rating before an American medical examining board. Not realizing what a horrible example I was, I had very little trepidation when, after having received my acceptance papers as a volunteer in the Foreign Legion, I was ordered to report in Paris for a medical examination.

I walked into a room partially filled with other tough-looking specimens of every race under the sun, including a couple of blacks and one or two whose real color I was unable to distinguish because of a most effective disguise of plain ordinary dirt.

My name was called, and I popped into a small office, occupied largely by various charts and a much harassed black-beavered, beetle-browed individual with a booming voice and the caduceus of the Medical Corps on the deep-red velvet tabs of his uniform collar. I blushingly complied with his order to strip. As impersonally as if I were just another horse, he gave me a short once-over and saw that I was equipped with the regulation torso, head, arms and legs. Satisfactory grunt. The first hurdle had been surmounted.

Then he laid a large dirty, grease-spotted towel on my lily-white chest, and I shuddered with the thought of how many chests like those in the anteroom that same towel had already covered. It didn't take me long in the French army to get over my squeamish ideas.

He ordered me to breathe deeply. I did, surprising even myself. Although my heart was beating like a triphammer, the long-drawn sigh had no trace of the heaves. With his ear to my chest, protected by the towel from contamination, he listened for waterfalls and volcanic upheavals, none of which, fortunately, were forthcoming at the moment. Briskly he nodded approval, and I drew another sigh of relief, to which, as luck would have it, he wasn't listening. A slight grating as of steel rails dragged across a graveled yard was produced by that exhalation.

But the most difficult portions of my tests were yet to come. Standing me off at ten feet in front of a chart whose letters looked as large as the Corticelli sign in Times Square, he commanded me to read.

"The second line," he'd say, "the third letter. I see there a B. What do you see?"

Sure enough, it was a B, and I'd say so.

"*Bon*," he'd explode enthusiastically.

Then we'd do some more of those silly exercises, he calling the letters as I checked up on him. He was right every time. He never tried to cross me by calling the wrong letter. He wasn't taking any chances I'd be wrong, and his "*Bons*" grew bigger and better with every answer.

Then we passed to the color charts, where we repeated the same delightful process.

"I see red. What do you see?"

"Red, Major."

"*Bon*. I see green. What——"

But why go on? In two shakes of a lamb's tail it was all over.

He gave me a friendly pat on the bare back that sent me staggering across the room and, signing his name to my papers with an official flourish, he congratulated me on being a perfect physical specimen and said that as far as he was concerned I could go out and get myself killed at any time "*pour la France.*"

I fooled him, though, and didn't get killed. Despite my tremendous handicaps, including the fact that my college education was of very brief duration, I served three years with the French pursuit and got more than my fair share of victories. The physical examination was a farce, and no mention was ever made of mental requirements. I couldn't even speak the language well at the time.

To the French, at least, it was a self-evident fact that a chap didn't have to be a genius or abnormally developed to be a war aviator. Generally the ability to understand words of two syllables was enough, and while good health was a great asset, it was by no means an absolute requisite. Bravery and marksmanship were much to be preferred.

Witness that beloved French ace, Georges Guynemer, the man whose memory is enshrined in the hearts of French, English and Americans alike. Frail, consumptive, half crippled, weighing less than a hundred pounds, he literally had to fight his way into flying. By the simple use of excellent marksmanship and unequaled experience in flying ships of various types, he made himself one of the most outstanding figures of the war in the air, knocking down fifty-four official German planes.

Seventy per cent of the aviators in the French army were noncommissioned officers, many peasants, some of them exceedingly dumb, practically none with anything remotely resembling a college education. And were *they* flyers? Their magnificent records speak for themselves.

As an example, there was René Fonck, the greatest ace

of the French army, with some seventy-five officially confirmed enemy planes to his credit and the Recording Angel alone knows how many more for which he received no credit. When the war flamed out, Fonck was a very sketchily educated young French peasant in Alsace. Grim, saturnine, phlegmatic, he actually fought his way to the top, pulling himself up by his own bootstraps.

In the Lafayette Escadrille, of whom I can truthfully say with great pride there were no better flyers ever weaned, it seemed fated that the best-educated men, the ex-college boys full of vitality, intelligence and the joy of living, were the first to go west.

Our greatest ace, Raoul Lufbery, gained practically all his education in his world-wide travels. Schools saw very little of him. He couldn't even speak good English, much less write it. Perhaps if he'd known more, he wouldn't have flown as much or gotten as many of the enemy. He finally joined the others in the Last Long Flight, but it took the enemy three years and the loss of more than twenty of their own side to get him.

The fearless Dud Hill was almost totally blind in one eye. Not having quite the sympathetic aid that I received from my doctor in his physical examination, Dud passed the eye tests with flying colors—by memorizing the letter chart and peeking through his fingers with his good eye when it came to the color chart.

He was not quite so successful in a second examination taken during his schooling, and his handicap was discovered. The machinery was started to take him off flying and reduce him to mechanic. Long before the papers came through, Dud brilliantly passed all the flight tests and was flying at the front. So they decided to let him stay, and

Raoul Lufbery (Courtesy Paul A. Rockwell)

Harold B. Willis (Courtesy C. H. Dolan II)

Dudley L. Hill (Courtesy Paul A. Rockwell)

Hill justified their confidence by making a glorious record in both the French and American flying forces.

In fact much later it was found, when an examining board came to look the Escadrille over with a view to determining their fitness to fly with the American aviation, that there wasn't even one fairly perfect physical specimen among us. Among the crippled misfits of survivors, more than half had no alma mater. Still our records showed that we did a pretty elegant job of what we set out to do.

From a chap's memory of the year Nero staged his whoopee party in Rome, or his profound knowledge of why 2X squared over BVD equals four quarts of scotch, who, except himself, is capable of telling what kind of a buzzard he'd be at fifteen thousand feet, with an enemy ship in his sights and a couple of others pouring lead into him from behind?

In a situation of that kind, which was not at all infrequent, his education made surprisingly little difference. He couldn't wave a college diploma at a homicidally inclined enemy and say sweetly, "Hey, you can't do that. Can't you see I'm a college man?"

War at best is a brutal thing, and when one is on his own, far up in the skies, fighting a savage leaden duel, with quick extinction as the penalty of the loser, the mantle of civilization slips from the shoulders of the social registrite and the college graduate just as quickly, if not more so, than from the boy from the streets.

Then it's only that intangible something inside, the stark naked soul of the man himself that brings him back to the well-earned sweets of victory or entitles him to a nice cozy spot where he can so comfortably use the fruits of his education in pushing up pretty daisies.

CHAPTER V

Breveted on Blériots

IT WAS AN INTRIGUING, but at first somewhat startling, new career that was opened to us, once we had so blithely signed our lives away on endless masses of meaningless papers at Legion Headquarters, been issued the usual misfit uniforms of a second-class French poilu and received transportation to a primary aviation school.

With carefree hearts, we drew black leather pants and jackets, goggles, gloves and crash helmets, prepared to demonstrate immediately that eagles were only sissies.

However, it took some little time before we gave the birds any real competition, even though the French had perfected a splendid, simple and decidedly novel system of training.

Incredible as it may seem, from the moment that a nervous youngster first slung his leg over the edge of a cockpit till some gold-braided, high-ranking brass hat clapped him on the back and said, "*Mon enfant*, you're a pilot," the fledgling never had anyone with him. There was no dual control. He was strictly on his own.

Of course there were instructors. Older pilots, worn out with the strain of war flying, or perhaps convalescing from wounds received at the front, who sat calmly on the ground, explained clearly what had to be done, then sent us up to do it.

When something was wrong, they pointed out the mistakes when you came down and sent you right up to correct them. Nothing seemed to escape the eagle eyes of these *moniteurs*.

By easy stages, thoroughly learning every basic principle as we went along, we absorbed everything that anyone knew about flying, maneuvering and acrobatics. With each successive stage, we gained more confidence in ourselves, because we were doing it without dependence on anyone else, so that when we were finished we had laid a foundation that was as solid as the Rock of Gibraltar. We could never forget it or violate any of its precepts.

As a consequence, the pilots turned out under this system were the finest in the world. Just as a self-made man who rises in his business from the lowest to the highest position knows every last detail, so these men knew their ships and their air.

But the greatest advantage of this method was the almost total absence of fatalities. Considering the types and worn-out conditions of the training planes, it was nothing short of miraculous. I spent nearly three months at Buc, one of the biggest preliminary training centers in France. In all that time and with all the men there in training, some three or four hundred, practically none of whom had ever been in the air before, only one man was killed.

Poor Dennis Dowd, the brilliant young lawyer from Brooklyn, who, having enlisted in the Foreign Legion on account of a shattered romance, served gallantly until he was badly wounded in the second battle of Champagne.

After convalescence, he transferred to the aviation and met his untimely end in one of the old Caudron G-3s. We all thought that, his health shattered by his hardships in the trenches, he fainted in the air. His ship went into a spin at three thousand feet and never came out. He had previously shown promise of being an excellent flyer.

Not one of the Frenchmen was either killed or badly hurt, an amazing record in view of the terrific handicaps they had to overcome.

The school at Buc, near Versailles, where most of the Lafayette boys were breveted, was a training center for pilots who would eventually go to pursuit squadrons. If a man didn't make a good showing, he was eliminated and either sent back to his regiment or to another school for training in observation or bombing, but these men were few and far between.

Nearly everyone who got to Buc finished with honors. There were sixteen in my class to start. Fifteen of us got our brevets. Just one man was eliminated, and they found out pretty quickly that he wouldn't make a pilot if he lived to be a million.

However, French training schools were no bed of roses. We were up every morning before dawn, with only a cup of lukewarm chicory, masquerading as coffee, to sustain us till the first meal at eleven o'clock. Daylight found us shivering at our various fields, awaiting our turns on that fearful and wonderful contraption known as the Blériot monoplane.

Taking the early wartime ships as a whole, I am inclined to shudder just a wee trifle as I think about some of them, wondering where we ever found the nerve to take them into the air at all, much less to do battle with them.

Ignorance was certainly bliss!

We didn't know any better, so we thought everything was perfectly all right. Away back in the dark ages, M. Blériot himself had flown one of them across the English Channel. If he could do that and still be in good health, we failed to see where we had anything to fear.

Nevertheless, in anything except the most favorable combination of circumstances, such as a perfectly perking motor (a great rarity) and absolutely calm air, without a trace of wind or heat bumps, keeping a Blériot under perfect control presented somewhat of a problem to the student pilot. Consequently, during our training, practically all flying with them ceased at ten o'clock in the morning, when there was likely to be a breeze and the air a little bumpy from the heat of the sun, and wasn't resumed till late in the afternoon, when the breeze died down and the air was presumed to have calmed off. The Blériots were not rough-weather ships by any stretch of the imagination. As a matter of fact, they would have made excellent museum pieces or a fine background for posing for photographs on the ground, but they were just a trifle unstable and dangerous in the air. Probably very fortunately for our healths, we never had to fly them at the front, but there were plenty who did in the earlier days. They did it not only cheerfully, but with great success, and to those men who flew them as weapons of war we bow in deep reverence for their heroism.

In itself, the construction of the Blériot was a source of never-ceasing wonder. With only slight exaggeration, it seemed as if they were merely gathered-up odds and ends of wood, discarded matchsticks and the like, which were wired together, catch-as-catch-can fashion, with bailing wire, to form the fuselage. Then old handkerchiefs were sewed together to cover the wings and that part of the fuselage around the pilot's seat. The remainder of the fuselage was left naked, which gave the ship a sort of half-finished appearance. We were undoubtedly wrong in thinking it was left naked because, with true French thrift, they wanted to save on fabric. More likely it was to facilitate replacement of brace wires, which had an uncomfortable habit of snapping when any particular strain was put on them.

The landing gear was fairly solid, with junior bicycle wheels at the end of each axle, wrapped with a couple of turns of light rubber cord.

Despite all rumors to the contrary, the motors weren't taken from discarded motorcycles. They ranged from the three-cylinder Anzani, the Italian radial motor, which also had seven and nine cylinders and was the forerunner of the present-day Curtiss and Wright radials, to fifty- and sixty-horsepower Le Rhone and Gnome rotary motors.

This latter motor always presented elements of surprise, for it was a single valve with no carburetor. Raw gas was fed directly into the cylinders, and with a very disconcerting habit of popping one of those valves quite frequently, fire generally resulted, which was likely to cause the pilot considerable embarrassment.

The stick in the Blériot had an odd feature. It had a triangular-shaped grip on top, with a contact button on one side so that the motor could be blipped on and off. Instead of grasping the stick like a broom handle, the pilot curled his fingers around the top bar of the triangle, like the handle on a pail.

There were no ailerons, the wings, owing to their light construction, warping quite easily.

The unfortunate pilot sat with half his body projecting above the fuselage, with no protection against the full blast of the propeller stream. The whirling stick was only a couple of feet in front of his nose.

Adding to the intricacies of flight in the Blériot, French regulations, strictly enforced in the schools, required that embryo pilots must wear a marvelously constructed Tower of Babel, known as a crash helmet. Sometime I should like to meet, in private, the massive-brained gorilla who designed the thing and, now that it wouldn't mean another eight or ten days of prison, tell the brass hats who made us wear them just what, in unexpurgated terms, I think about that ponderous headgear. It's a certainty that the engineer and the draftsman who drew the plans for it never had to wear one. It was built in layers, like a Chinese pagoda. It weighed just short of a ton. In it was an arrangement of springs and cork. It had an elastic chin band which was supposed to hold it in place. The theory was that if one overturned or suddenly stopped and got pitched out on the topknot, the crash helmet would prevent a fracture of the skull. A broken neck from the weight of the thing was much more likely to result. I have never known of an instance where it served any practical purpose.

Apparently they came in only two sizes—too large and too small. Under no circumstances was one ever known to fit anybody's head. They either perched up there like a wart on a nose or else settled coyly down over nose and ears. As a consequence, on the ground and while climbing into a ship, they could be precariously balanced, but the minute the full blast from the propeller hit them, they were either blown right back, hanging like a sunbonnet, or else slewed around at various odd angles on the head, interfering with vision and otherwise becoming a general nuisance. To me, at least, they caused more worry in the air than the Blériot itself, which was plenty.

Being of such light construction, the plane had plenty of give in the air. Frequently, in making a tight bank, I have looked back and seen the tail whipping around after me, bent in a perfect arc. It seemed as if I could almost reach out and grab the tail surfaces and rudder.

Heaven forbid that I ever had any desire to do so. I was just tickled to death that everything was hanging together.

However, despite all their little peculiarities, these little planes were far from being death traps. On the contrary, while we never took them very far from the field (for motors were too unreliable) and while we never went very high (as altitude goes nowadays—six or eight thousand feet was about the ceiling), we did everything in them that is done with present-day ships. We even looped, and one or two of the more hardy souls actually spun them and came out safely without any casualties except the near heart failure of those on the ground watching them.

Paradoxically, while they seemed most flimsy to look at, they were in reality fairly strong. They had to be, for until the boys got used to them they received plenty of rough usage.

When a student was first learning to crow-hop up and down a field, he'd take off, rise about ten or twenty feet and then bring the ship down almost flat, hardly peaking at all, by blipping the motor on and off. About four or five feet off the ground, the amateur eagle just let her drop ker-wham.

The sound was the general effect of an earthquake in a hardware store, but the miracle was that the ship seemed to suffer no particular ill effects. A tire here or a couple of wires there would go, or perhaps a shock-absorber cord, but nothing happened to render the ship unfit for further use.

I very much doubt that heavier ships could have absorbed all the punishment the Blériots were forced to take so nobly.

Our first training stage was, of course, on the little clipped-wing Blériots known as the Penguins. Their wing length was cut to about five feet, so there wasn't enough surface with the underpowered motors, generally the three-cylinder Anzani, to carry them into the air—that is, to stay.

Once or twice I got quite a thrill. When rushing down the field with a little breeze under my tail, I'd hit a bump and rise a foot or two before I sat down with an awful smack.

The Penguins had a slightly widened, strongly reinforced landing gear for running along the ground. It was basic training to teach the fledgling to handle the stick and motor, get accustomed to the noise and wind blast, learn to raise the tail in flying position and, by correcting the rudder for the motor torque, run in a straight line, just as he would take off later in the higher-powered, full-winged ships.

What a beating those Penguins took! They were possessed of the devil, anyway, and showed almost human intelligence in thinking up dirty tricks to play on their unsuspecting passengers. Start two at opposite ends of the field with practically the entire width of the field between them, and somehow or other they'd run together in a horrible collision in the center of the field. That is, it always sounded horrible, but usually repairs could be effected by the phlegmatic, betel-chewing Annamite mechanics within a very few minutes.

Then there was the bugbear of ground loops, or *chevaux de bois* (wooden horses on the merry-go-round), as the French so aptly named them. Once the Penguins started to turn in a ground loop, nothing could stop them except coming to a full stop with completely retarded motor. They'd whirl round and round like a dog chasing his tail. Then the red-faced, cursing neophyte would have to climb out, point his nose in the way he wanted to go and start all over again. It took plenty of trips up and down that long field before a boy learned how to straighten out one of those perverse little animals and keep it straight. But once he learned on a Penguin, he could handle any ship in the world with no fears. It was exceedingly rare at the front to see a ground loop by a Blériot-trained pilot.

To add zest to the performances, while the field was reasonably smooth, still there were plenty of rough spots, and something was always dropping off the Penguin or coming unstuck. We usually started out in the morning or afternoon with four, and by the time class was over we'd be very fortunate to have one in running order.

However, the Annamites were patient folk. They'd put Penguins together again almost as fast as we could wreck them. We had to help them, and it was swell training, for we learned to spin propellers and do all kinds of rough mechanical and construction work.

Someone was always in trouble in the Penguin class, and there were plenty of funny incidents to help pass away the hours while one was waiting his turn to get into difficulties. One of the most ludicrous happened to a very sincere and earnest young Frenchman, who was having a bit more than the ordinary difficulty in running a consistent straight line. He seemed fated for hard luck, for if he wasn't ground-looping and appeared in a fair way to make a full trip up and down in a reasonably straight line, something always went wrong with the Penguin or the motor.

At the end of the field was an old, disused reservoir, which had evaporated so that there was about three feet of evil-appearing, very gooey brown mud at the edges of a still considerable body of water. One morning the young Frenchman started out with a do-or-die expression on his face. He pursued a weaving and tenuous course to the far end of the field, with his tail dragging most of the way. Then he turned and started back toward us, and a miracle happened. He got his tail up and came booming along without a variation. There was a slight tail wind, and his motor was barking steadily. He was making excellent speed and a fine *ligne droite.*

He got so intrigued with it all that, as he came closer, he forgot all about stopping. It was his first successful attempt, and he was bubbling over with enthusiasm. We saw him coming and scattered just in time. He might have been going yet if the reservoir hadn't interfered. As it was, he hit the mud full tilt, then his whirling prop bit into the water and over he went. His body sticking out like a sore thumb above the fuselage, his head was jammed into the mud.

Nearly exhausted from paroxysms of laughter, two or three of us formed an extemporaneous lifesaving crew and dashed into the water. Hastily we extracted him from his perilous situation, pumped a little of the foul water out of him and sat him right side up. He blew out a mouthful of slimy mud, wiped one eye clear and opened it to look at the *moniteur* who was on the point of exploding.

"Well, anyhow, Sergeant," he asked anxiously, "I made a good straight line, didn't I?"

The sergeant's voice trembled with suppressed emotion as he answered that of its kind he had never seen a better. His heart filled with sympathy over the woebegone appearance of the unfortunate youngster, he sent him back to the barracks for dry clothes without giving him the bawling out he so richly deserved.

As soon as we were able to give a fairly consistent straight-line performance on the grass-cutting Penguins, we were advanced to the next class of fifty-horsepower, standard-winged Blériots.

There we did more *lignes droites* on the ground, then the little crow hops, up ten or fifteen feet, soar awhile, then blip her down.

Soon we learned to push the nose down a bit, then level off for a landing, just as if we had come in from a long flight instead of twenty feet. With a Blériot, that's all there was to learning to fly, except of course the next step, which was to take two or three times the altitude we had taken on crow hops and, instead of coming right down, go on around the field, making a *tour de piste* with flat turns, and then come down just as we had been doing.

With the confidence attained in several such tours, we were taught to use the stick to warp the wing and bank in the turns to prevent skidding, and there we were. It was an exceedingly simple, efficient method, and despite the fact that, up in the air, the wings looked to the worried young eagle like a couple of sheets of newspaper and the light ship quivered under every bump and breeze, the ship practically flew itself.

But the fledgling pilot never thought of that. Once he had made his *tour de piste* he modestly took all the credit to himself. He strutted his ability as a flyer, looking on the poor groundlings with a haughty eye, without giving any prestige to the plane itself, which after all had done substantially all the work. Sometimes, in fact, students in the crow-hop class went right ahead and flew a *tour de piste* without meaning to, long before they were considered to be ready for any such venture. Like the youngster in the Penguin class, they'd get so intrigued with actually being in the air that, instead of coming down before they'd reached the end of the field, they'd find they were still up in the air with a whole flock of tallish trees right in front of them. Preferring to risk a bawling out from the *moniteur* rather than a sure crack-up in the woods, they kept right on going around, sometimes making two or three tours before they could get enough nerve to retard the motor, turn the nose down a little and come in for a landing.

Since they always got away with it and they were only beating the gun by a few days, the *moniteur* gave them a bawling out with his tongue in his cheek and promoted them to the next class: the final class in Blériots, with the big, powerful sixty-horsepower motors which would hurtle a Blériot through the air at the breath-taking speed of about sixty miles an hour; that is, if all the cylinders were hitting and there was a tail wind. However, it seemed plenty fast to us at that stage of the game.

Despite the absence of casualties, I don't want to give the impression that everything went along smoothly and simply, without trouble or crack-ups. Far from it.

After a full day's training, partially wrecked Blériots lay all over the various fields. Bad landings which even a Blériot couldn't take, motor failures in very embarrassing spots, and the general uncertainty of the new pilots themselves spread the little ships all over the surrounding landscape. There was a boneyard of Blériots, smashed beyond hope of repair, which must have chilled the hearts of the French ministers of the war budgets.

But it was wonderful how many bad crack-ups there were without injury to the pilots. The planes themselves dissolved in splinters, simply disintegrated, but the high-hatted, disgruntled pilots always disentangled themselves from the wreckage and walked calmly away. The lightness of the ship's construction seemed to absorb all the heavy shocks before they got to the pilot.

In some of the schools, as at Buc, the Blériot was used only for preliminary training. More advanced training, including the necessary tests for the military brevet, was taken on other types of planes. At one or two centers, however, the whole course was given on the jittery little ships, including the three long cross-country flights which were the final tests. With the flimsy little planes and unreliable motor, I can condole with and admire the hardy souls who can say, "I was breveted on Blériots." They don't have to take off their hats to anyone. Having made a Blériot eat out of their hand, flying any other plane would be just like shooting fish in a glass bowl.

One aspiring young cloud hopper, however—the only one in my class who failed—became convinced quite early in the game that he was never cut out to be a fearless aviator. On his first wabbly *tour de piste,* he completely misjudged his distance when he was ready to come down. He had to cross a tree-bordered main highway, and he shut off his motor far too quickly, with the consequent result that he came firmly to rest in the top of one of the tallest trees.

The ship was tightly wedged—so tightly that the mechanics had to take it all to pieces to get it down, but this intrepid aviator didn't know that. He sat up there for four mortal hours, not stirring a muscle and scarcely daring to breathe for fear of disturbing the delicate balance. There was no ladder at the school long enough to reach him, and he screamed with terror as the tree shook when short ladders were placed against it.

Everybody at Buc took the occasion to come and console him, some shouting up exceedingly ribald advice, others offering to rescue him with balloons or at least drop wine and cigarettes, since he expected to be up there the rest of his life. He was too scared to make any response—he simply sat there with stony face, staring straight ahead.

Eventually the firemen came out from Versailles, ten kilometers away, and raised an extension ladder, but by that time our hero was thoroughly convinced. If a thing like that could happen to him in a Blériot, he had no difficulty in visualizing the possibilities offered by other and faster planes for a boy to lose his life. He asked for a transfer back to his original infantry regiment, where he could be safe.

CHAPTER VI

Château Breakdowns

WHEN THE MONITEURS decided that we had done everything on Blériots that we could safely do, we were sent to continue our educations on the sixty-horsepower Caudron G-3.

It was a far heavier ship, a biplane instead of a monoplane with more than twice the wingspread of the Blériot. Although in most cases they used practically the same motors, the Caudron actually flew higher, faster and longer than the Blériot. But unlike the Blériot, with its openwork fuselage from the cockpit back to the stabilizer, the Caudron had no fuselage at all—that is, in the usually accepted meaning of the term "fuselage."

Between the upper and lower wings was suspended the motor, and attached to it, projecting out a foot or two behind the wings, was a sort of bathtub in which the pilot and observer sat. Of course in training and on cross-country hops we didn't have any passenger, but a place had been provided for one for service at the front.

Like the Blériot, the Caudron had no ailerons, but the whole wing warped. It required just a little heavier hand, but the response was almost as quick.

About three feet on each side of the bathtub, a long spar ran down at a sharp angle from the top wing. Corresponding spars ran straight back out from the landing gear, and, where the upper and lower spars met, the stabilizer, elevator and rudder were suspended.

The lower spars rested on the ground when the Caudron was at rest and formed the drag on landing. They lifted about a foot off the ground when the ship was in flying position.

What the Caudron lacked in fuselage, it certainly made up for in wires. There were brace and flying wires of every description, size and kind around, between and through those spars. The effect bore a strange resemblance to a chicken coop. The mechanics used to say that the only way to tell if a wire was broken or missing was to put a bird inside. If the bird could escape, then a wire was gone somewhere.

The Caudron's rate of climb was slow and its ceiling under twelve thousand feet. Its top speed under the most favorable conditions could hardly have been above eighty-five miles an hour. However, slow and awkward as it was, it was a pretty fairly dependable ship in all kinds of weather—that is, if the motor held out. It landed fairly slow, for it had considerable wingspread in proportion to its weight.

After we had shot the works in the Blériot and graduated to the Caudron, it was a considerable change for the better. The heavier construction and greater wing surface gave us a feeling of having something solid under us in the air, a comfortable feeling sadly lacking in the Blériot.

It was an easy transition from the Blériot to the Caudron, but I can certainly see where a reversal of the process might have been fatal. The Blériot was as sensitive to controls as a high-strung filly, while piloting the Caudron was like driving a sturdy old draft horse. A fairly heavy rein was needed.

At first we did nothing but get our hands in: take off, fly a couple of *tours de piste* and land. Not very difficult, but it certainly had its thrills. The ships were old and fatigued. They had seen plenty of service at the front in all kinds of weather.

And the motors! None too reliable to start with, they all had long gray beards by the time we got to use them. Every successful flight was an epic achievement.

The field at Buc was large, fine and level. But surrounding it on all sides was farm land, most of which was in wheat, which brought on many distressing complications.

I shall try to clarify the situation for those who have never had the doubtful pleasure of landing in a wheat field or something similar with long, tough, high stalks.

When a quick forced landing is necessary, a green wheat field presents from the air a level and inviting appearance, but it is in reality an octopus-infested trap for the unwary.

"Swell," buzzard says to himself as his motor fizzles out. "Absolutely providential. Nice smooth field. I'll take it."

He carefully maneuvers for the spot and only at the moment of sitting down, far too late to do anything about it, is rudely disillusioned.

Underneath the even green stalks, the ground is quite likely to be furrowed and ridged. But even if he could avoid that peril and land lengthwise of the furrows, his goose is cooked.

The tender green stalks catch hold of the propeller and landing gear and wrap themselves around them with tentacles of iron. The forward course of the speeding plane is rudely halted, and, the next thing the bewildered pilot knows, he has done a neat nip-up and is hanging head down, wondering how in tarnation he got there. I speak with deep feeling, for the only crack-up I had in all my training until I got on cross-country flights was caused by that selfsame wheat.

When it came my turn to take out one of the Caudrons, the student who had just brought the ship in warned me that the motor was on its last legs. However, it seemed to rev up all right on the ground, so I started gaily off.

About the time I got to the edge of the field, the tachometer dropped to eight hundred, barely flying speed, and despite all I could do, kept right on dropping. I was only about two hundred meters up, and I tried to hold her in the air, but it was no go.

I suddenly began to feel the old bus wabble from lack of speed. Instinct, rather than knowledge, told me that I'd better do something about that and do it in a hurry. So I did the only thing I knew. I poked the nose down, and as I did so I saw a grand level green field dead ahead of me.

I came down like a bat out of hell under the impression I was going to make a marvelous landing. I picked up enough speed to bring the old Caudron out of the wing slip she had started when it began to wabble.

I leveled out just over the tops of the waving stalks and confidently waited for the Caudron to settle down in this magnificent landing I had been contemplating. It was all over in the flash of an eye, and so was I.

Hanging head down, I managed to get the safety belt unbuckled and fell out on the ground in the middle of a wide swath of newly mown wheat, which I presume the French government had to pay for. I stood for a moment, contemplating the wreck of my hopes with a sad and disillusioned eye.

Suddenly, hearing the wail of wind through taut wires over my head, I looked up. Another student with a G-3 from our class had started out soon after me and had watched me go down and turn over. He retarded his motor and came down to take a look-see to find out if I'd been hurt.

Unfortunately, as soon as I had waved to him that I was all right and able to walk, when he tried to put his motor back on, he found there was no soap. Might have been either flooded cylinders or ignition trouble. In any event, he couldn't pick it up and conked down not a hundred yards from where I had done my somersault. Of course he achieved the same result.

I hurried over to him, found he was scared but unhurt, and while we were condoling with each other another curious buzzard came down for a look, lost his motor and "capoted" a couple of hundred yards on the other side.

All these mishaps occurred within ten minutes of each other, and it seemed as if the good old rule of three were still holding good.

It was one of the rules of the school that, in case of a crack-up or forced landing away from the field, a pilot had to stick with his ship till the wrecking crew came. While we three were waiting, curiosity got the better of a fourth eaglet about thirty minutes later, and he plunked down to join us in the wheat field. Between the planes and the wrecking crews, we certainly put a considerable acreage of wheat on the blink that day.

Some time later, very much crestfallen, our quartette, none of whom felt like rendering "Sweet Adeline," rejoined the class to take what was coming to us. Our *moniteur* was a young sergeant named Prieur, who had had quite a number of hours at the front. He romped up and down the spines of the three curiosity seekers, and I shivered in anticipation of what he must be going to tell me, the cause of it all.

Much to my pleased surprise, he had nothing but praise; told me he knew my motor was bad and he was very happy that, badly as it had turned out, nothing had happened to me personally; informed me that I had done exactly the right thing in landing at once instead of trying to regain the field, a very natural instinct. I didn't tell him that I had no choice in the matter; that I had already started to slip, and the only way I kept from killing myself was to pick up the slip and land. Then he went on to tell me a thing that made a deep impression and has always stuck in my mind, particularly since I have seen so many others go to unnecessary deaths by violating it.

"As you know," he said, "the greatest strain comes on motor and plane just as you leave the ground, before full flying speed is attained. If you ever have motor trouble on taking off or at low altitude, turn your nose down instantly and land straight ahead. It doesn't make any difference if it's in a wheat field, ditch, woods or the roof of a house. Then at least you've got a chance. If you lose your head or try to be smart and turn back to the place you've just left, you won't have speed enough, and a fatal wing slip will almost invariably result."

Prieur knew what he was talking about, for he had seen it happen so often, as I did in the years to come. That one crash in the wheat field and Prieur's wise advice may have saved my life a dozen times, since I never forgot it.

As soon as we had gotten used to the feel of the Caudron, we were advanced to the higher-powered classes, with eighty- and ninety-horsepower rotaries and the Anzani 110. There we learned to handle them almost like pursuit ships. All our tests for fitness for a military license were performed in them: spirals to right and left, figure eights, dead-stick spot landings, which must be within a fifty-meter circle from an altitude of three thousand feet, and an altitude test of over two thousand meters for an hour. To nurse one of the grunting old mills up to that height, which was higher than most of us had ever been, and keep it running for an hour, was in itself quite a stunt.

It was very warm on the ground the day I went up for my altitude test, and I dressed in a pair of light cotton coveralls without even wearing gloves. I found by the time I got up to seven thousand feet that the air was decidedly nippy, and I was practically a congealed corpse by the time I came down.

We didn't need a great deal of practice on forced landings. We got plenty of those in the course of routine training.

When all the preliminary tests had been completed, there remained only the three cross-country triangles. We had only map and compass to guide us. We carried a sealed barograph, which showed our time and altitude, and papers that had to be signed at each control stop. They weren't taking any chances that we'd come down somewhere and complete our voyages by automobile.

The triangle was Buc-Chartres-Evereux, or vice versa, a distance of about three hundred kilometers. Rarely did anyone make the three triangles in uninterrupted succession. I leaped off six times before I finally completed three. With student after student using the same ships, motors were inclined to let one down in most unfortunate places.

The combination of unreliable motors and cross-country hops gave rise to that good old Eskimo custom known as *pannes de châteaux*, meaning château breakdowns. A pilot would disappear for anywhere from three days to a week and come back with a smug face and a tale of having made a forced landing, but fortunately, oh so fortunately, near a big château, where he was royally entertained and lived on the fat of the land all the time he was waiting for the repair crew.

Some of the alibis for château landings were works of art. Dirt in the carburetor, wing flutter, rainstorm, anything served. Of course, motors *were* bad, and there *are* a lot of châteaux in France, but it was a strange coincidence that when a pilot had to land, it was always within easy hailing distance of a château.

To count on your brevet, a cross-country had to be completed the same day, but I don't know of a case on record where there was a forced landing near a château where repairs were made the same day and the voyage continued. The stricken pilot's mechanical knowledge appeared to have mysteriously evaporated the minute he touched the ground.

It got so prevalent that the brass hats began to regard even the legitimate breakdowns with a fishy eye. I was made well aware of their attitude and silently resented it, for I had a couple myself. Needless to say, mine of course were absolutely legitimate. It was merely one of those coincidences that they both happened to be in the neighborhood of a château.

However, there was an order posted once at the school, which forbade any pilot to land under *any* circumstances away from an airport. The massive brain who wrote that order didn't mention what he expected us to do when the motor stopped completely. Perhaps, we decided, we could use sky hooks to stay up there until we were rescued by a Zeppelin, or get out, flap our arms and carry the ship in on our backs.

My first cross-country hop with an eighty-horsepower Le Rhone Caudron G-3 ended in a flat failure less than three quarters of an hour after I had left Buc for Evereux late one afternoon. To demonstrate how little I contemplated a forced landing, I hadn't shaved for two days and wore only a sweater and a smelly, oil-stained leather flying suit, long britches and jacket. Not altogether what the snappy, well-dressed aviator should wear when being entertained by one of France's foremost citizens.

I dropped three cylinders, one after another, losing altitude all the time, and finally had to come down in a field among some haystacks, ending up with my propeller buried in one of the stacks and my wing tips touching two others. Fortunately, the field was right beside the luxurious summer home of a Paris perfume manufacturer named M. Bagot, who had just arrived with his family the previous day. He nearly busted a gusset trying to entertain properly the brave young American hero who had come to save France. I was a little embarrassed an account of my clothes and general appearance, but I managed to bear up bravely until the repair crew arrived three days later. They had to take the ship down to get it back to Buc. My gracious host became my firm friend and, when I went to the front, sent out enough toilet goods every month to supply the whole Escadrille.

My other *panne* was the culmination of a series of bizarre incidents and resulted in practically the only casualty I experienced during my entire service. The day after my return from my visit with M. Bagot, I started out again, this time planning to make Chartres my first stop. Much to my pleased surprise, I perked along without trouble until I got there. Then, in landing, out in the center of the immense field, which was the Farman school and even bigger than Buc, my motor died just as I hit the ground. I sat there quietly for some time waiting for the usual mechanics to run out and do their duty.

Nothing happened, and finally I stood up in the cockpit and waved. Whereupon a gentleman in a blue uniform mounted a bicycle and pedaled out to me. He informed me that since it was Sunday, flying was suspended and all the mechanics were on leave. He was one of the soldiers on guard duty, and though he was not a mechanic, he offered to help me out. He grunted and perspired, pulled the prop through twenty times, but couldn't get a single pop out of the old mill.

Finally I got fed up and told him I'd take a whirl at it myself. I set the gas lever up a couple of notches, left the switch on and hopped out. I guided my willing helper through the wires, showed him where to stand on the step outside the cockpit and what his part of the entertainment was when and if I got the motor going. All he had to do was push the gas *manette* back to idling speed. He seemed none too bright, but I thought he was capable of that. Naturally, believing my boy pal knew his onions, I didn't trouble to put any chocks under the wheels. That was my mistake.

I spit on my hands, spun the prop and with inanimate perverseness the old Le Rhone caught the first whirl. It went off with an awful roar.

The noise and the wind blast sent my helper into a panic. He never touched the gas, but simply jumped off the step and scuttled through the wires like a frightened rabbit. The Caudron jumped forward and started to move down the field.

As it went by, I grabbed the end of a wing and hung on for dear life. The plane was moving at a pretty good speed by this time. It went fast enough to rise a foot off the ground and come down with an awful smack. My weight on the end of the wing and the propeller torque caused it to turn in a great circle. Hanging onto the wing, I was making tremendous kangaroo leaps, but I dared not release my clutch. If I lost that ship, I could see my career as a French airman going right up in smoke.

Two complete grand circles of the field we made, my Caudron and I, half on the ground and half in the air, before I was able to work my way along the back of the lower wing, get on a spar, work my way through the wires and up to the cockpit, where with practically my last breath I got hold of the gas.

When we came to a stop, we were less than ten feet from where my valuable assistant had parked his bicycle. He had completely disappeared.

Taking time to recover a bit of my poise and breath, I reluctantly taxied into the line amid raucous jeers from several officers who had delightedly watched my mad dash around the field with my pilotless plane.

I dug up a sergeant mechanic who looked over my bus and found a short circuit in the ignition somewhere near the switch. He wasn't enthusiastic about repairing it, and I was in a hurry, so he simply cut the switch out, bridging the gap between magneto and distributor plate direct. It simply meant that ignition was on constantly and I'd have to cut off the gas to stop. That would have been all right, only he didn't do a very good job of wiring.

As a consequence, about halfway to Evereux, while at about two thousand feet over the great forest of Dreux, the ignition just cut out for good and all. The main bridging wire shook loose.

Hastily, I looked for a place to sit down. All I could see was an immense sea of tall trees. There didn't seem to be an open field anywhere in sight. I figured I was finished. I resigned myself to hanging in a treetop and perhaps starving to death should I escape instant annihilation.

Suddenly, just underneath me I saw, with a heartfelt sigh of relief, a noble tower topping a good-sized red building, set in a little spot of green no bigger than a pocket handkerchief. It was the park of a château and, being my only chance, I took it.

I got into it all right, but the place was so small that before I could slice in over the treetops and set the ship down, I picked up such speed that I shot clear across the park and went into the underbrush and trees on the other side in a grand crash. A nicely placed tree on each side took off my wings, and the underbrush caught the landing gear. I immediately did another nip-up. This time I was hanging head down about seven or eight feet off the ground, and all my weight was on my safety belt. The safety belt had a trick clasp. One was supposed to punch it to make it break, but with my weight on it, it held like concrete. I had nothing to hang onto or with which to brace myself to ease the strain. The inventor had made no provision for upside-down business, and I struggled futilely to get loose.

Suddenly a bearded, smocked French peasant, crawling on hands and knees, stuck his head under the wreck and casually inquired if I was dead. He seemed very pleasantly surprised when I told him decidedly not, but I needed plenty of help.

I explained very carefully that he was to put his hand on my shoulders and push up till my weight was off the belt and I could break the clasp. He said he understood perfectly, and I suppose he did, but his understanding lacked imagination.

He pushed up all right, but as soon as I cracked the belt, he hastily ducked from under and let me drop squarely on the back of my neck. It telescoped two vertebrae and knocked me out for fifteen minutes.

I awoke with my head in the lap of a charming and very beautiful English girl, whose husband, a French officer at the front, owned the château.

I was there for several days till the wrecking crew came. Then they had two wrecks to take care of. I was the other.

Having had such bad luck with Le Rhones, I wept such copious tears when I got back to Buc that I was finally promoted to an Anzani. With it in the nose of my G-3, I perked around those cross-country triangles in short order.

But the day I got my wings and said au revoir to the

Caudrons, as I hoped forever, I breathed a sigh of real relief. Any kind of trick could be done with them; they'd never lose their wings; they'd fly and glide like a bird, with or without a motor, but I'm mighty happy I never had to use one as a pursuit ship at the front, even though plenty of the boys did great work with them in 1915 and 1916.

I'm still very proud that I was breveted on one. After the Blériot and the Caudron G-3, nothing with wings could ever cause any misgivings in my heart. When a buzzard tamed those two ships, if he was still alive and not a nervous wreck, he could fly anything.

When all our tests had been satisfactorily completed, we were pilots, got our French army brevets and International Aeronautical Federation licenses, four days' leave and automatically achieved the exalted grade of corporal.

From then on, all we did in progressive schools was to learn to fly pursuit ships, smooth out our air work and landings, learn gunnery, acrobatics, formation flying, attack and balloon hopping.

When we were ready for the front a couple of months later, we were pretty well heeled as fliers. And except verbally, no one had ever shown us the way. We taught ourselves, and it made a splendid solid foundation, with loads of self-confidence to back it up. There was never any inferiority complex. We thought we knew all the answers, and it wasn't until we got to the front, with flaming death menacing us on every side, that we learned, through bitter experience, how little we actually knew.

CHAPTER VII

Raoul Lufbery, the Inscrutable

On April 20, 1916, the American Escadrille had its actual formation as a unit at the flying field of Luxeuil-les-Bains in the Vosges Mountains. It was a vision come true after nearly a year and a half of unremitting toil, delays, discouragements, disappointments and actual opposition.

There were seven pilots who first got their orders and went out to form the original squadron. They were Thaw, Bert Hall, Cowdin, Norman Prince, Kiffin Rockwell, Chapman and McConnell, of whom only Hall is still alive.

The Vosges was an extremely quiet sector, and the boys were sent there primarily to acquire the teamwork necessary to a flying unit. Then, too, the new pilots needed the baptism of anti-aircraft artillery, or "Archie," as it came to be more familiarly known, to acquaint them with the business of aviation over a battlefield or alien territory, without too much of the added menace of enemy airplanes.

Each man was assigned his own sleek new plane, a speedy little Nieuport single-seater pursuit ship, powered by a ninety-horsepower Le Rhone rotary motor and equipped with a single forty-seven-shot Lewis machine gun mounted on the top wing. The synchronized gun that

April 1916. The first four pilots to report to the Escadrille and their Commanding Officer. Left to right: James McConnell, Kiffin Rockwell, Capt. Thenault, Norman Prince and Victor Chapman. Only Thenault survived the war. (Courtesy Paul A. Rockwell)

Left to right: Kiffin Rockwell, Capt. Thenault, Norman Prince, Lt. de Laage de Mœux, Elliot Cowdin, Bert Hall, James McConnell and Victor Chapman. (Courtesy Soubiran Collection)

fired through the propeller had not yet made its appearance on the Allied side, although the Germans had a crude one developed by Anthony Fokker. The Nieuports were the last word in speed and manueverability, with a ground speed slightly in excess of a hundred miles an hour.

The mechanics, of whom there were two assigned to each pilot, were all French, and they were the salt of the earth. Each one took as much pride in the plane and his *patron* as if he were doing the actual flying. He would brag about the exploits of his pilot and defend to the death any aspersions that might be cast on the pilot's courage or flying ability. The mechanics were in charge of Sergeant Chevalier, an English-speaking, red-headed French reservist from San Francisco, who was a master hand at both French and American profanity. He not only ruled the mechanics with an iron hand, but most of the pilots as well, including the French officers. No one ever tried more than once to put anything over on Chevalier, and he was idolized by pilots and men alike.

In addition to the little fighting planes, all the other equipment for the Escadrille was brand-new as well, from the fifteen battleship-gray Fiat trucks to the office, armory and rest tents.

Including the mechanics, chauffeurs, armorers, motorcyclists, telephonists, wireless operators, Red Cross stretcher-bearers, clerks and orderlies, there was a nonflying personnel of seventy-odd assigned to the squadron —practically ten men for every pilot. No wonder pursuit pilots felt like prima donnas!

Two regular French officers, Captain Georges Thénault and Lieutenant André de Laage de Mœux were in command. Bill Thaw, already commissioned second lieutenant on account of his previous service and brilliant exploits, was the only other officer. The remaining pilots were either sergeants or corporals.

Every volunteer in the French army started as a second-class soldier, and although on getting his brevet as a military aviator he was automatically named corporal, he had to earn the rest of his stripes. The French didn't believe in passing out commissions indiscriminately. They had to be earned either by meritorious deeds or length of service. Raoul Lufbery was the only other American volunteer to gain a French commission while serving in the Escadrille.

It was a somewhat flattering and entirely new life that opened for these pilots when they arrived at the front. During the training period, they had been subject to rules and regulations as stringent as those of any ordinary soldier in barracks. But, once at the front and assigned to regular flying duty over the lines, they received the same treatment accorded to officers, no matter what their grades. Their time was their own, outside of regular assigned duty, to do with as they pleased. There were no roll calls or other military frills. Instead of the hard chicken-wire bunks they slept on as student pilots, each man had a soft bed and was entitled to the services of an orderly.

They were treated with great respect by nonflying officers of much higher rank and, being volunteers, they were shown the greatest consideration by the extremely generous French government, who saw to it that they had the best of everything.

All the pilots messed together regardless of rank, but while stripes were forgotten, discipline was never allowed to suffer. Thénault, De Laage and the other French lieutenants who succeeded him were always cordial and

Capt. Thenault directing a lineup of Nieuport 11's at Luxeuil, May 1916. (Courtesy Paul A. Rockwell)

Nieuport 11's on the field at Luxeuil, May 1916. (Courtesy Paul A. Rockwell)

Nieuport 11's on the field at Luxeuil, May 1916.
(Courtesy Paul A. Rockwell)

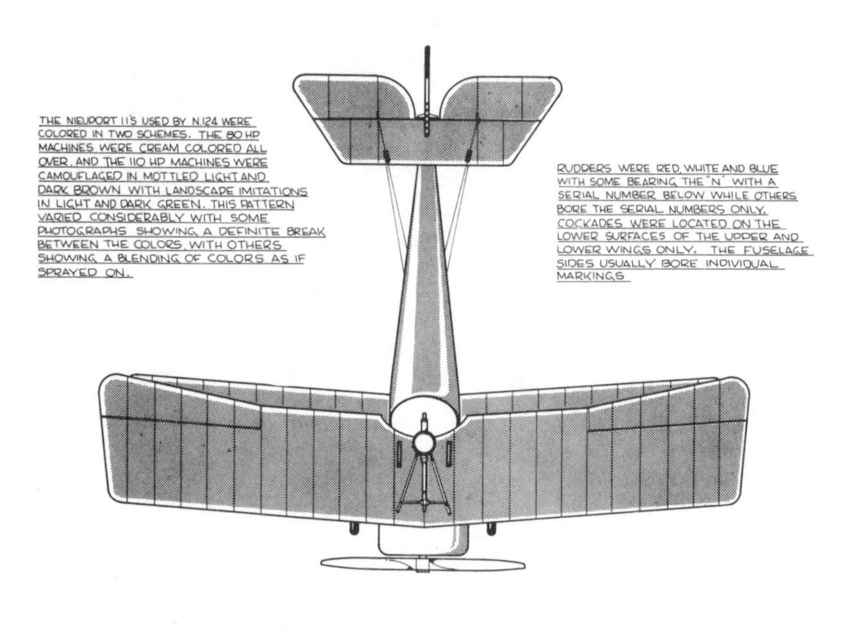
THE NIEUPORT 11'S USED BY N.124 WERE
COLORED IN TWO SCHEMES. THE 80 HP
MACHINES WERE CREAM COLORED ALL
OVER, AND THE 110 HP MACHINES WERE
CAMOUFLAGED IN MOTTLED LIGHT AND
DARK BROWN WITH LANDSCAPE IMITATIONS
IN LIGHT AND DARK GREEN. THIS PATTERN
VARIED CONSIDERABLY WITH SOME
PHOTOGRAPHS SHOWING A DEFINITE BREAK
BETWEEN THE COLORS, WITH OTHERS
SHOWING A BLENDING OF COLORS AS IF
SPRAYED ON.
RUDDERS WERE RED, WHITE AND BLUE
WITH SOME BEARING THE "N" WITH A
SERIAL NUMBER BELOW WHILE OTHERS
BORE THE SERIAL NUMBERS ONLY.
COCKADES WERE LOCATED ON THE
LOWER SURFACES OF THE UPPER AND
LOWER WINGS ONLY. THE FUSELAGE
SIDES USUALLY BORE INDIVIDUAL
MARKINGS

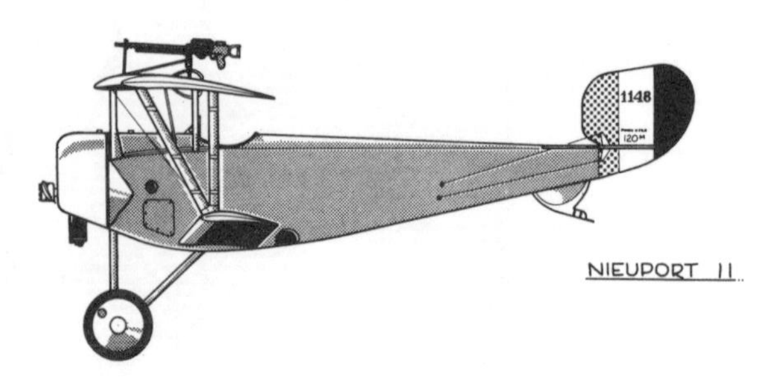
1148
120M
NIEUPORT 11

friendly, but never forgot, nor allowed us to forget, that they were our superior officers when military necessity demanded. It was a delightful combination.

At Luxeuil, the boys were quartered in a luxurious villa close to the warm baths and messed in the best hotel in town. There was always a staff car at their beck and call to carry them to the field, and while they were waiting for their planes to be completely equipped they were taken on long drives through the Vosges Mountains and on into Alsace to acquaint them with the very few places where a forced landing could be safely made in that rugged terrain. It was a war de luxe for them.

But one of the first men to whom they were introduced was the famous, black-bearded Commandant Happe of the Luxeuil bombing group, on whose head the Germans had set a price. On the desk in his quarters were eight little boxes containing medals. Proudly, but sadly, he pointed them out to the curious pilots.

"For the families of the men I lost on my last raid," he explained briefly. "I'm glad you're here. The Boches are plentiful, and we shall welcome your protection."

The boys' faces had a thoughtful look as they took their leave of the doughty commandant. Life at Luxeuil was most delightful, but it occurred to some of them that it bore a strange resemblance to the old Roman custom of fattening up the sacrifice and giving him a royal time before the appointed day.

However, this delightful life of ease was fated to be of short duration. The day following Rockwell's spectacular victory, the first and only one of the Escadrille at Luxeuil since its formation, they were ordered to Verdun. On May 19, the night before they left, the Germans flew over and delivered a few packages of farewell gifts. Four tractors were destroyed and six men were killed. It aroused the boys to fighting pitch, and they were determined to square accounts in their new sector.

On May 20 they were installed on their new field on top of a large hill overlooking the Meuse Valley and the town of Bar-le-Duc. A magnificent villa halfway between the town and the flying field was assigned to them for living quarters. On the ground it was still a war de luxe.

But as they took their place on the schedule with other fighting units, each of which had its specified flying hours, rotating so that there was always an *escadrille de chasse* over the lines, the boys began to get a real taste of war in the air.

They began to come in closer contact, too, with the tremendous scale of operations on the ground. Even as far behind the actual battle lines as Bar-le-Duc, they could sense their proximity to a vast military operation, which later proved to be one of the greatest battles of history. The endless convoys of motor lorries and horse-drawn vehicles, the never-ceasing flow of horizon-blue-clad troops and the distressing number of ambulances brought realization of the near presence of a gigantic struggle.

Shortly after the Escadrille's arrival at Verdun, they were joined by Raoul Lufbery, who was shortly to become the first American ace and one of the most tragically outstanding figures of the war in the air. To me, Luf was one of the greatest mysteries of the war. No man alive can truthfully say that he knew him. I ate, slept, drank and fought beside him for months on end. I discussed combat tactics and played bridge and went on binges with him. He saved my hide once when I was a very green young

View of the field at Behonne, near the town of Bar-le-Duc. Chouteau Johnson's Nieuport 11 in background.
(Courtesy Paul A. Rockwell)

Left to right: Didier Masson, Stephen Bigelow, Chouteau Johnson, William Dugan and Raoul Lufbery. (Courtesy Paul A. Rockwell)

Chouteau Johnson in his Nieuport 11 equipped with anti-balloon rockets. (Courtesy Paul A. Rockwell)

Raoul Lufbery in his Nieuport 17 C.1 at Behonne, Winter 1916-17. (Courtesy Soubiran Collection)

The Lafayette Escadrille at Behonne, July 1916. Left to right: Lt. de Laage de Mœux, Chouteau Johnson, Lawrence Rumsey, James McConnell, William Thaw, Raoul Lufbery, Kiffin Rockwell, Didier Masson, Norman Prince and Bert Hall. (Courtesy Paul A. Rockwell)

pilot, and in grateful appreciation, through carelessness, I very nearly caused him to be brought down some months later.

I was in daily contact with a figure of flesh and blood, but know him? Not a chance. In contrast to him, the Sphinx was a child's primer. He kept his real self shut up like a clam in a shell. He was a man seemingly devoid of fear or, in fact, emotion of any kind. But what a man he was in the air! He had forgotten more about combat flying than most men ever knew.

Broad forehead, deep-set eyes, squat, chunky figure just a trifle over five feet six and muscles of steel. He rarely ever talked, but when he did, it was with a strange accent that had traces of every nationality with which he had been in contact. Where he went, what he did, what lay behind that broad forehead and those inscrutable eyes, no one ever knew. I only know one certain thing about him. Raoul Lufbery flew, fought and died for revenge.

Luf was born in France, but when he was just a little shaver his mother died and his father remarried, emigrating to America and leaving Raoul with his grandparents. After a very brief schooling, Luf became innoculated with the wanderlust bug, and the dust of many countries rested on his shoes. He had been almost everywhere and done almost everything. One had but to mention a place, no matter how remote, to find that Luf had been there, absorbed a considerable amount of the national drink, knew the mayor (Luf had a penchant for knowing mayors and mayor's daughters intimately) and was a walking meteorological chart on flying conditions, prevailing winds and when bad weather might set in.

He had been a sailor in the German merchant marine,

waited on table in a Greek restaurant, soldiered in the Philippines with the United States army, collected customs duties for the Chinese and taken tickets on the Indian railways.

In the midst of his wanderings, he made a visit to Wallingford, Conn., where he expected to find his father. Fate was against him. Unwarned of his son's imminent arrival, the elder Lufbery had departed on a visit to France just a few hours prior, and their paths were never again fated to cross.

After a few months' employment in Wallingford, Raoul again yielded to his itching feet, and it was while he was in Calcutta, out of a job, that he met the man who was to shape his entire future life.

It was 1912, and the daring French aviator, Marc Pourpe, with a flying partner, was giving exhibition flights with an old Blériot. Luf had always been interested in aviation, ever since the pioneer days of the Wrights. He rushed out to the field to greet the intrepid flyer and satisfy his curiosity. He found Pourpe in all sorts of difficulties, trying to erect a hangar with coolie labor.

Luf immediately proffered his experienced services, which were gratefully accepted, and by dint of a liberal use of harsh language, profanity (of which he was a past master) and hard work, Luf and the coolies got the hangar up on time.

From that time on, Pourpe and Lufbery were inseparable. They were a living reincarnation of Damon and Pythias. Pourpe became enshrined in Luf's heart. To him, he gave all the affectionate worship of the father who had been denied him all his life.

When Pourpe's flying partner was killed in an accident

and his mechanic became ill and returned to France, Pourpe broke in Luf as his mechanic, and for the next two years they traveled throughout India and the Orient, having all sorts of glorious adventures.

Luf was always reticent, but once in a while, under the warming stimulus of wine, when the hangar yarns were flying, he would unbend and give us just a peep into the past. I think one of the few times I ever saw him laugh was the night he told us of their narrowest escape.

They were in a small Chinese village. Pourpe had just given an exhibition, and after examining the Blériot, the Chinese decided their reputations as master kite builders were endangered. They constructed an exact reproduction of bamboo sticks and gaudy paper. It soared through the air beautifully, but it lacked one essential detail. It would not sing.

Since nothing but an exact copy would satisfy them, they filled a large box full of angry bees and attached it to their model. It made a splendid buzzing sound close at hand, but their infantile brains failed to comprehend why it wouldn't make the same noise in the air as the musical box on the kite of the foreign devils. They became enraged and credited the white men with sorcery. Several hotheads suggested killing the sorcerers and taking possession of the evil kite. Warned by a friendly servant, Pourpe and Luf were forced to make an indecently hurried exit from the village, barely eluding the savage mob howling for their blood.

Then came Pourpe's epic flight from Cairo to Khartoum in Egypt and return. Lufbery followed or preceded him on every stage of the journey, traveling by Nile steamers and cargo rafts, on camels and donkeys, by train and many times on foot, with his tools and a little food on his back.

In the summer of 1914 they returned to France to get a new plane, and while they were there war was declared. Both immediately enlisted, Pourpe as a military aviator and Luf as his mechanic.

Then, one day, Pourpe failed to return from a flight over the lines. He met his death in one of the first air battles of the war. Luf received the news with stoic calm, but he was burning up inside. There existed no doubt in his mind as to his course of action. He swore a great oath of savage, unrelenting vengeance and, as the first step toward his goal, applied for and immediately received a transfer to a military school for pilots.

He learned to fly quickly and was first assigned to a Voison bombardment squadron. In this nerve-racking work in the slow-flying, unwieldy old crates that so much resembled flying baby buggies, he acquitted himself nobly, but it was only a means to an end. It offered few, if any, chances for personal contact with the hated enemy. Luf demanded a transfer to pursuit. His commanding officer, loath to relinquish a good bombing pilot, approved the request only after a long and passionate appeal, in which Luf's desire for revenge played a prominent part.

Then occurred a curious (in view of later developments) paradox. Luf was a complete failure as a student on the tricky little pursuit ships. He was heavy-handed and cracked them up regularly. His instructors despaired of him, said he would never make a pursuit pilot and tried to send him back to bombing. Luf fought for further chances and clung to it with dogged determination. He gritted his teeth and in the face of all opposition overcame his deficiencies and became a complete master of acrobatics and combat flying.

It was unquestionably the burning urge for revenge which aided him to overcome every obstacle to fulfill it, for, aside from that, every other emotion in Luf seemed to have died with Pourpe, leaving only the empty shell. Certain it is that he showed no affection for anyone else.

Without exaggeration, those of us who flew and fought with him and appreciated his dexterity believe that few could equal and none surpass him. His air work was incomparable. It didn't come easily, for he wasn't a natural-born flyer. He gradually and literally "pulled himself up by his bootstraps" till he became the master craftsman. Then his plane became a part of himself, a thing that can be said of but few airmen. He flew as the bird flies, without any thought of how it was done. His record of seventeen official victories is impressive, but it represents only a fractional part of his actual destruction. Many of his combats and victories took place so far back of the enemy lines that no official confirmation was possible. With his plane showing the evidences of a savage leaden duel, the lone eagle would glide down from the cloud-flecked skies, make a terse report, and that would be the end. He cared little for the credit, but there was certainly an inner satisfaction that he must have felt, but never showed, that he had chalked up another victim of his vengeance.

When he himself "went west" in a blaze of glory, he was the oldest American pilot on the front and one of the greatest of all aces. His name glows in fiery letters across the pages of history with those of Guynemer, Fonck, Bishop, Barker and Richthofen.

He had no particular method of attack. He flew alone

a great deal and waited patiently for opportunities. He not only waited for them but worked for them as well. Except in emergencies, when he gave or accepted combat he was in the most favorable position.

Having been a mechanic, he gave his motors his personal attention. He spent hours at the butts, firing and regulating his guns, so there would be no jams. He had his cartridges triple calibrated, thus eliminating to the greatest possible extent the chances of an oversized shell case sticking in the breech block.

In a patrol, Luf was always on the job, and many a youngster like myself has him to thank for his continued existence. He had a happy faculty of being on the spot at the right moment to rescue some unhappy buzzard who had gotten himself into a jam. His cool head, steady nerve and unerring aim were worth a whole squadron.

Ofttimes sacrificing a sure kill of his own, with his uncanny faculty for watching everything that transpired in a dog fight, he'd swoop through the lead-filled sky to some isolated spot where a desperate youngster was waging a losing fight. Making a lightning decision as to his best method of attack, he would dart here, there and everywhere, till it seemed as if the whole sector were full of Lufbery-piloted planes. Twisting and turning in a succession of amazing acrobatics, firing a short burst at one, then another, he bewildered and confounded the enemy hornets. No odds were too great in an emergency.

Luf joined the Escadrille on the 24th of May 1916, but it was not until July 30 that he scored his first official victory in a single-handed combat to the east of Etain on the Verdun sector. Flushed with success, he went out again late the same day and, in almost the identical spot, scored

Raoul Lufbery after a fight over the Verdun sector.
(Courtesy Paul A. Rockwell)

Raoul Lufbery and his Spad 7. (Courtesy Paul A. Rockwell)

a second victory, the first double ever recorded in the annals of the French army!

Day after day he haunted the lines, returning only when his fuel was exhausted or not a bullet remained in his drums. He was a vengeful terror of the skyways. But on the ground he was as phlegmatic as a carved Buddha. He showed very little elation in victory and no disappointment in defeat. He was apparently without fear or imagination. Death held no terrors for him.

However, he was no phantom of the air. Many times he came back from a hard combat with his ship a bullet-ridden sieve. Sometimes he had gotten his quarry, more often not. He complained bitterly that he thought the Germans were either armor plated or using sky hooks to stay up with, for when he had filled them full of lead they still refused to fall.

During his remorseless hunt, he encountered the first of the great German aces, Oswald Boelcke. They engaged in a desperate hand-to-hand struggle. Roaring through the heavens, these two masters of the craft poured deadly streams of hot lead into each other. Back and forth, up and down, around and around they thundered in great surges of speed. Red-hot gun barrels spewed out a ceaseless stream of deadly, leaden death. Black holes appeared in Luf's wings, wires twanged as they snapped, and struts vanished like magic in thin air. Two bullets went through Luf's flying suit and one through his fur-lined boot.

They fought to the point of exhaustion, till every slug had been fired—then, with gestures of mutual respect, they parted.

His whole ship quivering with the strain and threatening to fold up at any minute from the mortal wounds it had received, Luf tenderly nursed it back to the field. As he sat it down on the tarmac, the strain was too much, and the shattered, bullet-riddled plane collapsed under him.

Shooting down an enemy plane in those early days was no mean feat. The pivoted Lewis gun on the top wing was exposed to the full blast of the propeller slipstream. Owing to the wind pressure on the drum, jams were frequent and ofttimes permanent. To hold a vibrating, bucking ship steady on a long power dive or in acrobatics, meanwhile trying to aim and fire a gun on a darting target, required the craftsmanship of a magician.

Despite these handicaps, Luf scored another victory on August 4, the enemy plane falling at Abancourt, near Verdun. On August 8, he shot down an Aviatik, which fell in flames near the Fort de Douaumont. Meanwhile, before he obtained his fifth official victory on October 12, he had several more successful fights so far back of the German lines that there was no possibility of confirmation, but which were undoubted losses to the German Air Corps. He was certainly beginning to get a full measure of revenge for Pourpe.

With his fifth victory, he took his place among the immortal air heroes of France and America, for he was the first American ace, a distinguished representative on the pitifully small contemporary roster of aces.

Unless an enemy plane was brought down on our side of the lines, requirements for confirmation in the French army were exceedingly strict and most difficult to obtain. It was the only army requiring three impartial witnesses to the successful conclusion of a combat. Even the testimony of your squadron mates wasn't considered as anything but additional proof. Reports and confirmations had to come from balloon and ground observers, and weather conditions or any number of other reasons might have hampered visual substantiation of the outcome. One of the main reasons for such a strict ruling, I presume, was that about 75 per cent of the French pilots were non-commissioned officers, while in other armies practically the entire flying personnel were officers. As such, their commissions stated that they were gentlemen. Since a gentleman does not falsify, their doubtless sincere, but frequently erroneous claims were not to be questioned. Hence the French scores didn't mount to such staggering totals, but every one was an established and fully witnessed victory.

In his consuming passion to destroy enemy planes, Luf had many narrow escapes. One of his closest was on the day he got his fifth official. It was while he and other members of the Escadrille were acting as protection escort for the first big concentrated daylight bombing raid made by the French and English on the Mauser factories at Oberndorf on October 12. Single-handed, Luf attacked and brought down a three-place Aviatik.

It was a hard nut to crack. He was under fire from practically every angle. The Germans in the triplace were flushed with victory. They had just brought down a Voison bomber and considered themselves impregnable. Through a lashing hail of bullets, Luf sliced calmly under the tail and ripped a line of lead up the belly of the big ship. High above, a protecting Fokker spotted the audacious lone eagle and sliced down on him in a screaming dive.

Lead sang a mournful dirge in his ears; his Nieuport staggered from the shock of direct hits, but through it all Luf held his difficult and dangerous position.

Holding his dancing plane steady with his left hand, he pointed the muzzle of the Lewis high and, with fingers frozen to the trigger, fired a full rouleau without a jam. The forward gunner couldn't get his Maxims into range, but all this time Luf was under a savage, devastating fire from both the rear gunner of the Aviatik and the Fokker pursuit pilot.

As his unerring aim ripped up and down the length of the Aviatik's fuselage, the rear gunner folded up in his cockpit like a closed jackknife, and at the thirtieth bullet the head of the pilot fell forward, lolling grotesquely on his chest.

The Aviatik listed and fell off on a wing. It slipped a few hundred feet and snapped into a tailspin, whirling with ever-increasing speed. A thousand feet below, one wing, then a second tore off and floated away. The stripped fuselage of the great ship plummeted to earth like a rock.

Holding his stick between his knees, Luf stood up in full view of the anxious Fokker pilot and changed his empty drum for a full one. Then he turned and attacked the Fokker with savage fury. For a few seconds the German made a futile attempt to fight back. Luf got on his tail and hosed a steady stream of flaming lead at him.

The Fritz couldn't stand the pressure, got panicky and, standing his ship on its nose, dived full power into his own lines, happy to have escaped annihilation. Luf made no attempt to follow. He had another job to carry through. He calmly ground up to continue the protection of the bombers and escort them safely back across the lines.

When he landed at Luxeuil, there were four neat bullet holes in his instrument panel, two on each side of his body, so perfectly in alignment that a deflection of a fraction of an inch either way would have put them squarely into his brave heart. Luf always said that he was glad he didn't take a deep breath at the wrong time. In addition, there were twenty-two more neat holes stitched in his wings and fuselage.

So it can well be seen that Luf was no wizard. His success was simply the result of great care and forethought, plus hard plugging and brilliant piloting developed through hundreds of hours of grueling flying and, overshadowing all, a burning ambition.

He received many decorations and citations, but of them all, the finest tribute was given him at this time in his citation for the Médaille Militaire, the most prized and the most difficult to win of all French decorations. It read as follows:

> LUFBERY, RAOUL, SERGEANT PILOT OF ESCADRILLE N-124
> Model of skill, of sang-froid, of courage. Has distinguished himself by long-range bombardments and daily combats in which he has engaged enemy planes. The 31st of July, he did not hesitate to attack at close range a group of four enemy planes. Brought down one of them in close proximity to our lines. Succeeded in bringing down a second the 4th of August. This citation carries with it the Croix de Guerre with palm.
>
> [Signed] JOFFRE.

One of the finest of all Luf's qualities was his simplicity. He knew, of course, that he was a national hero. The papers, both in France and America, were full of his exploits. There was seldom a *prise d'armes* at the aerodrome when he was not one of the pilots to be decorated. But he never boasted or took credit to himself. He counted his success as three fourths luck and was always surprised that so much of it should come his way. He disliked flattery, even though he had to take a lot of it. It had no unfortunate effect on him. He was always the same old Luf.

But, outstanding as Luf's exploits were, each one of the other boys was doing his full share to put America on the air map of the war.

CHAPTER VIII

Bill Thaw, Iron Man

FOLLOWING Lufbery to the Escadrille came Chouteau Johnson and Clyde Balsley, who had been night flying on the Paris Air Guard, a nasty job. In fair weather or foul, night after night, one heard them circling the staggering old Voisons over the city, guarding against possible enemy air raiders.

In utter blackness, with their slow old crates, their success in repelling attacks would have been more or less questionable, but by their very presence they instilled a feeling of security in the hearts of the French people.

A few days later came Dudley Hill, Didier Masson, Larry Rumsey and Paul Pavelka. It was an audacious and formidable aggregation who took up the gauntlet against the enemy over the inferno that was Verdun.

From the Argonne Forest to the S bend in the Meuse River in which nestled the shell-torn city of Verdun and on to the broad plains of the Woevre ran a desolate, wide brown band that only a short time previous had been a peaceful French countryside adorned with farms, villages and verdant forests.

There, Nature had been ruthlessly murdered. Every sign of humanity had been swept away. Roads had vanished, and forests were fire-blackened stumps. Villages were gray smears where stone walls were tumbled together. Only the faintest outlines of the great forts of Douaumont and Vaux could be traced against the churned-up background. It was impossible to distinguish any separate shell crater, for they were so closely interlocked that they merely blended into a great mass of troubled earth. Only broken, half-obliterated links of the trenches were visible.

Over it all hung a constant pall of smoke rising to an altitude of more than a thousand feet, fed continuously by new columns as high explosives tore deeper into this ulcerated area.

Except for the throbbing overtone of the great guns, felt rather than heard, the Verdun battle seen from the skies was a weird combination of stillness and destruction, for in a plane practically all noises are deadened by the sound of the motor.

In green patches on each side of the brown belt myriads of tiny flashes told where the guns were hidden; and those flashes and the smoke of the bursting shells were all that could be seen of the titanic struggle on the ground.

However, as they began to cover themselves and the name of the American Escadrille with glory, the boys had little time for sight-seeing or worry as to what was going on below them.

Hardly had they arrived at Bar-le-Duc when Bert Hall scored the second victory for the Escadrille by crashing a German two-seater observation plane, and Bill Thaw started to build his iron-man reputation.

I can never speak of or write about Bill without a certain feeling of awe, amounting almost to reverence. I am certainly proud to have been his flying mate and his friend.

William Thaw (Courtesy Paul A. Rockwell)

The desolation of Verdun from the air, 1916.

When the gods that be finished making Bill, they broke the mold.

He went through the whole bloody business right from the beginning, always in active service, part of the time in the trenches as a common poilu, the remainder as a war bird on the wing. He raised himself, by dashing service and glorious exploits, to lieutenant colonel, and with this exalted rank he covered himself with glory and achieved practically every decoration in the power of the grateful Allied nations to bestow. He never lost, except by death, a friend once made, man, woman or child. With a magnificent record he emerged from that seething caldron without a trace of swelled head, still just "plain ole Bill." It is hard to write about Bill Thaw without becoming maudlin.

As with whisky and soda or ham and eggs, one must associate Bill Thaw and the Escadrille. Their names are practically synonymous. Thaw was the only American to be with the Escadrille from the day of its inception to the time it passed into history, transferred from the French army and lost its identity in the American army under the official title of 103rd Pursuit Squadron.

Most of the time he was in practical, if not nominal, command and handled with unfailing tact and good humor one of the toughest jobs ever thrown on the shoulders of one man. It is reasonable to suppose, since he seemed to be doing all right before there was any such thing, that he could have gotten along without the Escadrille. But most certainly the Escadrille could never have gotten along without Bill. Many times he must have been seething inside, but he never showed it. He made a brilliant success of a job where most men would have gone mad.

Thaw's experiences as an aviator started long before

the war, when getting into the air was considered quite a feat and staying there came under the general heading of miracles. He owned a Curtiss flying boat which was just about able to stagger off the water if all conditions were just right. He did considerable flying around Southampton, his summer home on Long Island Sound, while he was still a student at Yale.

One day he suddenly decided to fly to Atlantic City. With another trusting youth as passenger, he pulled the rackety old plane off the water and confidently started down the East River. The ancient crate would never at any time make much altitude, and on this day in particular Bill was making heavy weather of it. However, everything went fairly well until suddenly the Williamsburgh Bridge loomed up out of the mist. Bill tried to pull her up and over, but he had no time. He saw he was never going to clear the bridge. So he did the next best thing and flew under it, probably the first man to fly under a bridge in any kind of a plane. Doubtless he was full of jitters, for there were less than inches to spare, but I'll wager he didn't show it. His passenger would never have known that it wasn't the most usual thing in the world; that flying under bridges wasn't a daily appetizer for Bill.

That was characteristic of Thaw. No matter what his private emotions might have been, he never showed perturbation. Nor did he allow obstacles to stand in his way. He simply ignored them. It was just that quality in him that made him one of the world's greatest diplomats. While he outranked every other American in the French army, no one was made to feel it. He was only twenty-three at the time, as young or younger than most of the men under his command. But his physical appearance, his keen judg-

Left to right: Robert Soubiran, Courtney Campbell, Kenneth Marr, William Thaw, unidentified, and David Peterson. Chaudun, July 1917. (Courtesy Paul A. Rockwell)

William Thaw's Spad 7 on the left, and Didier Masson's on the right. Chaudun, 1917. (Courtesy Paul A. Rockwell)

William Thaw and the lion cub, Whiskey. Paris, September 1916. (Courtesy Paul A. Rockwell)

ment, his tactful handling of men and situations all contributed to our acknowledgment of his fitness and right to be in the driver's seat.

Bill has never received the credit he deserved. He was in hot water most of the time. On one side were the high ranking officers of the French army, men with tons of gold braid, strict disciplinarians, fired with patriotic fervor and the best traditions of an army life which was their career. Men with a totally different language, background, customs and ideals to the bunch of grousing, hard-boiled, hell-raising adventurers that composed the Escadrille, to whom discipline was just another word to be found somewhere in the dictionary. No wonder there were clashes!

According to the French brass hats, all Americans were slightly "teched in the haid." The best proof was our being in a war where we had no business, and most of our daily doings seemed to bear out their contentions. But they also assumed that, since we were in their army, we should be subject to the same rules and course of conduct to which they were subjected.

We were as far apart as the poles, and it was Bill's superhuman task to act as a buffer and maintain some sort of cohesion and co-operation.

He was a burly brute with a splendid physique, thick black hair, snapping black eyes and a pair of flowing mustachios which were the pride of his heart. When they were waxed, Bill looked every inch the dapper officer, but when, as more often happened, they drooped, Bill had the benign air of a venerable walrus. With his quiet smile and surprisingly soft voice, Thaw could shove the applesauce down our throats and make us like it.

We took every advantage possible of our position. Any

buzzard who didn't overstay his leave by at least twenty-four hours was a sissy. Bill was constantly on the jump, squaring us with the brass hats; settling squabbles among the boys resulting from strained nerves or too much cougar milk; restraining some peevish egg from biting off the captain's ear by promising to do it himself when he found a spare moment; representing the Escadrille at reviews at the front or flag-waving affairs in Paris.

These last two jobs fell on him for two reasons. He was the head man in our outfit, and he was about the only one who had a regulation uniform. The rest of us went in for musical-comedy-style aviation uniforms, fearful and wonderful to behold; guaranteed to knock the not-too-difficult little mademoiselles right square on their backs. While the uniforms were entirely successful in their chosen purpose, they were hardly the thing for official inspections and always a bone of contention.

In addition to his diplomatic work, Bill's life was anything but monotonous. His days were full and most of his nights. He had to attend official conferences on tactics where he was the only American present. His squadron activities were numerous. Banking a roulette game, playing poker, keeping up with his drinking and incidentally taking out patrols of ambitious young eagles far into the Boche lines and knocking down plenty of the black-crossed ships.

Then there were his personally conducted tours of the front-line trenches when bad weather made flying impossible. He never forgot his comrades in the Legion, and whenever we were anywhere near the same sector Bill would gather up a gang of pilots, load up with cigarettes and hootch, grab off the light car and away we'd go. Sometimes we hunted in vain for long hours to find the regiment, but we always had the cigarettes and liquor, and it was about the only way some of us ever got to see what the war on the ground was all about.

On one of his trips, walking through the trenches, a dirty little figure in mud-stained horizon blue walked up and saluted.

"How are you, Lieutenant?" he rasped. "Remember me?"

Bill tried his best to pierce through the disguising mass of mud and sadly shook his head.

"Why, Bill, I'm Percy. Don't you remember the time you lost your belt and I had to lend you mine so you could stand inspection?"

Recollection dawned on Bill, and he grasped the hand of the little West Indian Negro in a grip of real friendship.

"Say, Bill, I'm awful fed up with this trench stuff, and my rheumatism is giving me hell. Can't you do something?"

Thaw went into conference with himself and emerged with a brilliant idea.

"Sure, Percy," he promised. "I'll fix it."

Bill was a fixer. He went to Percy's commanding officer and, working very diplomatically, then and there got Percy a transfer to the Escadrille as his own personal orderly.

Percy was absolutely devoted to Bill, and Bill's wants were always paramount, but he was most congenial with everyone and was always willing to lend a hand to put someone to bed. He was a splendid addition to the squadron personnel.

We never questioned Bill's decisions. We knew he'd give us better than an even break. We didn't squawk or alibi with him. His word was law, not because he was our superior officer, but because he was Bill. We would have been quick to resent the idea that a gold stripe gave him the right to lord it over us and get tough. It was a blind faith, and we did the things he said whether we liked it or not.

However, there wasn't anything paternal about Bill. He didn't try to reform us or guide our erring footsteps. On the contrary, if there was any drinking or gambling, he wanted to be in on it. If there wasn't anything doing, he'd start something. He didn't care where you went or what you did or how much you drank, just so you could show up for patrols and at least make a pretense of getting into the air.

Many times, through a dim haze, I have seen Bill led off to bed leaning heavily on Percy's shoulder at two o'clock in the morning when he was scheduled for a show at four. In the gray dawn, eyes red rimmed, and weaving a bit on unsteady legs, he'd be on his way to the hangars with a cheerful grin and an encouraging word for everybody, all set to hop in and lead a patrol. He would never ask anyone to do what he wouldn't do himself, and he'd do two men's work if necessary.

Thaw happened to be in Paris when the war broke out. He immediately offered his services in the aviation, but the French couldn't find any place for him, despite his previous experience. They had few military aviators and fewer ships. No one could foresee the part that aviation was to play in the next four years.

Bill was determined to get into the war, so he did the next best thing. With twenty-nine other adventurous

Americans, including Jimmy Bach and Bert Hall, he enlisted in the Foreign Legion. His regiment was sent to the front in every spot where the fighting was hottest. Death was rampant in a multitude of forms. It was cold, it was muddy, it was vermin infested. Second-class Soldat Thaw got what is technically known as a bellyful.

He had never given up the idea of flying. One day, when the Legion was in a rest area, Thaw, Bach and Hall got permission to visit the nearest aviation field. On it was the D-6, one of the first organized squadrons on the front. These hardy birdmen were flying the Deperdussin monoplane, a two-seater with an eighty-horsepower Gnome rotary engine. It was the fastest ship in service, capable of between eighty and ninety miles an hour with a good tail wind and a six-thousand-foot ceiling.

They contacted the officer in charge, Lieutenant Brocard. Brocard was the ultimate type of French gentleman. He later became the head man of all French aviation and proved himself a marvelous friend to all Americans. The three boys asked for his help in getting out of the Legion and into aviation. Brocard promised to do what he could. As a result, some weeks later, Bach and Hall were transferred, but no orders came for Bill.

He worried terribly, so much so that he sought and obtained permission to revisit the D-6. His regiment had moved, and Bill had to walk the thirty-two kilometers there and back. Nothing could have been so conclusive a proof of his earnest desire to become a military aviator, for Thaw's love of less exhausting modes of travel was almost a religion with him. To walk from the barracks to the hangars was almost more than he could bear, and if they weren't right beside each other, he generally found a means of conveyance. The lack of taxis at the front he considered as one of the hardships of the war. I have no desire to create the impression that Bill was lazy. Far from it. He simply wanted to conserve energy for more important outlets.

Lieutenant Brocard again gave an ear to Bill's pleas and heated up the wires to Paris. As a result, less than a month later Thaw was transferred from the Legion to the Escadrille D-6 as a *soldat mitrailleur* (soldier machine gunner).

The "soldier" part was all right, but the "machine gunner" was anticipating just a little. They hadn't even begun to mount machine guns in planes at that time. Observers took up a rifle, revolver or even bricks. While reconnaissances and raids over enemy territory were exciting enough with the possibility of a duel at close range, the casualty list was very low.

Picture standing up in a bucking, vibrating plane tearing along at eighty miles an hour, trying to aim a rifle or throw a brick at another fellow, passing at the same speed, with any idea of hitting him. All just in the spirit of good clean fun, particularly as it was always questionable as to how long a ship would stay in the air. Valves froze, motors caught fire, connecting rods broke and oil lines plugged up, freezing the motors. All sorts of unusual and unexpected accidents occurred, so that every flight had all the zest of pioneering. There was nothing monotonous about any flight. It didn't really need the final touch of machine guns to make it exciting.

Quite frequently the Germans and French would circle around each other for an hour or more, directing batteries and taking observations, occasionally taking a pop shot at one another just to keep up the interest and then part with an airy wave of the hands.

There wasn't enough action in it to suit Bill, and he soon got fed up with being just a passenger. With his customary tact, he soon convinced the gold braids that they were losing an unparalleled opportunity by not letting him pilot. He was sent to the St Cyr aviation school to demonstrate his ability.

Although his piloting experience had been confined to hydroplanes, Bill told them that he was a master hand at any type of ship. He inspired confidence to such an extent that they soloed him immediately on the old Caudron G-2, the flying chicken coop, considered as a very speedy ship and exceedingly difficult to handle.

He got away with it in great shape and before long was taking up officer student observers. With their sublime ignorance of flying, they thought he knew all about it and put blind faith in his ability. They never knew how scared he was, and no one ever had any cause to doubt that he knew all he claimed to know.

This was in March 1915, and Bill was raised to the exalted grade of corporal pilot. Simultaneously, Norman Prince was beginning to get some definite reactions from the French war ministry towards the formation of a squadron of American volunteer airmen. There were six men available, which at that time was the ordinary flying personnel of an escadrille. Thaw was one of the six to be ordered to Pau for further training.

But Bill was altogether too smart. He had been long enough in the French army to know that dilatory tactics and the inevitable paper work were the delight of army administration. He had no desire to be mired in the rear areas, no matter how charming the spot.

He pulled a lot of wires and got an immediate transfer to the C-42, an escadrille of Caudrons in active service, commanded by Captain Thénault, who was destined a year later to take command of the American Escadrille. Thus Thaw, with the exception of Lufbery, was far ahead of every other American in flying at the front.

The C-42 was stationed at Nancy, and while Bill was with it he flew across the lines in every type of old crate in service. He was the first one to take across the twin-motored Caudron G-4, scathingly referred to as the "Flying Bathtub."

By May 1915 he was named a sergeant and cited once in army and twice in divisional orders for his exceptional courage. Most of his jobs were long-distance observation flights at low altitudes. While the planes weren't so hot, the enemy gunners on the ground didn't seem to lack much in ambition or skill. While trying unsuccessfully to end it definitely, they succeeded in making life fairly miserable for Bill.

One of his narrowest escapes came while he was taking his observer, Lieutenant Felix, on a long trip into Germany to get some absolutely vital information. The Boches seemed equally determined that he shouldn't get it, or at least get back with it. It appeared as if every battery on the front were directed against his ship. He flew for more than two hours through a perfect storm of shrapnel and, miraculously, neither he nor Lieutenant Felix was even touched. The devil must have had his arms around them both, for most of the fabric of the plane was in ribbons, four struts were completely carried away and two separate wires to the elevator hung by a single strand. The ship had to be junked on his return. It was so completely destroyed that repair was impossible.

Through this veritable inferno, Bill returned twice to his objective, fully expecting every minute that the plane would fall to pieces. They obtained all the information they sought and, by a feat of magnificent piloting, Bill was able to bring the wrecked ship back and land himself and his observer unharmed. He received the first of his many citations for bravery for this exploit.

His service with the C-42 lasted a full year, and in reward for his courageous and brilliant work he was made a *sous lieutenant* (second lieutenant), the first American to be so honored.

Then in April 1916 he was ordered with the six other Americans to Luxeuil to form the squadron for which he had worked so hard and long. There, for the first time, he learned to fly a Nieuport, but it wasn't till the Escadrille moved to Bar-le-Duc that he really began to strut his stuff.

May 24 was one of his busiest days and one that didn't conclude quite as he would have wished. Early in the morning he got separated from the formation with which he was flying. Hoping to locate them, he flew up and down the sector over the Meuse where they had been ordered to maintain an offensive patrol.

Suddenly he discovered another plane a few hundred feet below him that had mysteriously materialized out of the great open spaces. He started to go down and join forces, but decided on the way down that it might pay him to be a little cautious and see who the lone eagle was.

He swung around with the sun to his back, and as he

warily approached he discovered to his astonishment that the other plane was a Fokker. The Boche pilot discovered about the same time that Bill was no friend of his. He made a quick bank and fired a few rounds at Thaw.

Apparently it was only a warning, for the firing ceased, but the sound of whining lead around his ears had roused Bill's anger. He proceeded in a workmanlike manner to surround the Fokker, stitch his initials in the black-crossed wings and write his full name up and down the fuselage.

The jerry pilot fired a few more shots, but he wasn't doing himself a bit of good and, extremely disconcerted, he attempted to make a getaway. Bill continued to surround him and gave him the full works. Despite the frantic efforts of the enemy flyer, Bill sank nearly a full Lewis rouleau into the quivering ship and literally blasted him out of the sky. The Fokker, with a dead man at the controls, crashed in our lines near Douaumont.

It sounds fairly easy, but considering that Bill had to fly the erratic little Nieuport with one hand and aim the Lewis gun on the top wing with the other, meanwhile trying to keep a very scared but acrobatic-minded Hun in his sights, it becomes a real exploit. Thaw was plenty proud of his first official victory for the squadron, but he was no man to sit back and take bows.

He had tasted the thrill of battle, found it good and wanted more of it immediately. So he went out again that same afternoon and got himself in a swell mess. At about thirteen thousand feet, he found three Fokkers. If they saw him, they paid no attention to him, feeling secure in their numbers. Thaw laid out a plan of attack. He had no qualms of uneasiness as to the outcome. He had already put one Fokker away that day. His theory was that if one is easy, three ought to be three times as easy. There was where he made his mistake.

He took a little altitude and, swinging into the sun, screamed down on the three enemy planes, firing wildly. Taken by surprise and uncertain as to how many French planes were attacking them, the Fokkers dived. Doing his utmost to imitate a whole patrol in action, Bill drove them down to three thousand feet in their lines.

Then the Germans suddenly awakened as to what all the shooting was about. They had him where they wanted him. They turned and commenced a mass attack on Bill. They got him in a cross fire and hosed lead at him from all angles. It wasn't at all according to the schedule that Bill had laid out. He attempted to bow out gracefully and concede the field, but there was a wide divergence of opinion. Every way he turned, a snubby-nosed enemy poured flaming lead at him. Fortunately most of it missed him altogether or passed harmlessly through his wings.

But the unequal struggle couldn't go on forever. A whining slug finally got him in the arm, and Bill had to let everything go and run for home. He stood on his nose in a dive that whipped the breath from his lungs.

His ship was a perfect sieve, and blood was pouring from his arm, weakening him almost to the point of exhaustion, but Bill gritted his teeth and, cussing a blue streak, landed the wavering Nieuport in back of our third-line trenches. Still cussing, but too weak to get out of the plane by himself, he was tenderly lifted down by poilus and taken to a first-aid station, where he was bandaged up and sent back to the squadron.

Most men would have gone to a hospital and stayed there till the wound healed, but not Bill. He simply refused to be made an invalid. He spent a few days in Paris, explaining in various bars how it all happened, and then came back to the Escadrille with his arm in a sling. In addition to being able to instruct the other boys what not to do when meeting three Fokkers, he became the best and probably the only temporary one-armed pilot on the front.

Whether the bone was shattered, or never properly healed, or whether it was just force of habit from crooking it so much was never made clear, but the arm never straightened out completely, and he always carried it in first drinking position.

That one day's courageous exploits again brought him a signal honor. He was cited for the Legion of Honor, the first American in the war to receive it:

Inscribed on the special lists of the Legion of Honor and the Médaille Militaire the soldier whose name follows; to take rank the 18th of June, 1916, Chevalier of the Legion of Honor:

THAW, WILLIAM, LIEUTENANT OF ESCADRILLE N-124.

A volunteer for the duration of the war. A pilot remarkable for his skill, his spirit and contempt of danger. Has recently delivered eighteen aerial combats at short distance. May 24 at daybreak he attacked and destroyed an enemy plane. The same evening he attacked a group of three German machines and pursued them from four thousand meters of altitude down to one thousand. Painfully wounded during the combat, he succeeded, thanks to his daring and his energy, in bringing into our lines his gravely damaged aeroplane and landed normally. Already twice cited in the Order of the Army. This nomination carries with it the Croix de Guerre with palm.

[Signed] ROQUES.

Thaw got about all the decorations possible. He mentions several members of Escadrille who got Médaille,

Norman Prince for one. His complete accumulation at the end of the war consisted of the Distinguished Service Cross with bronze oak leaf, Legion of Honor with rosette and the Croix de Guerre with four palms and two stars.

He should have had at least one more medal: With Lufbery, he was the inventor and chief exponent of that very dynamic concoction known as the Lafayette Cocktail. It was composed of equal parts of brandy and champagne. This soothing mixture with the kick of a mule brought him and many another good man down where the Boche failed.

Bill was without a question the most striking and popular figure on the front. There was never a dull moment in his company. No matter where we were sent, Bill had generally been in that sector before. He always knew a houseful of more or less alluring young wenches in the next village or an attractive widow who owned a château with a grand wine cellar, and he was most generous about letting his friends in on his soft spots.

It seemed as if there weren't a man, woman or child from Dunkirk to the Vosges who didn't know "Meester Beel Taw"; not only know him, but love him.

At Verdun, the various escadrilles began to adopt their individual squadron insignias, which were painted in glowing colors on each side of the fuselage of every ship belonging to the squadron. Since the Indians were the original inhabitants of America, and the American volunteers resembled them so strongly in many ways, Bill suggested as most appropriate, and was largely responsible for, the adoption of the now world-famous squadron insignia of the Escadrille Américaine: the feathered head of a yelping Indian brave in all his war paint.

In addition, each member of the Escadrille assumed the

privilege of painting on his ship his personal insignia, according to his individual artistic taste or pet superstition. Aside from the pride that each one felt in identifying himself to the enemy gentlemen across the lines by his own distinctive marking, it was frequently most helpful in the air, where identities were difficult to distingush, to know by his insignia who was with you and in what position in a patrol or a dog fight.

Thaw had a huge letter T painted in red on his upper and lower wings; someone had a pair of dice with seven up; others had their initials in various scrolls and borders, while Bert Hall produced a bizarre effect by having his name BERT in large block letters on one side of his fuselage and the name reversed on the opposite side—so, he said, that an aviator passing him on that side with great speed would be able to read the name without difficulty!

CHAPTER IX

Victor Chapman

THE SAME DAY that Thaw was wounded, Rockwell's face was badly gashed by flying shards of an explosive bullet which hit his windshield during the course of an unsuccessful combat. He refused medical treatment and kept right on flying.

Then Victor Chapman bobbed up with one of his many heroic exploits. Chapman was a big man in every way, mentally as well as physically; a man who refused to recognize such an emotion as fear; who never asked for the best of anything or demanded odds; who would attack five Germans single-handed as quickly as one; a man who did more flying than all the rest of his comrades in the Escadrille put together. From the number of his combats and his indomitable courage in attacking against almost overwhelming odds, it is a miracle that he survived as long as he did.

The habits and characteristics of men are queer things. There are all sorts and kinds of men in any organization —some good, some bad, some well liked, some despised. In an outfit like the Escadrille, with its personnel drawn from the four quarters of the world, under the stress of war's duress and living in such close companionship, these qualities became all the more noticeable.

The greater part of the American youngsters who enlisted in the French army, first in the Legion and later in aviation, did it from a spirit of pure adventure, a desire to experience new thrills, despite all the hardships and dangers and probable death that they knew were in store for them. In the Escadrille there were one or two notable exceptions—men who enlisted from a sincere desire to be of service; to give unselfishly of themselves for what they considered to be a righteous cause; actuated only by the highest motives, even though it was for a country not their own. Such men were certain to stand out among their fellows. Living, they radiated unselfish idealism. Dead, their memories were a shining example to the faltering spirits of men lacking in their strength of character.

Such a man was Victor Chapman, Foreign Legionnaire and best beloved pilot of the Escadrille Américaine. Though he fought like a fiend incarnate when it was necessary to fight, he never went native. The mantle of civilization was never stripped from him as from so many others. Despite the searing horrors of war, his artistic soul was able to see the beauty in anything: in shell-torn earth, in ruined villages, in a sea of clouds, in the stark skeletons of fire-blackened forests. Just as in humans, he saw only the best in nature and overlooked the unpleasant.

He was just six feet tall, with a finely shaped head crowned by an unruly thatch of thick black hair. Deep-set, sparkling eyes shone beneath bushy brows, while in the generous mouth white teeth flashed in a frequent friendly smile. There was a deep timbre to his heart-warming voice, sincerity in every syllable that he uttered.

He had a profound love for France and an unbreakable determination to do more than his share against the enemy.

Chapman was the great-great-grandson of John Jay, one of the signers of the Declaration of Independence. His father, Mr John Jay Chapman, the essayist and poet, has been called one of the finest writers of the English language in the United States.

Victor was graduated from Harvard in 1913 and was a student at the Beaux Arts in Paris when the war broke out. With many other Americans he immediately enlisted in the Foreign Legion as a second-class soldier. He served France in the trenches for just a year.

For over one hundred consecutive days he was in the front-line trenches as loader for a machine gun. He was slightly wounded once while half his squadron were either killed or seriously hurt. But his idealism was so strong that all the killing, the mud, filth, gore and hardships meant nothing to him. It was just a means to an end, and that end was the triumph of France over her enemies.

Hard-bitten men of every nationality and every degree of life were his constant companions, and he was a friend to all. His greatest pleasure was to be able to do something for somebody. One of the machine gunners of his squadron, a former German, sought him out one day with a sad tale. It appeared that he was afflicted with some sort of a stomach ailment which required a milk diet, and unless he could have the milk the doctors intended to evacuate him to a hospital somewhere in the rear.

The Legionnaire was a real hero and told Chapman that it would break his heart to have to leave, and he meant it. But since there was no milk obtainable in the trenches, it seemed inevitable. Chapman told the man not to worry. He'd fix it.

That same evening, after *la soupe* Victor disappeared. Some hours later his section saw him returning, dragging a full-uddered cow along behind him. He had walked many weary kilometers to find the animal.

"I bought her so that you could have your milk," he told the sick machine gunner. "Now you can stay here with us."

Most tragically, both the machine gunner and the cow were killed a week later by the explosion of a big shell.

Despite his valiant services as a soldier, Chapman didn't feel that he was doing enough for France. It all seemed pretty futile just to stay in the trenches and take occasional pop shots at the enemy with rifle or machine gun. He was much too restless and eager to get into closer contact—something where individual effort would count to a greater extent.

Thaw, Hall and Bach had long since wangled their way into aviation. Rumors were afloat of the contemplated formation of the Escadrille. Chapman decided that his future lay in the air. An opportunity came for him to transfer, and after considerable difficulty he got his commanding officer's endorsement for his request.

He was terribly disappointed not to be sent at once to a flying school. He was instead sent to the Escadrille V.B.-108 as a machine gunner and bombardier. This was one of the famous day-and-night long-distance Voison bombing squadrons. Fortunately his orders came to transfer to actual flying after he had spent but thirty days as a passenger, making only one long-distance raid on which he acquitted himself nobly.

He was sent to the military school at Avord, and on the 9th of January 1916, after taking his instructions on the old Maurice Farman, he was breveted *pilote aviateur.*

Plans for the actual formation of the Escadrille were moving with agonizing slowness, so, with Kiffin Rockwell, Victor was sent to fly Voisons in the Paris Air Guard. There he stayed until the Escadrille became a reality, and he was one of the first seven to be ordered to duty.

As soon as the machine guns were mounted on the wings of the shining little Nieuports, Victor got into the air and stayed there. Flying was all that he lived for. He'd make a two-hour patrol, come back, gas up and go off again, alone or with anyone he could wheedle into going with him.

He was the first out in the morning, the last to come in at night. He grabbed meals on the fly and got very little sleep. He had an iron constitution. He didn't know the meaning of fatigue. The captain and the other pilots tried to get him to slack up a bit, fearing that he would wear himself out, but they had no luck. He gave himself without stint.

On May 24 he was cited for the Croix de Guerre with palm for his courageous attack on three enemy planes, in the course of which his clothes were pierced by several bullets and he was slightly wounded in the arm. However, citations and medals, while he was proud of having won them, didn't mean much to Chapman except that in winning for himself he was winning for France. It was the game that counted and he played it like a sportsman.

Then, on the 17th of June, he had an extraordinary experience and an extremely narrow escape from death. In his usual fearlessly reckless way, all alone, he attacked a formation of five enemy planes: two Aviatiks, coming over to take photos, escorted by three Fokkers for protection. He saw them almost as soon as they had crossed the lines, for they were bracketed by French Archie puffs. He circled warily over their heads for a few minutes, watching for an opportunity. The Huns, secure in their numbers, paid little attention to him.

It seemed like sheer suicide for a lone eagle even to consider attacking such a formidable armada.

The demands of his work carried one of the Aviatiks a little apart from his escort and directly under the circling Nieuport. It was just what Victor had been waiting for. With the swoop of a hawk, he dived. The Lewis gun blazed a message of death. The dismayed German, warned by the bullets that etched a line of charred holes in his wing, attempted to run; to slide under the protecting wings of the Fokkers. Too late. The keen-eyed Chapman clamped a steady, nerveless finger on the trigger trip. Without a miss or a jam, forty-seven leaden messengers, a full drum, found their mark.

The Aviatik whirled crazily; shuddered like a stricken animal. With the hand of a dead man on the stick and a white-faced passenger coughing blood, it plunged to earth in long moaning sweeps.

The amazed Fokker pilots immediately got into action. As the Nieuport dived on the Aviatik, they dived on him. Maxims and Spandaus beat a deadly tattoo. One of the Fokkers was painted in the flashing personal insignia of the famous Captain Boelcke.

As the machine guns cracked in his ears, Chapman realized that he had bitten off more than he could chew. He was a marvelous pilot, but he couldn't shake loose the killer on his tail. Holding his stick between his knees, he hurried frantically to change the drum of the Lewis. Without it he was helpless, at the mercy of the black-crossed plane. He knew there would be no mercy.

Slug after slug crashed around his head and into his instrument panel. Miraculously he escaped death time after time by the merest fraction of an inch. The fabric on his wings and fuselage started to rip and tear, shredded streamers flapping out in the wind.

Before he could get the rouleau clamped into place and turn to defend himself came the fatal bullet. It practically severed the metal aileron control on the right side, a foot from his head. Then it ricocheted and cut through his leather helmet, leaving a deep gash four inches long across his scalp.

With the right aileron flopping, half out of control, the Nieuport started to spin. Blood streamed into the intrepid pilot's eyes. He wiped it away with the back of his gloved hand, but the steady stream continued, almost blinding him. The Fokker was following him down, but the erratic course of the spinning Nieuport made it a most difficult target, and most of the singing lead went wide.

Chapman realized that his only chance to avert a fatal crash was to regain instant control of his spinning, battered ship. Seeing only dimly through a red haze, he calmly located and grabbed the severed ends of the aileron control and brought them together. Then he held them with one hand while he piloted with the other. Performing a series of remarkable acrobatics with his crippled plane, the daring pilot succeeded in evading his pursuer, who, seemingly satisfied that he had sent the Nieuport to a fatal crash, ground up to rejoin his comrades.

Bleeding badly and still holding the ends of his broken

control, Chapman landed at the little field of Froids. There he found some friends among the pilots of a French squadron. His wound was dressed, and he ate lunch. The mechanics wired the ends of the aileron control together, and later in the afternoon Chapman flew the Nieuport back to the Escadrille's field by way of the lines.

He thought nothing more of it; only smiled and considered it an interesting adventure. The other boys wanted him to go to a hospital or to Paris for a short rest, but he flatly refused. Wearing a white bandage instead of a helmet, he was in the air again, ranging the lines, just as quickly as he could get a new plane.

The next day, June 18, as is described more fully in the following chapter, the Escadrille suffered its first serious casualty: Clyde Balsley was brought down over Verdun and was carried to the Vatlincourt Hospital, where he was not expected to live. As soon as he heard the news, Chapman rushed over immediately. With his sympathetic nature, he was a constant visitor. He managed to get over to see Clyde at least once, sometimes twice, a day.

Clyde was burning up with fever. His greatest desire was for water, and all they would give him was a piece of muslin doused in water for him to suck. Barely able to talk, Balsley confided his burning thirst to Chapman, knowing that he could count on Vic to do something about it.

Chapman suggested oranges and bullied the doctor into approving, but there was nothing of the sort available to an evacuation hospital so near the front lines. Victor swore that he should have the oranges even if he had to fly to Paris to get them. He was just that kind of man, and he was like an angel of mercy to the poor pain-racked kid in the hospital.

Victor E. Chapman in Legion uniform. (Courtesy Victor W. Chapman)

Victor Chapman after the fight on June 17, 1916. Bandage, bullet-shattered windshield and torn turtleback attest to German marksmanship. (Courtesy Paul A. Rockwell)

After a long search, he found the oranges and, on the morning of June 23rd, put a bag of them in his ship to take to Clyde. They never arrived.

Just before he took off, a regular patrol of the Escadrille, consisting of Captain Thénault, Lufbery and Prince, started out for the lines. Chapman thought it would be a good idea to follow them along the lines for a while and see what happened, then take his gift to Balsley.

The regular patrol spotted two L.V.G. observation ships almost as soon as they got to the lines. The captain signaled for an attack, and the three Nieuports sliced in for a kill. They quickly found themselves in a bad jam. Three escorting Fokkers sitting overhead plunged down on the Americans. They were badly outnumbered and forced to run.

Chapman, some distance behind, saw their predicament and hurtled his Nieuport in to help them. Ignorant of his arrival, the three American flyers succeeded in fighting and maneuvering their way out of the trap and back to the French lines unharmed.

The odds were five to one against Victor, but he didn't hesitate for a second. He plunged into their midst. All five turned on him and caught him in a vicious circle from which there was no escape. A deadly cross fire raked his ship from all sides.

Without ever pulling out from his first dive, the Nieuport dashed full motor toward the ground. It disintegrated in the air before it struck. The hail of lead had cut several of the flying wires, and Chapman himself received a ball through the head and several through the body. As his inert body fell forward, it slumped against the stick.

Weakened by the severed wires, the wings were unable

to stand the pressure of that terrific power dive and collapsed. The fuselage plunged straight as an arrow into the torn-up welter of earth inside the German lines.

It was a glorious death, just as Victor himself would have wanted. He died as he had lived, with his face to the enemy, giving his all for his idealism.

The American formation returned to Bar-le-Duc unconscious of the tragedy, believing that Chapman had gone directly to the hospital. The first news they had was from a Farman pilot, who, having seen the fight from a far distance, telephoned that evening that, when the three Nieuports were attacked, a fourth had suddenly appeared, dived into the combat and gone to a glorious end.

It was nearly a week before the full truth was known, and it caused immeasurable sadness in the Escadrille. The most beloved of all was the first to fall in the squadron. He received a splendid posthumous citation:

CHAPMAN, VICTOR, SERGEANT PILOT OF ESCADRILLE N-124

A pursuit pilot who was a model of audacity, energy and spirit, the admiration of his comrades in the Escadrille. Seriously wounded in the head the 17th of June, he refused to interrupt his service. Several days later, he threw himself forward to attack several enemy planes and found a glorious death in the course of the combat.

Through a curious mischance, there was no report of his death from the Germans, nor, for over four years, was any trace found of his body or grave. It was a great mystery.

Strangely, he was buried and carried on the German records under the name of Clyde Balsley. The only identification he had on him when he fell was a letter from Chouteau Johnson addressed to Clyde Balsley, American Aviator, Vatlincourt Hospital. Somehow the Germans took it for granted that the dead aviator must be Balsley.

Then, in 1921, Frederick Zinn, an old comrade of Victor's in the Legion who, having transferred as an observer to French aviation, had eventually been given a majority in the American army, was sent to Germany as head of the American mission for locating graves of American aviators fallen in enemy territory. After a long arduous search, he located a grave near the moldering wreckage of a Nieuport. On a weather-beaten cross, almost obliterated by the elements, he deciphered the name of Clyde Balsley, together with the date, June 23, 1916.

The records were checked and the mystery was solved. It was the last resting place of Victor Chapman. His coffin now occupies niche number one in the crypt of the beautiful Lafayette Memorial at Villeneuve l'Etang, near Paris.

The Germans, through Major Zinn, returned to his father all that Victor had on his person, including the fatal letter and five hundred francs in money. Clyde Balsley, now in Hollywood, has the letter in his possession, delivered by Mr Chapman six years after it was sent.

It is an interesting sidelight on German honesty and thoroughness that, so many years after Victor had fallen, the money he carried should be returned intact.

It is a wonderful memory of a brave man that Victor Chapman left behind him. Kiffin Rockwell, his best friend and closest confidant at the front, who was soon to meet his own death from the blazing guns of enemy flyers, wrote to Victor's parents:

> He died the more glorious death and at the most glorious time of life to die, especially for him with his ideals. I have never once regretted it for him, as I know that he was willing and satisfied

to give his life that way if it was necessary; that he had no fear of death and knew there is nothing to fear in death. You must not feel sorry, but must feel proud and happy.

Chapman, beloved in his life as he was in death, deserves every tribute that can be paid to the memory of a fearless, splendid man who gave his all for his ideals.

CHAPTER X

Clyde Balsley

ON JUNE 18, as was mentioned in the previous chapter, the Escadrille suffered its first serious casualty. Clyde Balsley, the sunny-dispositioned ex-ambulance driver from Texas, was brought down, horribly wounded, in one of the closest escapes from death accredited to any aviator during the war.

The mere fact that he is still alive confirms belief in the ancient creed of our French comrades that there's *un bon Dieu* who makes it His special job to watch over aviators. All of us had need of this Watchman quite frequently, and Balsley got help when he needed it most. Of course, nobody just sat still and waited for matters to take their course; we did everything in our power to help, but it's a certainty we couldn't do it all alone. We had to have assistance, divine or otherwise.

Balsley is more or less one of the unsung heroes of the Escadrille, mainly because he was in action so short a time that he didn't have the opportunity to perform many of the sterling acts of valor of which he would have been capable and, as a consequence, lost the public acclaim and plaudits which were the reward of so many others less deserving than he.

Still, at the same time, strange as it may seem, by the mere fact of being wounded, he rendered a great service to his country, one far reaching in its ultimate effect. Balsley will always be remembered by Americans who were in France in the early days of the war as the airman *blessé*. For he was the only one who had been severely wounded in action at that time, and he helped to make clear and unmistakable to the French people America's friendship and desire to help.

Clyde had had three or four unsuccessful brushes with single enemy planes in the month he had been at the front, but he got his "blighty" in his first dog fight. In fact, it was the first real dog fight for any member of the squadron.

Some of them of course had had previous experience in bombing and observation work, and individual brushes with the enemy were frequent, but none of them, including the captain, knew very much about mass formations or combats. They were babes in the woods. They simply just got out and flew—against an enemy already equipped with faster planes and synchronized machine guns. It was inevitable that someone should be the first to get it, and it was Balsley's hard luck that he was the man.

He was one of the first Americans to transfer from the ambulance service and obtained his pilot's license in January of 1916. After his first tour of duty flying Voisons in the Paris Air Guard, waiting for the formation of the Escadrille, he was ordered to the front in May.

He arrived at about the same time as Lufbery and was assigned to billets with him. Clyde claims it was the biggest break he had in the war. The two boys were assigned to a little house near the flying field, owned and occupied by an old French couple. There was a lovely, sunny big front room with a luxurious feather bed and a dank, dark, cooped-up little back room with nothing but a hard cot.

When Luf and Balsley went to install themselves in quarters, Luf, who of course spoke perfect French, did most of the talking. Clyde chimed in occasionally with his halting speech and atrocious accent. Whereupon the motherly old French lady insisted that the brave American Balsley be given the comfortable front room and Luf the chicken coop, despite the fact that Luf rated the best, since he was already an adjutant with quite a number of decorations and Clyde only a corporal without a sign of a ribbon on his manly chest.

The old lady was a bit suspicious of Luf because he spoke such good French; suspicious that he was trying to put something over on her and in reality wasn't an American at all, while she was certain of Balsley on account of his bad French. She was so insistent that they finally had to agree with her arrangements to pacify her.

Then came the fatal 18th of June. Orders had been given the night before for a dawn patrol. Captain Thénault, Norman Prince, Kiffin Rockwell and Clyde were the pilots assigned. Lufbery's ship was out of commission, so he was grounded for the day. Chapman and McConnell were held on the *alerte* on the field to respond to emergency calls, a six-hour tour of duty that fell to all pilots in rotation.

With the night mists still thick on the ground, the four ships were lined up in front of the hangars in the half-light of early dawn. Their Rhone rotary motors turned over slowly with sharp barking explosions. There were shouted orders, a signal from the captain, and the four planes taxied slowly out to the starting line with a mechanic at each wing tip.

The captain waved his arm and throttles were opened wide. The mechanics let go and turned their backs as, with roaring motors, amid clouds of dust and bits of debris churned up by the flashing propellers, the four ships soared into the still air toward the first rosy flush of the coming dawn.

It is seldom we have the privilege of knowing the innermost thoughts of a man as he faces imminent death, but it was seared on Balsley's brain in letters of fire and his unforgettable story comes straight from the heart:

It was dawn, a Sunday morning in June 1916. Four of us left our field at Bar-le-Duc to make our regular patrol—Kiffin Rockwell, Norman Prince, Captain Thénault and I. We were flying 13-meter Nieuports with a forty-seven-shot Lewis gun mounted on the top wing. We had no regular formation, but flew fairly close together at between twelve and fourteen thousand feet. We made a long patrol from St Mihiel to Verdun, getting well into the German lines with the sun on our backs in the early morning.

Across from Hill 305, while still back within the German territory, I saw a German plane. Further on, I saw more Germans, and dimly, through the clouds, still more. Rockwell and Prince were flying together to my right. Pulling up close to the captain, I flipped my ailerons. From that he would know that I had seen a Boche.

Then I began to watch my man. Soon I saw him separate from the others. It looked like a good chance to pick him off. I glanced at the captain. He had started to dive. Evidently he was going after one of the other Germans whose presence I had signaled. Diving steeply, I swung to the left to get in line. Down—down.

As I came closer, I saw it was a two-seater. Probably it was

Clyde Balsley and his Nieuport 11. Behonne, Verdun sector, June 1916. (Courtesy Paul A. Rockwell)

Left to right: Clyde Balsley, Raoul Lufbery, James McConnell and Norman Prince. Behonne, June 1916.
(Courtesy Paul A. Rockwell)

an Aviatik. That meant he was as fast as I. One second I poised for decision. In that second lay my future. I would take him!

I kept on down. His observer hadn't seen me. I would pick them off on the way down and come up for a second burst. I held my fire—closer—closer. He was in my sights. His machine gunner was up in his seat. I fired once—twice. These were my first and last shots. My machine gun had jammed! Not a shot from his observer. Probably got him. I pulled away, caught my stick in my knees to reach for the collapsible mount to drop the gun and fix the jam, but a machine gun opened on my left, another on my right.

I was surrounded. No time for the gun. Two underneath and the one I had attacked behind. From the silence of my gun they would know there was nothing to fear. They would get on top of me. My fight was over. I was too far behind the German lines to dive to earth. I could only hope to outmaneuver. I pulled up for a renversement. I swung in every direction, then through a cloud. Bullets followed. Black patches on my wing. I sideslipped from that one and rolled over on my back. I was in another line of fire. The linen tore with the bursts. I was about twelve thousand feet up, and while I was completely over on my back something struck me—like the kick of a mule. I had the sensation as though my leg were shot away and put my hand down to learn if it was still there.

My safety belt held or the blow would have knocked me overboard. I cut the motor. My legs were paralyzed. Feet strapped to the rudder bar, my rudder went out of control. All controls reversed and legs paralyzed, headed down, I fell into a tight spin. Around and down, around and down. It was all over.

Soon I should hit the ground, as I had seen so many friends hit it. That would be all. How strange that I, the I that had seemed undying, should hit the ground like all the rest. I remembered the first man I had picked up. I should look like that. I remembered when I had picked up Captain Jolain. I had cried. Would anyone cry for me?

Around and down. Why—could this be death, this ease—almost this ecstasy—of giving up? There was no terror, no blankness; nothing but my clear mind following my body—following. Death could not be like this! That thought came thundering to me.

A second flash—France, my usefulness, my job. I was giving these up without a struggle.

"Stop yourself." I was shouting it out loud. "You're not dead. There *is* a chance. Don't quit."

In that second, I relived.

My mind cleared, and I tried to push my right leg into action. I worked with all my strength. My feet, strapped to the rudder bar, straightened it up. The ship was coming out. With the rudder bar straight, the spinning slowed. I pulled heavily on the stick. It came out slowly, but it came out. The spin was over. Where was I? My hand on my knee to keep the rudder straight, I leveled out. Crack—crack—crack.

Someone was still on my tail. My gun was still useless, my both legs were paralyzed. I could not maneuver, so down again I went, but this time under control. As I nosed over, I caught a glimpse of the river. French territory lay behind—I had my direction. I nosed over so far that a drum for the Lewis gun fell out. As it struck my arm, I thought I was hit again. Then they all fell out.

I looked at my altimeter. Only eight hundred meters up, but I kept on down to the treetops. I pulled out with an awful jerk. The wings stayed on. That last dive got me away. I put the switch on, my motor caught and I opened it up. The tachometer moved to the red; to the rupture point, 1500 revolutions a minute. It was my only hope. A long running drive to the lines.

Hand on my knee to hold that rudder bar straight. Fifty feet over the trenches—then, no longer trenches but broken shell holes. Blue helmets—France!

I was bleeding badly and faint. Field of green—could I swing for it? Stick in one hand, right hand on the knee, I worked my rudder, turned and slid in for the field. Too late, I saw it was filled with barbed wire. I was landing between the front line and the reserve. I pancaked in.

Wheels in the wire, the Nieuport turned over and crashed.

Gasoline was soaking me. I broke my belt and dropped out. Legs still paralyzed, afraid of fire, I tried to get to my knees. No hope. Caught onto the weeds, dragging myself along the ground like a dog with a broken back. Ten yards, no further. A burst of dust in the field, no sound. My ears were gone from that terrific dive. They were shelling the Nieuport. I lay there. I suffered so little pain that I knew that I was not badly wounded. This would mean hospital and Paris. Just a short leave and I would be back again. The 77's dropped all around me. A direct hit on the ship. The shelling stopped. Four French soldiers crawled out of their trench. They, too, had been waiting for the shelling to stop. Under the wire they came, caught hold of me and dragged me down. I had made my last flight for France.

So ends Balsley's own thrilling story of how he was brought down with a forbidden dumdum bullet in his hip, fired in direct violation of all the rules of international warfare. But it is far from the end of the tragic story of his harrowing sufferings resulting from that wound.

It was then about six in the morning. The sun, having driven away the mists, was flaming down on Clyde in the unshaded field. He sat up and took the shoe off his right foot. It was dripping red. He looked at it and then at his foot in dumb wonder. Somehow, he couldn't seem to connect that bleeding foot with himself. Yet he was there and the blood was there, so it must be all a part of him. Because he wasn't suffering much pain, he knew he couldn't be badly hurt, and it was certainly a marvelous excuse to get into Paris. He tried to move, but he was thoroughly exhausted by his superhuman efforts in dragging himself the ten yards. Intense thirst nearly drove him frantic.

He waited a few minutes longer. Then the four French soldiers came out from the near-by trench, crawling under the barbed wire to get to him. At their first touch, Clyde became aware that there was something more the matter than just a superficial wound. He'd stopped a bad one.

Learning from him that he couldn't walk, the four men dragged him like a sack of grain over, under and across the barbed wire. Under their rough handling, the numbed leg came to life, and the pain of that short journey was such torture that he nearly fainted. It was only a few short minutes, but it seemed centuries.

Finally they got Clyde to a first-aid post, where he was stripped of his fur combination and given a shot of anti-tetanus and a sedative, which helped in a measure to dull the pain again.

While he was waiting his turn for an ambulance to take him away, an ordinary touring car drove up, and a pilot from another squadron, who had seen the battle from the air and watched Clyde fall, came dashing in and offered him transportation.

Clyde wanted to be taken to the Escadrille headquarters at Bar-le-Duc, but the doctor in charge of the dressing station told the pilot that he could never stand such a long trip and to take him to the nearest hospital.

They loaded him, still on his stretcher, into the car, and the short trip over one of the roughest roads in France again nearly killed him. The stretcher jerked back and forth with the motion of the car, and every time they dropped into a shell hole, the pain was almost insupportable.

He was taken to the big evacuation hospital at Vatlincourt, where practically every man who was wounded at Verdun was brought before being shipped to the rear. Ten miles back from the front, it was near enough for the German planes to bomb it frequently.

There were only five women nurses for the whole hospital, all the rest being young medical students, each of whom acted as combination nurse and orderly. These young fellows were so inured to terribly wounded men and ghastly suffering that they were completely hardened and death meant nothing to them, except as surcease from pain to the man who suffered it.

There were thirty beds in the officers' ward where Clyde was placed, made of three rough boards on trestles, covered with a straw mattress and some dirty blankets. Never was a bed unoccupied for more than five minutes. Those who died during the night—and there were many—were taken out first thing in the morning and new patients brought in to take their places. During the day the change was constantly going on.

Twice, men on each side of Clyde died during the night, so that he was forced to endure the hot, fever-ridden hours of darkness with dead men beside him, less than an arm's length away, till daylight came and they could be carted off. There was a constant groaning, screaming and muttering of delirium, and the smell of gangrene and dirty, unwashed bodies in the airtight, closely filled room was horrible.

What really saved him was the fact that someone brought Balsley a large bottle of eau de cologne, with which he liberally doused himself and his blankets. There was a terrible shortage of water; bodies were never washed, and hands and faces only every other day.

The doctor took six pieces of the bullet out of Clyde on the first operation and brought them to his bedside, where Clyde put them in a tobacco sack to keep for a souvenir.

The second day after he was wounded, Balsley was decorated with the Médaille Militaire and the Croix de Guerre in front of all the other wounded in the ward. He realized during the ceremony, from his previous experience as an ambulance driver, that the decorations were given to him then because they expected him to die. It was such a shock that he made up his mind to fool them, and his will to live was stronger than any wounds.

Mme Ducroix, the motherly chief of the women nurses who became very fond of Clyde because of his youth and the fact that he was an American, opened a bottle of champagne after he was decorated, and every man in the ward, some of them barely alive, croaked their congratulations and drank to him.

Eventually Clyde was given vichy to drink, then coffee, but it was a long time before he could have any solids; for the same bullet which had exploded in his hip had pierced his intestines in a dozen places. His daily meal was a saline injection through his veins, a quart at a time. His skin at the point of injection would puff up as big as two fists till the heart would pump it through.

Every day, the boys from the Escadrille would come to see him, which was somewhat of an ordeal in itself. Clyde feels that he can never repay them—not in this life, at least, for all but one are dead—for in their life of hard service there was no conflict more exacting than the daily visit to that loathsome hospital.

After a couple of weeks, during which constant operations removed many additional pieces of lead, there came a change which made all his previous sufferings seem as nothing. His bed was continually wet from the heat, perspiration and solutions that were used, so that for days he would lie without moving an inch in a reeking mass. The skin about his hips broke out and festered. About once every four days, when his temperature went away above normal, they would change his dressings. It couldn't be helped.

All doctors and orderlies were working under tremendous pressure, badly handicapped, without proper equipment, for France had been caught unprepared for any such holocaust. Doctors operated twelve to sixteen hours a day, and orderlies were on duty twenty-four. They did all they could to relieve suffering, but it was so little against the tremendous wave that threatened to engulf them.

The doctors' surgery was of the roughest. They worked on the theory of "Do all you can for a man in a hurry; if he lives, send him back to the rear where he can have better treatment; if he dies, so much the better—for him."

And doctors and orderlies carried it out with superhuman heroism. If at times their treatment of patients seemed appalling, the strain on them was more appalling. Was it any wonder that in the hospital at Vatlincourt one lost all sense of the dignity of Death? It became a commonplace mechanism.

Clyde had to lie in bed with his leg doubled up and suffered such cramps that he begged for an operation to straighten it out. When the doctor consented to his plea, all his previous sufferings were mere discomforts. When the leg was stretched out for the first time, all the strands of the sciatic nerve, as big as a finger, which had been partially severed by the bullet, snapped off. A bullet exploding in the hip; that bleeding, bumping journey across the barbed wire on the day of the fight; probings, dressings, festerings, thirst—all these were mere discomforts compared with the pure agony that dragged him from under the sheltering oblivion of chloroform after that operation.

The doctor who had charge of Clyde was under the peculiar delusion that he alone could save the boy. So when he was ordered to Paris, he arranged that Clyde should be taken there, so that he could still be under his care.

Fortunately for Balsley, he was taken to the American Hospital at Neuilly, just outside Paris, and put into the hands of the head surgeon there, a man with a keen brain and a big heart. He saw immediately what was needed.

He put Clyde's leg in a suspension box with weights to prevent it from becoming any shorter than it already was —then in a plaster cast, in which he lived for many weeks. It was a tremendous change after the forced butchery at the evacuation hospital. Although abcesses made necessary half a dozen more operations, the Carrel system of irrigation, which saved thousands of lives, saved Clyde's life and leg.

The trained, constant and sympathetic care of women after the hurried attention of the poor driven orderlies; radiant cleanliness, the luxury of baths and snowy linen; delicacies to tempt his appetite; smokes to soothe his hours of pain—all of these made his year and a half at the American Hospital pass more quickly than the six weeks in the evacuation hospital.

Clyde always felt that he was going to get well, but he wasn't so sure that he was ever going to be able to walk. It was perhaps fortunate that he had that strong will, for I used to see him nearly every week at the hospital and wonder just how long he could last.

He was wasting away day by day, growing weaker and weaker, and would probably have died had it not been for the tireless, patient, splendid care of Miss Mary Wolf, his American nurse, who devoted herself to making him live. She pulled him through, and finally, late in 1917, nearly a year and a half after his combat, walking with a cane and a heavy limp, he was well enough to return to America, where he was commissioned captain of the U. S. Air Service in the Pursuit Division in Washington. He actually continued his flying during the war.

In the meantime, however, able to drag himself around with the help of crutches and a cane, he was occasionally able to leave the hospital and come into Paris for a glass of wine and a talk with some of the boys.

I ran across him on one of my more or less frequent trips to Paris, and on my return to the Escadrille I took Clyde out with me, and he spent a week with us at the front. I got nearly as much pleasure from it as he did, for I have never seen a man so happy, even though all he could do was look on, sniff the never-to-be-forgotten smell of burned castor oil and listen with avid ears to the daily first-hand reports of our scraps.

He even had the satisfaction of one more look at the lines from the air, for Lieutenant Plantié, a sympathetic French pilot hangared on our field, helped me boost Clyde, crutches and all, into a Farman and then took him over the lines. There were no Boches out that day, or at least they didn't see any, and they had no fights, which was perhaps a lucky thing for them both, although Clyde confessed he was much disappointed, for he'd have liked one more crack at them.

Although, after the removal of more than forty pieces of the bullet, plenty more still remain and he is badly crippled for life, Clyde is a real hero and never utters a complaint. The glorious record of his great adventure is compensation enough for him, for he knows that, despite pain and suffering as the first American aviator to be wounded, his services to France and to the United States were incalculable. The sympathy that he created cemented a bond between the two countries that can never be measured.

CHAPTER XI

The Eyes of the Army

Of course, in such a dangerous calling, where death was always just around the corner, casualties were to be expected, and while they were greatly saddened by the loss of their comrades, it served to spur the remaining boys on to redouble their efforts.

However, German guns were not altogether responsible for the gradual depletion of the squadron personnel. Ill health, induced by nerve strain, began to take its toll. Although each bore his share of the burden and bravely carried on during the wearying, devastating summer months, Rumsey and Cowdin were both on the verge of a complete breakdown. Will power and pure grit were the only things that kept them going.

Larry Rumsey was one of the first ambulance drivers to transfer to aviation, while Elliot Cowdin had managed to enlist directly in the French aviation in March of 1915. He had seen long arduous service in bombing squadrons and with a pursuit squadron, N-65, prior to the formation of the Escadrille. While with the N-65 he courageously attacked a formation of twelve enemy ships and brought one of them down, for which he was cited for the Médaille Militaire, the first man of the Escadrille to receive this most prized of all decorations. But the terrific reaction from the strain of his long service was beginning to make itself felt.

It's a great wonder that many more of the boys didn't crack up under the exacting demands of the war in the skies, particularly in the pursuit squadrons, for the scope of their operations and of the burdens thrust upon them was limited only by the needs of the moment. Each other branch of the aviation service had its own particular well-defined type of work to which it adhered to the exclusion of everything else, but pursuit pilots were, theoretically at least, the cream of the crop, equipped with the fastest planes and the best armament and might be called on for anything. Naturally they prided themselves on being the elite of the air, and in uniforms, messes and every other possible way they assumed all the prerogatives of pampered darlings, even venturing to sniff rather disdainfully at their unenlightened and less fortunate brother eagles, tolerating them merely as necessary evils. Social strata were quite definitely defined.

Lowest in the social scale were the bombing pilots, whom we scathingly referred to as "truck drivers." They were presumed to be persons of a very low order of intelligence, merely capable of taking a plane heavily laden with destructive explosives across the lines, day or night, in any kind of weather, to a far-distant objective under terrific anti-aircraft fire, drop their loads and return safely. We considered these semimoronic individuals as the type who never got over wearing the crash helmet even at the front and on leave would be likely to wear a regulation-issue uniform. We thought no imagination was needed in their type of work, and unless we very reluctantly were called on to accompany some mass formation of daylight bombers to some far-flung enemy objective—a very nasty, unnecessary job of protection, in our opinion—we of the royalty were hardly aware of their existence. Of course their work was no whit less dangerous than our own, but since at night they were in no danger of attack from pursuit planes, they were deprived of the opportunity for the spectacular air fights that were our daily meat.

Lumped together next higher in the social scale were the infantry liaison and artillery pilots. Infantry liaison was a really nasty bit of work. During a battle, under constant peril of an attack by enemy pursuit ships, exposed to intense fire from the ground, directly in the trajectory of shells of all calibers, they flew at low altitudes, blinded by dust and half suffocated by nauseous fumes, keeping in touch with the advancing infantry and wirelessing back positions, minute by minute, when all ground communication was impossible.

Frequently, during the course of an attack, one of these planes would completely disappear, disintegrate in the air, with no trace left of ship or crew. An explosive bullet from the ground might have caused the tragedy, but the probability was that the trajectory of some large-calibered shell had been rudely interrupted.

With all that vast expanse of space, it seems almost incredible that two such tiny objects as a plane and a shell should try to occupy the same place at the same time, but it happened fairly frequently. It becomes less amazing, however, if you draw a parallel between the air and the ocean and recall how often two ships have been known to collide in an apparently limitless body of water.

It still sends a chill up my spine to recall an incident

which occurred during an attack while I was patrolling at an altitude of about forty-five hundred feet. A hairs-breadth deviation might have had a tragic result.

I was inside the German lines, flying alone, headed toward enemy territory at my plane's top speed, probably in the neighborhood of a hundred and thirty miles an hour. Suddenly, out of the corner of my eye, first on one side, then the other, I caught a glimpse, not twenty feet from either wing tip, of two elongated, bottle-shaped black objects hurtling through the air and going in the same direction, passing me so fast that all I had was just a flash and they had disappeared. I got a tremendous bump from the vacuum created by their passage, but it was only a tiny thing compared to the vacuum that had been my stomach when I realized what those two objects were and what would have happened to me had I been a few feet to one side or the other.

The two shells must have been nearly at the top of their trajectory and at the point of inertia or I shouldn't have seen them at all. Consequently, except for some tremendous bumps, presumably created by the passage of some huge container of death, we never knew how many unseen shells passed us on their air passage to destruction or how close we were at all times to sudden and complete extinction by this particular method. It was just an added peril to keep us from being bored with life as long as we could retain it.

The duties of the artillery ships were only a trifle less hazardous than those of the infantry liaison. Unprotected for the most part, except for the armament they carried with them, they flew back and forth across the lines at a slightly higher altitude than the infantry ships, just right to offer a splendid target for a constant devastating barrage from enemy anti-aircraft guns every time they stuck their noses across the lines. Under these perilous conditions they soared back and forth across the lines for hours, directing and correcting the fire of a battery, or perhaps several batteries, of big guns on a particular objective.

Next higher were the long-distance reconnaissance and photo planes whose duties were quite obvious from their names. They penetrated far into the enemy lines, watching for troop and train movements and activity of every sort. Particularly in the early days of the war, the reconnaissance ships had the additional hazardous duty of landing and picking up spies.

Every foot of enemy territory was photographed by these hardy buzzards almost inch by inch and pictorial reproductions brought back to be studied at leisure under powerful microscopes, revealing the secrets of ammunition dumps, big batteries and all sorts of war concentrations. Cameras were so marvelously developed that many of the most detailed plates were taken at altitudes well above twenty thousand feet. At this altitude photo planes were reasonably secure, for with heavy motors and small wing surfaces, pursuit planes found considerable difficulty in efficient maneuvering over eighteen thousand feet.

Reconnaissance planes either went in groups, thereby being able to present a formidable defense, or else were given the additional security of an escorting patrol of pursuit ships. If photographs were demanded from a lower altitude, two or three photo ships were sent out with a pursuit escort on the optimistic theory that at least one of them might get back.

Then at the top of the scale came the anointed; the prima donnas who did all the spectacular work, got all the publicity and public acclaim and took all the bows for the hazardous drudgery of their less fortunate comrades. Now it seems hardly fair, but there was nothing we could do about it, and at the time we never gave it a thought or wanted to do anything about it, even had we been able. We were too cocky and proud to strut our stuff. Not without some small reason, we labored under the peculiar delusion at times that not only the aviation corps, but the whole war, revolved around us. Actually, although we participated in nearly all branches of activity, and some of our work was extremely hazardous, theoretically we were merely the guardian angels to make the productive work of the others as safe as possible.

We had two types of regular patrols, offensive and defensive. On the offensive, we were to go into the German lines, destroy, if possible, any and all enemy planes, keep them from coming across, harry them unmercifully and drive them from the skies.

On the defensive, we were to stay just on the lines, protect all our own planes and balloons, act as watchdogs and batter down any predatory attackers. Two hours over the lines was the time limit of our patrols, which usually consisted at first of at least four to six ships. However, owing to somewhat unreliable motors and pretty loose formations, these generally petered out to two or three planes that would stay the full time. We were given stated altitudes, type of work and definite sectors to work in, but our orders were very flexible, and plenty of latitude was allowed to meet any emergencies.

Patrols were staggered in altitude from low, around three thousand feet, medium, about ten to twelve thousand, to high, from sixteen thousand up. Taken in rotation, there was a patrol from each escadrille in a group (five to six escadrilles) on the front at each altitude every hour of the day from dawn to dusk, the relief patrol leaving the airdrome in time to arrive on the lines just as time was up for the patrol on duty.

Therefore each pilot generally had two two-hour patrols to make every day, and some of the more ambitious ones might even make a third voluntary patrol, either alone or with some other hardy soul. But a buzzard had to be mighty ambitious to want to make patrols for which he wasn't scheduled. The constant strain was pretty exhausting, and in four hours most of us could get all we wanted and maybe just a little bit more.

In addition, about every two or three days, a couple of pilots would be on six-hour *alerte* duty, which meant that, theoretically, they would be sitting in their ships in front of the hangars with motors warmed, champing at the bit, ready and waiting for an emergency call to hop instantly into the air and go after some daring enemy airman who had gotten by the front lines of defense. Generally the time was passed in the bar or in getting a little much needed shut-eye, for calls rarely came, and if they did, it was usually for some high-flying photo ship, which by the time we had gotten off and ground our way up to where it was last reported, was probably safely home. However, we had to be there on duty, which sometimes seriously interfered with some of the more intriguing features of the war.

But *alertes* and offensive and defensive patrols were only basic duties. We might be called on for anything and often were—such as protection flights for day bombers, reconnaissance and photo ships, involving long, tedious hops far into enemy territory, almost to the limit of our fuel capacity, with the attendant difficulties of trying to match our speed with the big-winged, slow-moving ships.

Or we might be ordered for one of the nastiest, most hazardous jobs of all: to knock down a specified *Drache* or observation balloon. They were tough to get, for they could be hauled down as fast or faster than we could dive. If we got within shooting distance, we might fill them full of holes and still not set them afire. They were ringed about with protective anti-aircraft and machine guns, and we'd have to fly through a barrage of shrapnel and singing bullets that would chill the stoutest heart.

Another specialized bit of unpleasant work was to be ordered to hang a couple of twenty-pound liquid bombs on a specially constructed rack in the cockpit, take off before daylight and streak across to German airdromes, try to blow up the hangars from a low altitude, then shoot the place up.

More hazardous and no whit less disagreeable was the duty of machine-gunning trenches and roads from a fifty-foot altitude, in which of course we were exposed to an intensive fire from the ground. A hit in any vital portion of the ship or a motor failure inevitably resulted in a crash, which ofttimes was fatal, but at best would mean that the unfortunate pilot would be taken prisoner and likely to receive some pretty rough treatment at the hands of his incensed captors, decidedly annoyed by having been machine-gunned from the air and quite actively resentful. They really couldn't be blamed, for it was not only annoying, but extremely destructive.

Frequently, too, in order to annoy the enemy to a greater extent, we equipped ourselves, upon direct request, with a sackful of Mills bombs, which in all probability annoyed us quite as much as it did the Germans before we were able to dispose of them. With a flat-winged ship tearing along above the trenches at high speed, being tossed about like a chip in a whirlpool in the disturbed air, pulling the pin on the bomb and getting it out of the cockpit before it exploded required considerable legerdemain. There was no opportunity for accuracy, and we couldn't stop to see the results, if by any chance there were any.

Sometimes, while in the execution of other duties, we also acted as messenger boys, carrying over tons and reams of printed propaganda with which we littered the sky above the enemy, hoping that it would have the beneficent effect for which it was intended when and if it reached their hands. I have the distinct impression that it was very rarely read, but used for more practical purposes, similar to the use we on our side of the lines made of much of it, for paper at the front was at somewhat of a premium.

No matter what our mission was, we were supposed to keep close watch on everything that transpired back of the enemy lines, fires, trains, convoys, flashes indicating new gun emplacements, and activities of all kinds, making an accurate report on our return. However, our information, if any, was generally fairly sketchy, for trying to keep formation, ducking Archie, watching for the safety of our own planes and attacking enemy formations, meanwhile guarding against surprise attacks on ourselves from above, behind and below was guaranteed to keep us fairly well occupied without worrying very much about what the Fritzies were doing on the ground. The observation and artillery ships and the sausages whom we were protecting were perfectly capable of telling Headquarters all about it much more accurately than we could hope to, for while we were all alone in our tiny planes with everything to watch and take care of, the other ships always had two-men, sometimes three-men crews: a pilot who had nothing to do but run the plane and keep a weather eye out for trouble; an observer or photographer who, unless they were attacked and he had to man his machine guns, could devote his whole attention to his business, and in ships which were built to include a third man, he too had nothing to do but watch and fight if need be.

Thus aviation was and is actually the eyes of the army, for in modern warfare land troops would be helpless without it. The army whose aviation corps could drive the enemy airmen from the skies would conquer quickly, for it would be similar to a man in possession of all his faculties fighting a blind man.

That was our job, and we did it to the best of our abilities with the rather flimsy tools we had to work with. The bombers wreaked untold damage both materially and morally; the other branches contributed their own invaluable specified services, while we in the pursuit not only participated in all their activities, but acted as general nursemaids and guardian angels as well.

We weren't exposed to the misery and suffering of the men in the trenches, nor to their terrific physical discomforts. We had our trick uniforms and our bars and our wenches; we slept comfortably, if not always luxuriously, and lived like kings while we could, for to paraphrase an old wheeze, our life in the air was likely to be a short but not particularly merry one. There were many times when the great adventure distinctly palled.

CHAPTER XII

"Skipper" Paul Pavelka

FIRE WAS THE HORROR most dreaded by every war aviator. Picture the soul-sickening sensation of a man thousands of feet in the air with his plane afire, the terrific blast of searing heat beating back into his face, the roaring flames eating into fabric and woodwork, the agony of helplessly facing a torturing death; no parachute, no way of escape, no chance of subduing the roaring inferno. Generally there were only two solutions, neither one very pleasant to contemplate. Either stick with the ship and suffer the agonies of a slow roasting death, or to jump into quick and merciful oblivion, a crushed and broken mass on the hard, unyielding earth. Few men have lived through this soul-searing, terrifying experience to tell the tale.

But Paul Pavelka, the ex-Foreign Legionnaire, affectionately known as "Skipper," was one of the fortunate ones. Skipper was one of the early gang to whom spine-chilling adventures and startlingly narrow escapes happened with amazing frequency.

Pavelka's home was originally on a farm in Madison, Connecticut. He ran away from home at the age of fourteen, because of difficulties with his stepmother, and like

Lufbery he had worked at many callings. He was a real adventurer who laughed at dangers.

He had been a cook in a sheep ranch in the West, a cowboy and an assistant nurse in a San Francisco hospital. Then he took to the sea and sailed on all the oceans—hence the nickname of Skipper. With a small band of comrades, after he had been shipwrecked, he once walked clear across South America. Going over the Andes, some of his companions, less hardy than Paul, died of starvation and exhaustion. He had been in Australia, the South Sea Islands, and had touched many European ports.

He was living in a sailors' home in New York when the World War started. He joined with a recruiter who took men to a Canadian port for a ship which carried over a load of horses for the British army. When he arrived in England, Pavelka first joined one of the strangest corps ever organized during any war. It was the "army" of the South American republic of Counani, with which he came to France in November 1914. The whole "army" of this mythical republic enlisted en masse in the Foreign Legion at La Rochelle. It was their only means of getting transportation to the war zone.

He went to the front in February of 1915, in the celebrated First Regiment of March of the Legion, and distinguished himself by his utterly fearless bravery in every one of the major attacks in which the Legion took part. He was wounded in June and, after his convalescence, returned to his regiment in time to take part in the Champagne attacks in October.

Toward the end of November, his hands badly cut from helping to erect barbed-wire entanglements, Skipper came to Paris on leave. Since before the Champagne offensive, he had not had the opportunity to change his clothes or wash up, and the mud of the trenches and blood of the battle-fields clung to his uniform. Almost a pound of shrapnel bullets were picked out of the lining of his greatcoat.

He pulled every wire that he knew and got all his friends to work for him, for he had put in his request for a transfer to aviation at the same time as his closest friend, Kiffin Rockwell, and he had been bitterly disappointed when Rockwell's request had been granted and his own refused.

When he rejoined his regiment on November 30, the order for transfer was there and the greatest desire of his life was realized. He trained on Blériots, taking his brevet in the latter part of February 1916. Then, on August 11, he joined Rockwell and the other Americans in the Escadrille at Verdun. He was assigned one of the newest Nieuports with a ninety-horsepower Gnome rotary motor. Just two days later, on his first flight over the lines, he had a horrible experience, a more terrible one than any he had known in the infantry.

He was just over Verdun, at nine thousand feet, when he saw black clouds of smoke rolling out of his motor and heard the roaring crackle of gasoline-fed flames. One of the combined intake and exhaust valves, peculiar to the Gnome motor, had broken and allowed raw gas to pour out into the metal cowling enclosing the whirling cylinders. It immediately caught fire, and Pavelka was helpless.

The heat was already intense, almost more than he could bear. There was nothing much he could do, but Skipper was determined to sell his life as dearly as possible. He closed his throttle and snapped off his ignition. Then, with a prayer in his heart, he turned the Nieuport on its side and, with a wing slip that literally sucked all the breath from his lungs, he slid to within fifty feet of the ground. It was a matter of seconds.

The rushing wind blew the flames away from his body, but the fire was eating into the wings and fuselage fabric. Paul was sure that he was going to be burned alive or killed in the crash that must follow, but calmly, with nerveless hands, cool as a cucumber, he brought the little plane out of the slip just above a great swamp. The heat roared back and seared his face and hands. He was ten feet above the earth when he pulled back on the stick and let the Nieuport drop with a sickening squash in the center of the swamp. Quickly he snapped his half-charred safety belt as the wheels touched and, rolling up in a little ball, he dived from the blazing ship into the cooling mud of the marsh. With mud dragging and sucking at his feet, he fought his way for fifty yards before the tank exploded, sending a shower of flaming debris high in the air. Skipper ducked low and stopped to rest his tortured lungs.

At this moment the German artillery, with the smoking pylon of the wreck to guide their aim, sent over a smashing barrage of large-caliber shells. They fell and exploded all around Pavelka, sending geysers of mud and water over him, but he was used to that and calmly sloughed his way through the whole barrage to safety. It was a combination of skillful piloting and rare good fortune that brought him through this near catastrophe unharmed.

Such an experience might have affected the nerve of most men, but not Pavelka. Although he was pretty well singed and all the hair burned from his face and hands, he was back in the air the next day, hot after the enemy.

Skipper was another of the most consistent flyers in the Escadrille. If there was a perilous mission to perform,

Paul Pavelka (Courtesy Paul A. Rockwell)

Paul Pavelka and Ronald Hoskier. Cachy, 1917.
(Courtesy Paul A. Rockwell)

Paul was the first to volunteer. Six hours a day in the air was nothing to him, and he often groused because the days weren't longer.

Despite his constant activity, Skipper was most unfortunate in that he was unable to knock down a Hun ship which could be officially confirmed. Time after time he landed at the field with his ship riddled with holes as the result of an encounter with some straight-shooting Boche. Somehow or other, the German ships could never be made to fall in spite of the hundreds of rounds of leaden slugs that he poured into them. By the same token, they could never get him to fall either.

The one time that he was able to bring down an enemy plane, he was so far back of the German lines and the visibility was so poor that the only witnesses were his comrades of the Escadrille. Even the balloon observers failed to see the combat and naturally couldn't furnish any information as to the results.

Paul was flying with Bill Thaw and Jim McConnell. They had made a tour of the sector without seeing a Hun. Led by Thaw, they penetrated about eight or ten kilometers in the German lines in their relentless hunt.

Suddenly Bill spotted a flight of seven Albatrosses streaking along below them. He gave the signal, and the three American boys fearlessly attacked. Although they were badly outnumbered, they had the advantage of altitude. Jim McConnell got his quarry on the first burst, but dived on down so far that, when he pulled out, two more of the sinister black-crossed ships were on his tail.

Thaw was in no position to come to his aid. He was playing ring-around-a-rosy with the leader of the patrol, having missed him on the first attack.

Skipper picked out his man as he sliced down through the murky air. After his first *rafale,* fired from less than seventy-five yards, he saw his enemy tumble out of the fight in a series of drunken acrobatics. He was certain that the Boche went down out of control. Then Paul saw the jam that Mac was in. The two Huns were sitting on his tail and had him in a deadly cross fire.

Skipper opened his throttle wide and roared to the rescue. He waited till he was less than fifty yards away from the nearer of the two killers and gripped his Lewis trip. He watched his tracers melt into the fuselage of the enemy ship.

Suddenly the plane sideslipped out of the fight, and Paul saw it dive almost vertically toward the ground. He banked hurriedly and came up under the belly of the remaining Hun. He pulled his nose up till he was hanging on his prop. His fingers curled once more over the trip. He fired four shots only, and then a cartridge crosswise in the block jammed the gun beyond repair. But it was enough.

A little jet of reddish flame sprang up in the oil-soaked belly of the gray-green ship above, which in a second burst into a roaring fire. Leaving a long streak of greasy black smoke in the gloomy sky, the Boche flamer plunged to his doom. The remainder of the enemy, badly disorganized, fled for safety. The three Americans had accounted for five of the Jerries, although they were probably not all casualties. Skipper and the man whose life he had saved, followed by Bill, sped for the lines.

Just as he got to the trenches, Paul's motor quit cold. He had plenty of altitude and volplaned down to a safe landing. He found his tank had been punctured in three places and the gas had slowly drained away. There were sixteen bullet holes in various parts of his plane, but except for those in his tank none of them were within four feet of his body. It was miraculous that his tank was not set afire, for a repetition of his previous experience might not have turned out so fortunately.

Bill and Jim did everything possible to get the Skipper's victories officially recognized, but although his name was posted in the order of the day as having successfully downed at least two of the enemy, no citation was forthcoming. There were no other witnesses except the members of his own patrol, and that was not considered sufficient in the French army.

CHAPTER XIII

Whiskey and Soda

EARLY IN SEPTEMBER, after the perilous, tiring summer months at Verdun, orders were received for the Escadrille to go to Paris, get new machines and report at the old headquarters at Luxeuil-les-Bains.

The new planes were officially known as the fifteen-meter, type-27 Nieuports. They were the same V-strutted ship with a slightly larger and flatter wing surface, powered by a 110-horsepower Le Rhone rotary motor, were ten to fifteen miles an hour faster, could climb higher much more rapidly and were extremely maneuverable. The ceiling was nearly eighteen thousand feet.

They were equipped with the newest innovation which the Germans had had for some time and the lack of which had proved somewhat of a handicap to the French flyers. It was the fixed, synchronized Vickers machine gun which fired through the propeller. The Vickers being stationary, one simply aimed the plane to shoot, whereas the Lewis, swinging free, had to be aimed while trying to pilot the plane. The first of these issues, until the bugs were out, were a bit unreliable, and most of the boys continued to keep a Lewis on the top wing for emergencies.

While the boys were in Paris, waiting for their ships,

another important addition was made to the Escadrille. A tiny lion cub, born on a French ship coming from Africa, was purchased for five hundred francs. He was a cute, bright-eyed baby who tried to roar in a most ferocious manner, but who was blissfully content the moment one gave him a finger to suck. He was promptly named Whiskey and became the original mascot of the Escadrille.

Whiskey got a splendid view of Paris during the few days he was there, for someone in the crowd was always borrowing him to take him some place. When it was suggested that he would eventually have to be caged, Jim McConnell popped up with the classic remark:

"Why put him behind bars? He'll see all the bars he needs, traveling with this mob."

So, during all the existence of the Escadrille, Whiskey was rarely confined, but roamed at large and romped with the pilots just like a big dog. Dogs for a long time were his constant companions, and Luf used to say that was one reason why Whiskey was so gentle—"because he didn't know he was a lion and thought he was just another dog."

Like all aviation squadrons, we had a plethora of pets and mascots who should have fitting mention and proper acknowledgment. On the front lines, within sound of the big guns, they were many and varied. Dogs of all breeds, descriptions and startling ancestry and one or two very mangy cats attached themselves to the outfit and in due time, if they survived the early perils of jealous indignation on the part of those who already belonged, became an integral part of the squadron life and took their places with the rest in the chow line. They even went so far as to give birth and raise their families in our mess hall.

Didier Masson once purchased a rather bedraggled-looking red fox from two itinerant poilus for fifty francs, bought it a collar and leash and started to raise it under the fond delusion that he could make a pet of it to rival Whiskey. The fox bit him several times, was extremely unfriendly and was a general nuisance around the camp.

Fram, Captain Thénault's big pedigreed police dog, developed an instinctive dislike for Masson's pet and was constantly sneaking around for a chance to tangle with it. One evening the fox slipped its collar and streaked out of camp like a flash of light. Masson, bemoaning the loss of his fifty-franc fox, offered a reward for its return. Two days later, the same poilus who had originally sold him the animal showed up with it again and collected the reward.

The following day, in an unguarded moment, Fram achieved his burning ambition. When he got through, the fox was no more. Masson, disgusted, gave the pelt to his mechanic, who sent it to Paris to make a fur neckpiece for his girl.

Adding to our collection, Bill Thaw and I, in a moment of artificial exuberance, bought us a very pretty little civet cat, all striped black and white. This little wood pussy is blood brother or sister, as the case may be, to a skunk. We were tearfully assured by the former owner that little Esther was fully housebroken and had had all smell-producing organs removed.

We proudly took our new pet home with us, only to have our trusting hearts broken the following day. Little Esther wasn't Esther at all, but a he-man of large attainments with all his faculties unimpaired. A broom handle in the hands of Sampson, our chef, put an end to the false Esther's odoriferous career while Thaw and I shed bitter tears over man's inhumanity to man.

Whiskey and Soda, the Escadrille's lion cubs. Whiskey was accidentally blinded in one eye. (Courtesy Soubiran Collection)

William Thaw holding Whiskey. Paris. (Courtesy Paul A. Rockwell)

Capt. Georges Thenault and his police dog, Fram.
(Courtesy Paul A. Rockwell)

Raoul Lufbery and his great friend, Whiskey.
(Courtesy Soubiran Collection)

But of course the very gentle and lovable Whiskey was the prize of our collection. His chief companion for almost a year was Carranza, a very nondescript white hound belonging to Masson, who had a great influence in making him believe that he was a dog. However, I always thought there was another reason, too, for Whiskey's gentleness. Through an accident, the poor chap became totally blind in one eye.

Like all animal cubs, he was most destructive. He loved to chew up blankets or curtains, not even disdaining a nice tasty uniform or kepi if he could get hold of it. These latter, in order to be really sporty, we bought ourselves, and they were quite expensive.

Whiskey was scolded and spanked, in hot water all the time, but he got away with it till he chewed to a mass of pulp a new kepi belonging to Larry Rumsey. Larry caught him just as he was finishing the job and, in a fit of anger, picked up a billet of wood and hit Whiskey over the head to make him let go. It wasn't a hard blow, but it must have ruptured one of the optic nerves, for a white film spread over the eye, and Whiskey had to cock his head on one side to see.

When Whiskey was a year old, we figured that it was only just and proper that he should have a wife, so after diligent search we found a little female, who quite naturally was promptly named Soda. Whiskey was as tickled as a kid with a new fire engine when he was introduced, and they got along famously, but Soda was never the pal with us that Whiskey was. She tried to imitate him in everything he did, except his friendly attitude. She had a mean disposition, always spitting, clawing and scratching and never wanted to be fondled like Whiskey, who adored petting.

While Whiskey recognized and was friendly to every man in the outfit, Lufbery was his special pet. Luf would romp with him for hours at a time, and Whiskey would follow him around with doglike devotion. No matter where he was, Luf had only to call, "Whiskey Man!" in a peculiar high tone, to have the big lion nearly wreck everything and everybody to get to his adored friend. Because of her lord and master's attitude toward Luf, even the malicious, evil-tempered little Soda accepted him with bored indifference.

It was Luf who taught Whiskey the famous trick that gave us many a laugh, for which we were deeply grateful, for laughs at the front were few and far between.

Hardly a day passed that we didn't have from twenty-five to fifty visitors, mostly poilus in rest camps and the like, curious to inspect the planes and attracted by stories of the Americans and their lions, stories which, before their arrival, few of them credited.

Luf would wait for a good opportunity, then send Whiskey around the corner of the barracks out of sight, while we lined up to see the fun.

His thoughts far away on other and perhaps more amorous matters, an unsuspecting poilu would stroll by the corner where Whiskey lay in hiding. Luf would give the signal. Whiskey, with a ferocious roar, would leap out, throw his huge paws over the shoulders of the victim and drag him to the ground by sheer weight.

In most cases the unfortunate soldier would be so petrified with fear at the apparition of this savage beast springing out on him so unexpectedly, that his knees would simply collapse under him. He'd go down and lie like a log, stark fear in his eyes, as Whiskey poised over him, apparently ready to tear him to bits.

Then Whiskey would put his head back and open his mouth wide, showing all his yellowed fangs in a silent laugh. At least, Luf always said it was a laugh, although privately I thought that Whiskey was just airing out his mouth after having gotten a taste of unwashed poilu.

Luf would quickly call Whiskey, and he'd come trotting over, purring about his achievement, begging for another victim. Sheepishly, the rescued victim would get up, come over and be urged to pet the savage-appearing but docile animal; which, if he did at all, would be done most gingerly and suspiciously. A tame lion was beyond the poilus' power of comprehension, but they were much too grateful to have escaped sudden death to be really angry at the trick. It was an unfailing source of amusement.

Unfortunately, when the Lafayette Escadrille was transferred to the American army, the higher-ups, not realizing what our mascots had meant to us, refused to let the boys take Whiskey and Soda with them. So the poor lions were sent to the Jardin d'Acclimatation, to be caged up in the Paris Zoo. Neither one lived very long. Their hearts were broken by separation from their friends and enforced captivity.

Life-size replicas of both lions are carved on the base of the enduring, magnificent Lafayette Memorial at Villeneuve l'Etang.

To all those dumb friends of ours, I, for one, am deeply grateful. They deserved a citation every bit as much as we humans, for they were our constant companions and comforts in all the black hours and endured every hardship with us cheerfully and uncomplainingly. Knowing that we loved and appreciated them, may their souls rest peacefully in the animal heaven.

CHAPTER XIV

Kiffin Rockwell

ON THE RETURN to Luxeuil, Robert (Doc) Rockwell joined the Escadrille. He had been a medical student prior to the war and, for over a year before his enlistment in the aviation, had volunteered his invaluable services as an interne in various French hospitals. Doc wanted a closer, more personal contact with the war, and he certainly achieved his ambition.

The personnel of the Escadrille at this time, in addition to Captain Thénault and Lieutenant de Laage, was Lieutenant Bill Thaw, Adjutants Norman Prince, Bert Hall, Lufbery and Masson, Sergeants Kiffin Rockwell, Dudley Hill, Pavelka, Johnson and Rumsey. Jim McConnell had been sent to a hospital at the end of August, because of a lame back resulting from a crack-up in a forced landing, and didn't return to the Escadrille for two months.

The rank of adjutant is more or less difficult to explain. In our own army, it corresponds approximately with sergeant major, or warrant officer in the navy. It is the highest noncommissioned rank in the French army, but only the thinnest of dividing lines separates it from commissioned rank. A gold stripe similar to a *sous* or second Lieutenant is worn with only a red thread drawn through it to distinguish its wearer as not quite commissioned. It ranks a salute and really carries considerable authority, particularly at night when the red thread can't be seen. The only difference is in the pay, and there a considerable disparity exists.

The boys were welcomed back to their old luxurious quarters, and as on their previous visit they had made many friends amongst the townspeople and French pilots stationed there, the older Americans were received with open arms and their new comrades quickly made to feel at home in the quaint Vosges town.

Their new planes were slow in arriving, and once again they lived the "life of Riley." Trout fishing, hunting and a continuous round of parties with about fifty English aviators whom, with their Sopwith two-place, one-and-a-half strutters and a tremendous ground personnel, the boys were greatly surprised to find quartered in Luxeuil.

There was no question but that there was a big hen on, but nobody knew what it was to be, and the Escadrille took full advantage of their leisure to enjoy themselves. As soon as the feeling of reserve had worn off, there was a continual exchange of dinners between the American and British pilots.

The latter hailed from every part of the United Kingdom, and most of them were soldiers by profession. They were all officers, but extremely democratic and diplomatic. As a result, in a few days, everyone was calling each other by some nickname and swearing eternal friendship.

One of the English lads paid the boys a very fine compliment when he said one day:

"We didn't know what you Yanks would be like.

Thought you might be snobby on account of being volunteers, but I swear you're a bloody human lot."

Which is extravagant praise for any Englishman.

But this life of gaiety and luxurious ease didn't endure for long, and it was for the last time. The pilots were really being fattened for the sacrifice. From now on, it was to become a war in all its grimness.

Kiffin Rockwell's new plane was the first to be ready, and on September 23 he took the air for the first flight of any member of the Escadrille since their return. It was like Kiffin to be first in everything, this well-beloved, capable, soft-spoken Southerner. It is probable that he was the first American to offer his services to France against the German aggressors; he was the first pilot to down an enemy plane in the Escadrille; likewise the first American in the Escadrille to be decorated with the Médaille Militaire and the first to be nominated an officer.

On August 3, 1914, the day before war was officially declared by France, he wrote to the French consul at New Orleans:

> I desire to offer my services to the French government in case of actual warfare between France and Germany and wish to know whether I can report to you at New Orleans and go over with the French reservists . . . or must go to France before enlisting. I am twenty-one years old and have had military training at the Virginia Military Institute. I am very anxious to see military service, and I had rather fight under the French flag than any other, as I greatly admire your nation. If my services can be used by your country, I will bring my brother, who also desires to fight under the French flag.

The Rockwells were born soldiers. They were proud of a trace of French blood in their veins, although the founder

Kiffin and Paul Rockwell in Legion uniform. September 1914.
(Courtesy Paul A. Rockwell)

Kiffin Rockwell in winter flying regalia. (Courtesy Paul A. Rockwell)

of the family, William Rockwell, came from England in 1630. Both of their grandfathers were officers of the Confederate Army, and a more remote ancestor was a captain on Washington's staff during the Revolution.

Kiffin's nature was made up of the simple virtues of a medieval warrior—pride amounting almost to sensitiveness, energy, determination, dauntless courage and unbounded faith in the justice of his cause. The flame of his idealism never for an instant flickered. Long after his enlistment, when he had come to know all the squalor and disillusionment of war, he wrote to his mother:

> If I die, you will know that I died as every man should, fighting for the right. I do not consider that I am fighting for France alone, but for the cause of humanity, the most noble of all causes.

Learning that they could secure passage on the American liner St Paul, sailing from New York on August 7th, Kiffin and his brother Paul didn't wait for a reply from the consul, but embarked for Europe, where they enlisted in the Foreign Legion on the 21st.

They were sent to Toulouse for training and, after about a month, a call was made for volunteers with previous military experience under fire to go to the front immediately.

All the Americans responded, and each man was questioned concerning his previous campaigns. One of the boys solemnly swore that he had served for five years in the Salvation Army. The old Legion noncom taking the information had never heard of that corps and just as solemnly entered it in his notebook. Kiffin and his brother, together with Bill Thaw and several others, claimed to have been in the Mexican army and, when their corporal commented on their awkwardness at drill, informed him that the fighting in Mexico was always guerilla warfare.

Kiffin was quickly sent to the front, and from the beginning his record of service was a splendid one. Months of dreary trench life with the infantry did nothing to diminish his enthusiasm or fighting spirit. His vivid description of an attack became a classic:

> There is nothing like it; you float across the field, you drop, you rise again. The sack, the three hundred and twenty-five extra rounds, the gun, have no weight. And a ball in the head and it is all over—no pain.

He was severely wounded in the thigh on May 9, 1915, when the Legion stormed La Targette, and after being discharged from the hospital he spent the month of July convalescing in Paris. There he ran across Thaw, who was already flying at the front and had come in for a new plane.

Kiffin's wound in the leg made it painful for him to make long marches, and Thaw suggested that he try for aviation. Rockwell put in his request for transfer, and after some opposition from the Legion chiefs, loath to lose a good soldier, his request was granted on September 2, a month after his return to the front.

He was sent to the school at Avord, where he took his brevet on the old flying chicken coop, the Maurice Farman, spending the rest of his time until the formation of the Escadrille perfecting himself on pursuit ships. Then he made himself famous by bringing down the first official plane for the squadron.

At Verdun, on May 24, the same day that Thaw and Chapman were wounded, Kiffin fought eight separate duels and was himself wounded, all in the space of two hours. He ran wild all over the front. It seemed impossible for one man to be in as many places at one time as he was. Seven times he either drove the enemy out of the skies or escaped death himself by the flicker of an eye.

Near the end of his gas supply, he ran across Victor Chapman flying alone. They joined forces and had only been together a minute when they spotted a seven-ship formation below them. Unhesitatingly the two youngsters attacked the enemy flight. Kiffin used his usual tactics of waiting till he was almost on the point of collision before firing. He had to dive through a hail of lead to get in his deadly attack. Chapman picked out the tail end of the flight for his meat, and Kiffin went for the one below, exposing himself to a merciless barrage.

Closer and closer he swooped without firing a shot. Lead whistled all around him. Suddenly there was a sodden "plunk" and an explosive bullet struck one of the wing supports near his head, spraying deadly slivers of wood and lead around his face. One piece ripped through his helmet and laid bare his scalp. Another chunk gouged out the flesh of his forehead. The blood gushed into his eyes, but he hastily wiped the flow away with the greasy back of his gloved hand and, sighting carefully, let fly at his enemy: one short burst at seventy meters and another long one at forty. The German ship quivered with the impact; appeared to hit a stone wall in the air, bounced back and stopped; then suddenly exploded. Kiffin slipped his ship just before the explosion and was showered with debris from the black-crossed plane. The whirling body of the pilot passed by him not twenty feet away.

It was his eighth battle of the flight and a grand climax. Practically out of gas, weakened from the loss of blood and shock from his wounds, his ship a perfect sieve, trembling in every spar, nevertheless he succeeded in winging his way back to the field at Bar-le-Duc and landing without harm. Chapman followed him in spouting blood. Both of them refused hospitalization, had their wounds dressed on the field and remained at the front.

In just recognition of his unexampled bravery, Kiffin was promoted sergeant and awarded the Médaille Militaire and Croix de Guerre with palm. His citation read:

ROCKWELL, KIFFIN YATES, CORPORAL OF ESCADRILLE N-124
A volunteer for the duration of the war, was first wounded May 9, 1915, during a bayonet charge. Passed into the aviation, he has there shown himself to be a skillful and courageous pilot. On May 18, 1916, he attacked and destroyed a German aeroplane. On May 24, 1916, he did not hesitate to deliver combat to several enemy machines during the course of which he was gravely wounded in the face. The aforesaid appointment carries with it the presentation of the Croix de Guerre with palm.

[Signed] ROQUES.

Kiffin was a demon in the air. He ranged far and wide in his search for enemy ships. In July 1916 he took part in forty officially reported combats; in August he fought thirty-four aerial duels. An excerpt from a letter to his brother Paul gives a glimpse of his extraordinary driving energy and determination:

I had thought beforehand that yesterday and today I would try my damnedest to kill one or two Germans for the boys (comrades in the Legion) who got it this time last year, but I had no luck. Am tired out now; have been out four different times today, all the time going up and down. Once I dropped straight down from 4,000 meters to 1800 on a Boche, but he got away. It tires one a lot—the changes in heights and the maneuvering.

When the Escadrille returned to Luxeuil, there was, as usual, very little fighting in the trenches, but, in direct contrast to their first tour of duty, a tremendous air activity. Owing to the French and British squadrons there and the threat their presence implied, the Germans had to oppose them by a large fleet of fighting ships. There were more than forty Fokkers alone in the camps of Colmar and Habsheim. Observation machines protected by two or three fighting planes ventured far into the Allied lines. It was something the Germans dared not do on any other part of the front. They had a special trick that consisted of sending a large, slow observation machine into the Allied lines, apparently alone, to invite attack. When a French plane would dive after it, two Fokkers that had been hovering high overhead would drop on the tail of the Frenchman, and he stood but small chance if caught in the trap. It was the first time the decoy system had been used.

Just as Kiffin was about to take off on September 23 for the Escadrille's first flight, Luf's plane was finished, and they left the ground together. Luf developed motor trouble, and Kiffin continued on alone, a foolhardy piece of bravery in that sector, but Rockwell cared nothing for danger. He had escaped death by such a narrow margin so many times that he had become a fatalist. He knew they wouldn't get him till his number was up. But on this flight, his short but splendid career was fated to end in a glorious death, struck down in the heat of battle, ten thousand feet above the ground. The circumstances were almost the same as the day he brought down the first victory for the newly formed Escadrille.

Just before he got to the lines, he spied a German ship

under him. It must have been a great satisfaction to him to at last catch an enemy plane in the Allied lines. He had fought more combats than all the rest put together, but all the planes he had shot down had fallen in the enemy lines. This was his first opportunity of bringing one down in his own territory.

In his daring, reckless fashion, he sliced straight down at the enemy, paying no heed to the steady stream of hot lead being hosed at him by the desperate German gunner. Rockwell didn't open fire till he was so close that observers on the ground thought a collision was inevitable. Then his gun coughed briefly, and for a second it seemed as if the German were falling, but almost instantly the Nieuport turned its nose down, and the wings of one side broke off and fluttered in the wake of the plane, which plummeted earthward at terrific speed. It crashed to the ground in a small field—a field of flowers—only a few hundred yards back of the trenches. It was not more than two and a half miles from the spot where Rockwell's first victim had fallen.

The Germans immediately opened up on the wreck with artillery fire. In spite of the bursting shrapnel, gunners from a near-by battery rushed out and recovered poor Kiffin's broken body. There was a hideous wound in his chest where an explosive bullet had torn through. A surgeon who examined the body testified that if it had been an ordinary bullet, Rockwell would have had an even chance of landing with only a bad wound. As it was, he was killed the instant the unlawful missive exploded.

With his death, France lost one of her most valuable pilots, and no greater blow could have befallen the Escadrille, for in addition to being a rare combat pilot, he

Kiffin Rockwell prior to going up in Bert Hall's Nieuport 11, on the field at Behonne.
(Courtesy Paul A. Rockwell)

Funeral of Kiffin Rockwell. (Courtesy Paul A. Rockwell)

was beloved by everyone for his chivalrous and romantic nature. Kiffin was imbued with the spirit of the cause for which he fought and gave his heart and soul to the performance of his duty.

His funeral was the most noteworthy of those of American airmen during the war. All the English pilots and eight hundred R.F.C. mechanics, a regiment of French Territorials, a battalion of Colonials and hundreds of French pilots and mechanics formed the cortege.

His valedictory by Captain Thénault at the grave was worthy of Kiffin and his life and death:

"When Rockwell was in the air, no German passed . . . and he was in the air most of the time. The best and bravest of us is no more."

CHAPTER XV

Norman Prince

ON OCTOBER 12, the big mystery was uncovered. It was a gigantic, concentrated daylight bombing raid on the Mauser Amunition Works at Oberndorf by the British in their Sopwiths and the French bombers under Commandant Happe. The Escadrille formed part of the aerial guard for the big armada.

The attack was a complete success, and the Mauser works were laid in ruins. The Germans were taken by surprise and were slow in getting their defense ships into the air. Nevertheless, on the return voyage, the bombers were attacked by large formations of the aroused hornets, and the French lost six planes, but the English escaped unscathed.

Four pilots of the Escadrille, De Laage, Masson, Prince and Lufbery each scored a victory, but in the midst of their jubilation tragedy again struck at the squadron, not in the heat of battle, but as the result of a most unfortunate accident.

The popular and enthusiastic Norman Prince, to whom more than any other one man must be given the credit for the existence of the Escadrille as a unit, was the tragic victim of the calamity. His loss was all the more keenly felt, for without his dogged persistence in overcoming every obstacle, there might never have been a Lafayette Escadrille. His was a fighting spirit that refused to yield until he had achieved his objective.

He was slight and a comparatively short man, with broad, powerful shoulders, blond hair, blue eyes that needed glasses, and a flowing, straw-colored mustache. His expressive face was rarely without a genial smile. He was sparing of speech, but he fairly oozed personality, and his energy and enthusiasm were unbounded. In his short but brilliant career, in addition to his great service in gaining permission of the military authorities for the organization of the Escadrille, his name stands out with a scintillating record of individual achievements.

His idea of a formation of American volunteer flyers to fight for France dates almost from the beginning of the war. Prince was at his home in Pride's Crossing, Massachusetts, when the war broke out. He had only just returned from France, where for many seasons he had gone to enjoy the hunting in and around Pau in the Basses-Pyrénées. Naturally, he had many close friends among the French and spoke the language perfectly. He felt that he ought to offer his services to the war-stricken country he had grown to love and admire almost as his own.

He was a real sportsman and although, like so many others, he might have gone over to enlist in the Legion or ambulance service, he had become interested in flying and thought that, if he became a pilot before going over, his services might be accepted in the Flying Corps.

With this object in view, in November 1914 he enrolled in the Burgess Flying School at Marblehead, Massachusetts, learning to pilot hydroaeroplanes.

Here he came in contact with another royal sportsman, Frazier Curtis, and between them they conceived the idea of getting enough American flyers together to form a squadron to fight for the Allied cause. Curtis had already tried to enlist in the Flying Corps of the British army and had been refused. He had returned to America to learn to fly so that he could go back and offer his services as a full-fledged pilot. He heartily approved of the idea of the volunteer squadron, but since he didn't speak French he was afraid that his ignorance of the language might prove a handicap. He suggested that Prince go ahead with the scheme while he tried once more to get into the Royal Naval Air Service.

Prince sailed for France in January of 1915, and on March 4 he signed enlistment papers in the Foreign Legion. By pulling a lot of wires and on the strength of his pilot's license from the Burgess School, he got himself transferred to aviation immediately and was sent to the military aviation school at Pau for further training. But in the five weeks which elapsed between his arrival and his enlistment, he hadn't been idle. He worked day and night to interest the French in the project. He was joined by Curtis, who had been once again rejected in London for the Royal Naval Air Service because he refused to give up his citizenship. The two Americans found themselves up against a tough proposition. Repulsed by the French, they appealed to Americans in Paris to help them pull wires. Curtis in the meantime followed Prince's footsteps and joined the French army.

Most of the Americans to whom they applied for help were either definitely against the idea or didn't think it particularly feasible. The situation for nearly six months seemed almost hopeless, but Prince and Curtis were not discouraged. Through the De Lesseps brothers of the Paris Air Guard and two sympathetic American residents of Paris, Mr Robert Bliss and Mr Robert Chanler, new avenues of approach to the French military authorities were constantly opened. At the same time, Curtis obtained the co-operation of Dr Gros, who gave unsparingly of his time and energy to the formation of the Volunteer Corps.

In the meantime Prince was actively engaged in flying at the front. As a result of his crash at Pau, Curtis's health broke, and he was forced to stop flying, but all of his time and every spare moment of Prince's were engaged in pulling wires to make their dream come true.

Norman was breveted in May 1915 on the Voison at Pau, and he was immediately assigned to Escadrille V.B.-108, a bombardment squadron. Voisons were slow, steady old crates with tremendous wingspread and great carrying power. They were used all during the war as day-and-night bombers and, until 1917, night flying on the Defense of Paris. Renault motors from seventy horse-power up were generally used. They were single-engined pushers and without fuselage. Pilot and passenger rode in a sort of overgrown baby carriage which projected some distance out in front of the wings. To prevent nosing over on a bad landing, there was an extra pair of light landing wheels in front of the cockpit which added to the baby-buggy resemblance.

In the early days of the war, their armament consisted only of rifles and shotguns, but later a Lewis gun was mounted in front for the observer. In the late summer of 1915, Prince was transferred to the V.B.-113, which were equipped with one-pound cannons in place of the machine gun.

While great things were expected of the Voison cannons, they proved to be a sad disappointment. There were no great casualties inflicted on the enemy, but they proved fairly dangerous to the passengers in the ship. The cannon was none too reliable and had to score a direct hit to do any damage. Voison fuselages, too, were never constructed to take care of the recoil. They were quickly discarded.

Day and night, Prince staggered across the lines with these heavily burdened crates loaded to capacity with high explosives. The great weight and tremendous wingspread, coupled with a low-horsepower motor, effectually prevented getting up to any great altitude. Consequently every voyage meant passing through a wicked barrage of anti-aircraft, shrapnel and machine-gun fire. The big ships were too clumsy to maneuver or change direction rapidly, and their slow speed offered an almost perfect target for the Hun ground gunners, even at night. It was not an intermittent barrage, but a nearly solid wall of flying metal which greeted them as they crossed the lines and never ceased till they had dropped their eggs and, only slightly higher, gotten across the lines on the return voyage.

It took "truck drivers" with plenty of guts to face that type of flying day after day and night after night, sitting on a ton of high explosives, not knowing what second some one of the bombs might be set off by a stray bullet or a piece of hot metal—then a blinding flash and extinction; never knowing when flying wires might be cut or motor hit—then a forced landing in the dark in strange territory, where, if a crack-up resulted with a full load, the result was nearly always the same. Slow-flying, clumsy, with bad blind spots in the rear, stragglers were cold meat for Hun pursuit pilots. Their greatest and practically only defense was close formation. That kind of work took guts.

For eight long months Norman Prince smiled quietly while Death rode like a grinning ape on his shoulder. Long-distance raids were his dish. Day after day he came back with his ship nearly torn to pieces by shrapnel. One of his gunners was killed and another badly wounded. Prince's helmet showed the scars of flying lead, while great gashes in his fur-lined combination demonstrated the narrowness of his constant escapes from death-dealing slugs. He escaped every injury.

He had a tremendous faith in his own personal immunity. Instead of becoming worn out by the terrific strain, he eagerly sought more opportunities. The more dangerous, the better he liked them. He excited the envy and admiration of all his comrades and commanding officers. It is more than probable that their reports on his bravery and that of the two or three other Americans who were distinguishing themselves in other French squadrons had a great deal to do with overcoming the reluctance of the French to allow more American volunteers to enter the aviation service.

Then, after his leave to America with Thaw and Cowdin which nearly resulted so disastrously, Prince was sent with Rockwell and McConnell to the Reserve Group at Plessis-Belleville to perfect himself on the Nieuport while awaiting orders for the actual formation of the Escadrille for which he had labored so hard and so long.

From the very first at Luxeuil, Prince was on every scheduled patrol and many voluntary ones, for he passionately wanted the honor of being the first to bring down an enemy plane in the squadron which he had fathered. When the plum fell to Kiffin Rockwell, Prince hid his disappointment with a smile, and his congratulations for Kiffin's exploit were heartfelt and sincere.

At Verdun, Norman was out on every patrol, striving desperately to shoot down a black-crossed ship to add his name to the fast-growing list of official victories for the squadron. But he seemed to be jinxed. Something always happened just at a crucial moment. Either a jammed gun or an unreliable motor let him down. It nearly drove him to distraction, for he felt that, since he had been the real creator of the Escadrille, he ought to set the pace.

Time after time he came in, his ship riddled with holes, to report failure, while the others, one after another, chalked up a score. He kept smiling and he kept right on trying. Eleven victories were officially credited to the Escadrille before fortune smiled on Prince. Then he performed a feat previously unheard of in the annals of war aviation, which more than made up to him for his previous disappointments.

He was out on a lone-eagle patrol when he spotted a single German two-seater some two thousand feet below him regulating artillery fire. Suspicious of a trap, for this enemy plane looked very similar to the decoy planes the Germans were putting out to trap the unwary, he hesitated for a moment before he sliced down to attack. However, unable, in a quick and searching survey of the sky, to locate any lurking pursuit ships, he plunged down in a long dive, and his first burst killed the observer.

Voison bomber of the type flown by Norman Prince prior to his Lafayette Escadrille service.
(Courtesy Paul A. Rockwell)

Funeral of Norman Prince. (Courtesy Soubiran Collection)

He rose in a zoom behind the tail and pumped a ripping *rafale* into the fuselage of the Aviatik. With the observer dead and no protection from the rear, the slower German ship was at his mercy. The pilot attempted to dive, but Prince fastened on his tail like a leech and ripped burst after burst through the wings.

Terror-stricken, the German pilot leveled off the Aviatik and stood up in the cockpit with both hands over his head, begging for mercy.

Remembering his fallen comrades, Prince's first impulse was to give no quarter; to shoot him down in cold blood. But he was over ten kilometers in the enemy lines. It was his first real chance, and confirmation might be difficult. If he could bring the German home, there could be no question.

Norman pointed toward the French lines, and the German pilot nodded and sank back in his cockpit. Firing a warning burst every time the German showed any inclination to get out of line, Prince herded the scared, unwilling Jerry back across the lines and forced him to land in a meadow outside of Verdun.

It was the first German ship brought down by an American on our side of the lines, and Prince had to go over ten kilometers into Germany to get him. He had broken the ice, and he was on the honor roll at last. He was raised from sergeant to adjutant, the last step before getting a French commission.

Apparently he had thrown off the jinx for good, for on September 9 he attacked, single-handed, a patrol of three Fokker monoplanes. Except for the fury and recklessness of his attack, the outcome might have been disastrous, for the Fokkers were equipped with synchronized Spandaus, while he was still using the cumbersome and unreliable Lewis.

Diving on the three ships out of the sun and catching them unawares, he came so close to the rearmost that he nearly collided before he opened fire. He ripped in a long burst and set the Fokker afire before the others knew what had happened. They turned to fire on him, but it was too late. He was far below, shooting like a streak of silvery light for the French lines. The confirmation of his victory was telephoned to the Escadrille before his wheels touched the tarmac. His citation for the Médaille Militaire followed this last victory:

PRINCE, NORMAN, ADJUTANT OF ESCADRILLE N-124
Voluntarily engaged for the duration of the war, has given proof under all circumstances of the finest qualities of bravery and audacity, engaging daily in numerous combats in the German lines. The 23rd of August, 1916, forced an enemy plane to land and brought down a second on the 9th of September.

On the 10th of October, Prince got another while flying with Lufbery. They went over the German aviation field at Habsheim and circled low, daring the Boche aviators to come up. The Boche took the dare in two layers, and the reckless Americans had to battle their way to safety, winning through by an extremely narrow margin.

Luf was forced to land just back of the French lines. Three bullets had entered his motor, two had passed through his combination, one of his flying boots was ripped wide open, and his elevator was in ribbons. But he had gotten two of the enemy.

Prince landed at Luxeuil with his ship cut to pieces. It was miraculous that it didn't collapse in the air. An explosive bullet had broken the main spar of the lower wing, and another had shattered the supporting mast of the upper center section just above his cockpit. Several wires were cut through, and others held by a single strand. The ship had to be junked, but Prince was more than content. In addition to a sense of personal satisfaction, he felt that he was evening up the score for Chapman and Rockwell.

Then came the fateful 12th of October, the tragic day which was to cut short the brilliant career of this intrepid young ace.

The fuel capacity of the Nieuports did not permit their going all the way to Oberndorf with the bombers. They were forced to turn back at the Rhine and come back to the French lines for more gas. Late in the afternoon they took off again to clear the air of enemy planes hovering in wait for the returning raiders.

Darkness came on rapidly, but Prince and Luf remained in the air to the last possible moment to protect any stragglers of the bombardment fleet. Just at nightfall Lufbery made for a small emergency field near the lines, known as Corcieux.

Slow-moving ships with great planing capacity could be landed in the dark, but to try to feel for the ground with the fast landing speed of a Nieuport was to court disaster.

Luf landed a bit bumpily but safely, and ten minutes after he had wheeled into the hangars, Prince decided to make for the field. He spiraled down and leveled off over the trees surrounding the emergency field. His eyesight was none too good, and in the dark he failed to see the high-tension cables that stretched just over the treetops.

The landing gear struck them at high speed. The ship snapped forward and hit the ground on its nose. It rolled over and over. Prince's safety belt broke, and he was thrown far from the wrecked plane. Both his legs were broken, and he suffered internal injuries.

In spite of the shock and his intense pain, Prince did not lose consciousness. His first thought was always for others. He heard the hum of a motor and, realizing that another plane was in the air, told the mechanics who had run to pick him up to leave him and light some gasoline flares.

"Don't let another fellow come down and break himself up the way I've done," he begged.

Luf went with Prince to the hospital at Gérardmer. As the ambulance rolled along, Norman sang to keep up his spirits. He spoke of how soon he could get well and return to service. No one thought he was mortally hurt, but the next day he sank into a coma. A blood clot formed on his brain.

The French commander of aviation at Luxeuil hastened to his bedside. Prince was named a second lieutenant and decorated with the Legion of Honor. His citation was read to him as he lay half conscious. His face working with emotion, the commandant was hard put to it to control his voice as he paid the final tribute:

> PRINCE, NORMAN, ADJUTANT PILOT OF ESCADRILLE N-124
>
> For nineteen months in escadrille has distinguished himself by a bravery and devotion beyond comparison in the execution of numerous bombardments and pursuit work. Has been grievously wounded the 12th of October, 1916, after having brought down an enemy plane. Already has the Médaille Militaire.

They were the last words Norman heard on earth. He died three days later, on the 15th of October, with the same sweet smile on his face that had characterized him while he was alive. His record is one of imperishable bravery, and the history of the glorious exploits of the Lafayette Escadrille is a fitting memorial to the vision that he conceived and executed in such an undaunted spirit.

On May 31, 1937, his body was, by permission of the French government, brought back to America by his parents, Mr and Mrs Frederick H. Prince, of Boston, from the Lafayette Tomb at St Cloud, outside Paris, where it had rested since 1916, to be entombed in a memorial chapel in the National Cathedral at Washington, D. C.

CHAPTER XVI

Didier Masson

ON THE SAME RAID that cost the heroic Prince his life, another of the Escadrille pilots, Didier Masson, pulled an extraordinary exploit that marked him as either the most adept or the luckiest man on the front, perhaps a combination of both. The Grim Reaper rode close beside him, but, more fortunate than poor Norman, he was able to outmaneuver his gruesome companion.

Masson's background was most colorful. He was a real adventurer in the true sense of the word. He was unquestionably the first war aviator and without doubt the only man alive who has comprised in his own person the entire air force of a nation. When he joined the Escadrille, he had seen more war flying and probably more hours in the air than all the rest of the gang put together.

Soft-voiced, reticent and unassuming as Masson was, it was difficult to credit the story of his hectic career. He was five feet six of human dynamite, characterized by an iron nerve and an innate courage that laughed at danger. His calm, even disposition, unfailing good humor and keen judgment in a crisis made him a favorite with everyone.

There was nothing spectacular about his war flying: no

fancy work, frills or brilliant acrobatics. But you felt absolutely certain that when you started out on a patrol with Masson, you'd never be deserted. No matter what happened, Didier was going to be there till the last dog was hung. He always seemed to be calm and unworried, no matter what his private emotions might have been.

His written official reports to the operations office, of which the following is a fair sample, were models of brevity and modest claim. Quoted from official squadron records:

> Saw 2 enemy aircraft vicinity of Anizy at 23 hours 10. Accompanied by Sergeant Parsons and Corporal Dugan attacked at once. Combat endured for five minutes. Fired twenty rounds at close quarters with Rumpler. Observer was killed by first burst. Motor was hit and plane went into spin. Final result—one enemy aircraft observed to crash and burn in vicinity of Longpont at 23 hours 20, the other disappeared at low altitude in his own lines. Confirmation requested.

There are just the cold hard facts as Masson wrote them; but one had to see him in action to realize the drama that lay behind that brief, phlegmatic report. The superb daring of his attack, his close watch of his comrades to see that nothing happened to them, his magnificent maneuvering, his unerring aim—those are the details of which no mention is made.

It is rather difficult for most of us to realize that, up to a comparatively few years ago, the use of airplanes in war maneuvers was merely the idle dream of a few crack-brained enthusiasts. Carrying bombs through the air and placing them at will in the enemy's territory was the height of the ridiculous. It took Masson to show the world what could be done by a daring pilot.

Masson started to fly in 1909, when a fifty-horsepower

motor was considered the last word. Planes came down on skids, for landing wheels were just experiments. The pilot sat away out in front with his feet on a distant rudder bar and nothing between him and eternity. A passenger was forced to sit on the edge of a wing and hang desperately onto a strut. The motor was mounted back over their heads in a choice spot to become an integral part of the pilot's skull in case of a bad landing. The aviators were fully exposed to all the elements, as there was nothing to break the force of the wind. A sustained flight of half an hour without a forced landing was sufficient to put a man in the ace class.

Masson learned to fly in France, principally on the old Antoinette monoplane, which Claude Grahame-White later made famous. Masson was known as the "Rubber Man" on account of the numerous spills he took and the bad crashes from which he escaped uninjured.

Didier is of French parentage, but his home was actually in Los Angeles, where, from 1911 to 1913, he continued his aeronautical researches. Having decided that he had conquered all the air in California and that exhibition flying, while it had its moments, was far from being the ultimate adventure, Masson looked for new fields to conquer.

At the moment Mexico seemed the best solution for a boy really searching for thrills. The Mexicans were in the midst of one of the periodic guerilla wars for the possession of the country. General Huerta was in the driver's seat for the moment, but the seat was rocking badly. General Obregon was hot on his tail, with Zaragosa, Carranza and Villa looming in the background. Airplanes were unknown; in fact, cannon were almost a curiosity.

Didier Masson (Courtesy Soubiran Collection)

The Spad 7 flown by Didier Masson. (Courtesy Paul A. Rockwell)

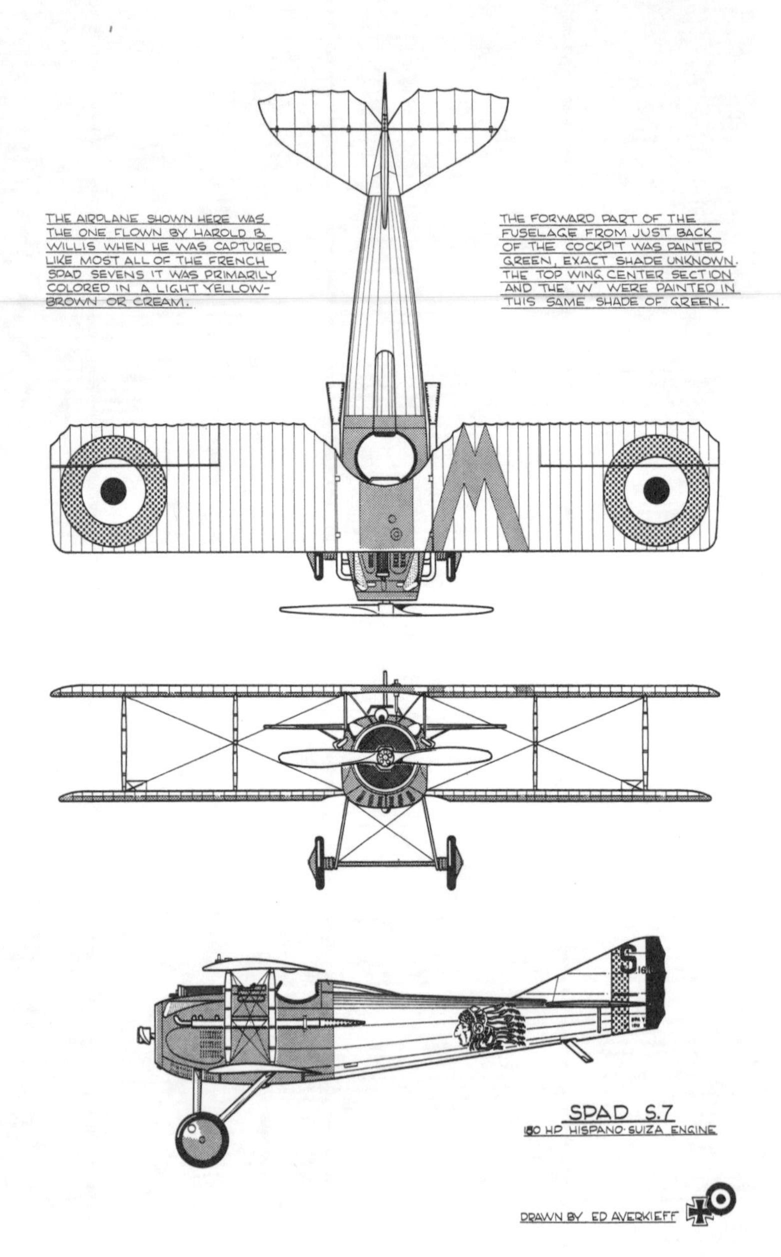
THE AIRPLANE SHOWN HERE WAS THE ONE FLOWN BY HAROLD B. WILLIS WHEN HE WAS CAPTURED. LIKE MOST ALL OF THE FRENCH SPAD SEVENS IT WAS PRIMARILY COLORED IN A LIGHT YELLOW-BROWN OR CREAM.
THE FORWARD PART OF THE FUSELAGE FROM JUST BACK OF THE COCKPIT WAS PAINTED GREEN, EXACT SHADE UNKNOWN. THE TOP WING CENTER SECTION AND THE "W" WERE PAINTED IN THIS SAME SHADE OF GREEN.
SPAD S.7
180 HP HISPANO-SUIZA ENGINE
DRAWN BY ED AVERKIEFF

Most of the battles were merely incidental, resulting from a surprise meeting between enemy troops, neither one of whom had had any idea the other party was anywhere in the vicinity. There would be a great deal of excited shouting; running to and fro; a few shots fired with practically no casualties and the battle was over. Such was the atmosphere in which Masson found himself in the early part of 1913.

General Pesqueira, a loyal Obregon man, then acting governor of Sonora, had seen airplanes in flight on one of his visits to the States. As he was above the average in intelligence, the idea occurred to him that possibly planes might be used for scouting duty in locating the troops of that ingrate and arch fiend, General Huerta, who stood in the way of Obregon's presidency. Nothing was said about bombing. It never entered his head.

He got hold of Masson and an English mechanic by the name of Tommy Dean and sent them to join Obregon's army. By the use of a considerable amount of ingenuity, Masson succeeded in getting a Curtiss plane of a long-forgotten model smuggled across the border. It was entirely knocked down and transported a piece at a time into Mexico on muleback. Considerable time was lost in rounding up the various parts of the plane. One wing and the prop were missing for several weeks. Masson was given the rank of major and constituted the whole Obregon air force; in fact he was the only aviator in Mexico at that time.

Aerial bombs were unheard of,* but once Masson had the ship finally assembled and in the air, he suggested that great execution could be performed on the opposing troops if they could only drop some high explosives.

**Further research has shown this impression of the author's to be incorrect.*

Tommy Dean, who was rather a clever youth with a flair for inventions, proceeded to experiment. He put some high explosives in tin cans and tied them up with bailing wire. He succeeded in fashioning a very deadly sort of bomb, one that was lacking a percussion cap, but was almost sure to explode if dropped from a considerable height. While his experiments were highly satisfactory, Tommy lost part of one finger from a bomb that exploded prematurely.

Together, the two of them rigged up a crude bomb rack under the wing and arranged a slip wire that would permit Masson to release the deadly load from the pilot's seat. Everything looked shipshape, but there was some question in their minds as to whether or not the bombs would clear irregularities in the field before the ship got into the air. Masson finally prevailed upon the young mechanic to take a position on one wing where he could watch the deadly load and note the amount of clearance while the ship taxied slowly.

Then Masson played a sort of a dirty trick on his young assistant. By leaning far out, Dean could see the bombs and was assured that there was a safe margin of clearance. He was about to signal this fact to Masson when, to his supreme horror, the ground below dropped away. Masson had taken off!

Dean went white as a sheet and froze to a strut with frantic fingers. It was the first time bombs had ever been taken aloft, and Dean was making his first flight. It was another case of the man who had never ridden a horse riding a horse that had never been ridden.

Masson was enjoying the joke keenly, but not so Dean. Eventually, though, he got the feel of the plane and his fright left him, although he was still a bit nervous.

An old, deserted adobe house jutted from the floor of the desert, and Masson picked this as the first target in all history to be attacked from the air. He flew low and pulled the trip wire. Down hurtled the clumsy bombs. A couple of them made a direct hit. The house disappeared in a cloud of smoke and debris. Tommy had done his work well as far as the construction of the bombs went, but there was a slight slip-up in the bombing rack.

Dean, holding onto the strut with a death grip, peered under the wing. To his horrified surprise, he saw that one of the bombs—the one farthest away—had failed to clear the clumsy rack. There it hung, a rough can filled with dynamite, potential death if they were forced to land with it under the wing. It was hanging so far down that it was certain to strike the ground at approximately the same time as the plane. Tommy had seen what the other cans had done to the adobe house.

He turned anguished eyes toward Masson, but Masson was having troubles of his own; troubles that had nothing to do with the can of dynamite. The fragile motor was coughing as if it had asthma. It appeared as if a forced landing were due at any minute. Masson was working frantically with adjustments trying to keep the old mill perking. Tommy shouted a warning, but his words were lost in the sputtering explosions of the engine. It was a moment that called for a big decision from Tommy Dean.

Should he relinquish his iron-fingered hold on the strut and attempt to release the bomb? Should he feature his first flight with an exhibition of wing walking?

There wasn't any real choice if both he and Masson were to continue as the Obregon air force. He carefully inched his way along the main wing spar, gripping stays and struts, his heart in his mouth. Lying full length on the wing, he reached under and after several heartbreaking failures, in which the death-laden can just swung away from his fingertips, he managed to poke the bomb loose just as the wheezy motor gave up the ghost and the sun-baked terrain rose swiftly up to meet them. They were nearly capsized by the force of the explosion, but Masson managed to land intact. It was the first he knew of the trouble. He had seen Tommy squirming along the wing, but had been much too occupied with his own problems to pay much attention. He and Tommy both tried to laugh the whole affair off, but their laughs were pretty shaky.

However, they deserve a lot of credit, for with their crude experiments they pioneered the way for the intensive bombing of the great war which was so soon to follow.

Part of Masson's subsequent duties were to attack single-handed the entire navy of his chief's implacable foe, General Huerta. However, this was not a deed of such reckless daring as might be supposed, for the Huerta navy, in the matter of equipment was quite on a par with the Obregon air force. One ancient gunboat, with engines capable of developing about four knots under forced draft, manned by beachcombers and other nautical soldiers of fortune, kept the sea lanes open after a fashion for the Huerta gunrunners.

Didier's first appearance above this antique tin pot caused an immense stir. It was the first time these wild freebooters had ever seen a plane, and Masson was at least successful in badly shaking whatever morale they possessed. He dropped tin can after tin can filled with high explosives around the tin-pot gunboat, even making several direct hits. All the direct hits unfortunately failed to explode, so the net result was merely a lot of badly scared sailors.

Masson was able to do his valiant work of observation and bombing without hindrance except for a few wild rifle shots from the ground, because for nearly a year there was no opposing air force. When he later transferred his allegiance and flew for Carranza against Villa, there was another complete armada of one ship arrayed against him, consisting of my commanding officer and myself, but the two machines were rarely, if ever, in the air at the same time.

It was a rare quirk of Fate that after we had been so bitterly opposed, although never coming in direct contact with each other in one war, two years later we should be fighting side by side in a common cause. We had many a laugh swapping experiences and shuddering over our narrow escapes from having to bring each other down.

But when the Big Scrap started, Masson was fairly well fed up with tin-pot revolutions and immediately resigned his Mexican commission to hustle over to France, where he offered his services as a pilot. It was some time before the French found out what Masson already knew: the great part that aviation would play and the dire need for experienced military aviators. So in the meantime, Masson's services were accepted and he was shoved into the infantry. Here, as a second-class soldier, he saw plenty of action in the first hectic months, but his old luck was still with him, and he miraculously escaped time after time from being wounded.

Then he was transferred to aviation and, after a brief refresher course at Pau, was sent to the front in September, first as an observation pilot flying the single-motored

Caudron, then with Escadrille N-68, the first squadron to be equipped with Nieuports, where he stayed until the formation of the Escadrille.

He did splendid work all during the summer months at Verdun, but it was not until the Oberndorf bombing raid that he made his great bid for fame. He was one of the patrol of four from the Escadrille who hurled themselves into the wildest, most desperate dog fight of the war up to that time.

As the multitude of heavily laden bombers plowed their way over on their destructive mission, there were no signs of enemy defense ships, but coming back, the slow-moving armada was attacked again and again, before it reached the Rhine, by the enemy hornets they had stirred up. The Fokkers were determined and aggressive. The massed bombers presented an excellent defense, but despite their heroic efforts, one and then another of the big Voisons went hurtling down to destruction. It began to assume catastrophic proportions.

Then the four Nieuports of the aerial guard roared on the scene and, thanks to their determined efforts, not a single one of the remaining bombers was harmed—they were escorted back across the lines in perfect security. Time after time, the cool-headed, daring pilots of the Nieuports dived in and broke up the Fokker attacks. They swooped on the enemy ships from every angle, bewildering them by clever tactics.

The Fokkers outnumbered them three to one, but the Americans put up such a valorous and brilliant attack that numbers counted for nothing. De Laage, Lufbery and Prince performed miracles. Their air work was superb. Fokker after Fokker was forced to quit the attack under the death-dealing menace of their guns. It was a veritable mad, macabre dance of death.

In the midst of it all was Masson, swooping down and zooming up on the sinister black crosses, hosing out a continuous stream of flaming lead. There came a brief moment when, almost hanging on his prop, he got a black belly fair in his sights. His hand clamped over the trip of his Bowdoin control. A second more and he had a sure kill.

Without warning, his purring Le Rhone suddenly stuttered, missed a few beats, then ceased with the suddenness of a chopped scream. Masson looked down. His eyes bulged. The fuel gauge showed zero. He was entirely out of gas, and there was no reserve tank. The French lines were barely in sight. With a lot of luck, if he could stretch his glide, he might be able to get back.

But his intended victim was on the alert. He saw instantly that Masson was in trouble. He turned from the attacked to the attacker. Lead began to whistle around Masson's head. A line of black holes stitched themselves in the silvery wing over his head, then traveled back along the fuselage. The German became bolder and more vicious in his attack. He knew that he had Masson at his mercy.

Didier had been in plenty of tough situations before, but this was the worst. However, he never for a moment lost his head. He was in a bad spot to defend himself without the aid of a motor. But he had ideas that were decidedly averse to getting washed out or spending the rest of the war as a prisoner.

Handling his motorless ship with the skill of a master, he started on a long, easy glide. He and the German were alone, far below the vicious fighting which still continued unabated in the twilight skies over their heads.

The German, his motor functioning perfectly, sliced in heedlessly in a long screaming dive, anxious to make his kill. It was apparently cold turkey. But he had reckoned without his host. He became overconfident and careless. He dove in on Masson's tail, firing a long *rafale* from his Spandau that ripped Didier's instrument panel into splinters. Whizzing slugs fanned Masson with their deadly breath, but by a miracle he wasn't touched.

Then the Fritz passed underneath and started to zoom in front of Masson's nose. Didier was waiting for just such an opportunity. He stood the Nieuport on its nose and followed it by a tight bank. Letting go his stick, he grabbed the handle of the Lewis and took steady aim. There wasn't much wind pressure on the drum and he squirted out a long, flaming *rafale* from the black muzzle without a jam. Ten shots—twenty. His tracers were spraying the slate-colored fuselage of the Fokker. He changed his range to the little streamlined spot in back of the cockpit.

A white face with square-cut goggles framed in a black helmet turned toward him with a look of hurt surprise. Then the head sagged, and with the deliberateness of a picture in slow motion the lone figure folded up like a jackknife and slumped down in the cockpit almost out of sight.

The Fokker started to whirl; faster and faster it went, with the stiffening hand of a dead man holding the stick, till it spun out of vision and merged with the dull monotone of the earth below. Three minutes later it piled up in an unrecognizable heap of wreckage behind the third-line trenches and burst into flame. A leaping tongue of fire and a tall column of greasy black smoke marked the funeral pyre.

Masson had accomplished the impossible. In a motorless glide, helpless to maneuver, he had not only escaped the almost certain death for which he had been fated, but in addition he had gotten his man. It was one of the greatest feats performed during the war, for it was against an enemy who held all the advantage.

But he was far from being out of the woods. He had lost altitude rapidly while he was in the spiral, bringing down his enemy. He was far below his comrades and the massed cloud of mighty bombers. The trenches were but a brown line in the dim distance. Underneath him were the eager hordes of the enemy, hopefully waiting for him to come down.

Masson straightened out and held his glide almost level till his wings wavered from loss of speed. Then he dipped his nose slightly to pick up speed and straightened out again in a series of Russian mountains. Up and down, up and down endlessly, straining tensely to gain every possible foot. Those brown, crawling lines that spelled the difference between despair and happiness were still so far away.

A friendly up current of warm air carried him a kilometer without loss of altitude. He urged the little ship on with the motion of his body, even talked to it as he would to a faltering horse. The Nieuport seemed to understand and gave its best efforts. Down and down he went, with the reserve trenches beginning to pass under his wheels.

He had scarce fifty meters of altitude as he approached the German first lines. Bullets from trench machine guns and rifles pierced his fluttering wings and whistled around his head, but again his luck held, and he passed through the hail of fire without a scratch.

His wheels skimmed across the churned welter of no man's land and almost hooked onto the barbed wire in front of his own trenches. He pulled the little ship up and over with his last remaining bit of flying speed. Across the trench line and down he squashed to a landing just behind a little mound of earth that momentarily hid him from view of the German front-line trenches.

He was surrounded by deep shell craters, barbed wire and communication trenches, but the Nieuport was undamaged. Not even a tire was blown. There wasn't one drop of gas left in his tank, nor a single cartridge in the drum of the Lewis gun on the center section panel.

Grabbing what undamaged instruments he could carry, Didier scrambled hurriedly from the cockpit and dived into a communication trench. He was well aware of what was going to happen. The first shell exploded near the ship just as he dropped into the trench, and in a minute the air was thick with bursting shrapnel and rolling clouds of smoke.

In five minutes the Nieuport was blown to bits by a direct hit, but Didier was safe in a post of command, receiving the congratulations of the French infantry officers on his narrow escape and sensational victory, all of which they had witnessed.

For this exploit, Didier was cited on November 8, 1916, for the Médaille Militaire, and the citation is a tribute to a real hero:

MASSON, DIDIER, ADJUTANT PILOT OF ESCADRILLE N-124
Very old pilot; after having taken part in numerous flights of artillery regulation and reconnaissance, has participated valiantly in the pursuit operations of the Verdun group. The 12th of October, 1916, during the protection of a bombardment, brought down

an enemy plane. Accomplished his mission to the finish, despite fuel exhaustion which befell him over the German lines and forced him to return by volplaning. The above citation carries with it the Croix de Guerre with palm.

The General Commandant in Chief

[Signed] JOFFRE.

In view of the Germany of today, it is a rather ironical angle that Masson's personal insignia on his ship all during the war was the swastika. It carried him triumphantly through all sorts of hard-fought combats and perilous situations.

CHAPTER XVII

Death of Paul Pavelka

THE EXPLOITS of these adventurous young Americans began to appear daily in the papers, both at home and abroad. Suddenly, much to their gleeful surprise, the boys awoke to find themselves greatly publicized heroes.

Naturally they refused to take it seriously, and it was merely a source of tremendous amusement to think of themselves in heroic roles, but all the publicity served a very useful purpose. It fired the imaginations and ambitions of scores of other young Americans, and although many never got beyond the stage of talking about it, there was a constant stream of new enlistments. More than twenty-five were in training in the schools during the summer of 1916.

Two days after Norman Prince's death, the Escadrille was ordered to Cachy Wood, on the Somme front near Amiens, and the war de luxe was finished. Before leaving, the English boys gave the Escadrille a farewell banquet which will go down in history as probably the greatest binge of a war which saw an astounding number, particularly in the aviation corps. It practically wrecked the whole outfit for a week, but the Britishers were extremely grateful for the protection they had received from what

Left to right: Robert Soubiran, Didier Masson, Whiskey and Raoul Lufbery in Nieuport 17 C.1, Cachy.
(Courtesy Paul A. Rockwell)

Frederick H. Prince and Nieuport 11 while instructing at Pau.
(Courtesy C. H. Dolan II)

Head-on collision of two Nieuports at the Pau training area.
(Official U. S. Air Force Photo)

they called their "guardian angels" which had enabled them all to return safely from the bombing raid and they wanted to show their appreciation. For a few days, the guardian angels felt they had overdone it just a trifle.

En route to Cachy, the squadron was strengthened by the arrival of three new men. Freddy Prince, brother of Norman, who made only a brief stay; Willis Haviland, the handsomest man in and the Beau Brummel of the outfit, who had transferred after splendid work as an ambulance driver in all the most dangerous sectors, and Bobby Soubiran, the lion-hearted, ubiquitous kodak demon, who after brilliant service with the Legion had succeeded in wangling a transfer to aviation when he was wounded in the second Champagne attack. Thanks largely to Soubiran's efforts with the forbidden camera, a complete photographic record of the Escadrille is preserved for posterity.

It was most fortunate that replacements were slowly filtering in to the squadron, for the personnel and morale were both extremely low. There were even rumors of filling it up to active strength with French pilots, for it was difficult to muster enough men to fly all the scheduled patrols.

Chapman, Rockwell and Prince had been killed. Thaw and Balsley were wounded, and Jim McConnell was in the hospital with his wrenched back. Rumsey and Cowdin had left for hospitalization on account of ill health. It threw an intolerably heavy burden on the rest of the gang, but they carried on uncomplainingly.

Bert Hall transferred, soon after the arrival at Cachy, to a French escadrille with which he had formerly served for a brief stay, then departed on some mysterious mission to Russia, which ended his participation in the war.

The following summer, he returned to America by way of the Orient and spent the rest of the hostilities in the United States.

In place of luxurious villas and tasty, well-cooked hotel food, the Escadrille was assigned with five other French escadrilles to portable barracks, erected in a sea of mud. Cold and damp fog penetrated every crack and crevice, and these big sheds were anything but watertight. There were no arrangements for cooking, and for some time the boys had to depend on the hospitality of the other squadrons, who generously saw that no one went hungry. There weren't enough blankets and everyone had to sleep in his fur-lined flying suit.

In desperation, many nights I slept with Whiskey, taking him to bed with me to try to keep me warm. Anyone who has never tried sleeping on a folding canvas camp bed with a half-grown lion has a neat thrill in prospect. From my point of view, it wasn't an unqualified success. I always put him down at the foot in an endeavor to keep my feet from freezing, but sometime during the night he'd work his way up, and I'd awake in the cold gray light using him for a pillow and my mouth full of evil-tasting lion fur. I guess perhaps lions aren't supposed to smell like the perfumes of Araby. In any event, Whiskey smelled pretty bad. He wasn't any too careful about his bathing or personal hygiene, and in addition, he had a remarkably well-developed case of halitosis. Still, I couldn't complain, for a lion should smell like a lion, and he did help wonderfully to keep me from freezing.

Bill Thaw and Masson, who was unanimously elected to the thankless job of *chef de popote*, or mess chief, went to Paris and brought back a complete kitchen outfit and, more important, materials for an excellent bar, which did a tremendous business from the moment of its installation.

Masson held the job of *chef de popote* until September of 1917, when he left the Escadrille for a well-earned rest as instructor in one of the American aviation centers at Issodoun. When he departed, the job was handed to me, and I had a chance to find out what grief really was. We used to ride Masson's tail something scandalous, but when I assumed the responsibility I was sorry for everything I had ever said. I found he had been doing a swell job working under the handicaps he had.

An ex-sauce cook, who had once worked in the Ritz in New York, was installed to preside over the pots and pans. His name was Sampson, and he was a honey when it came to preparing succulent food. He knew about ten words of English, mostly profane, and used them for everything. But no man is altogether perfect and without reproach. Sampson's morals were a bit flexible.

There was only one thing Sampson couldn't resist. That was temptation. It was part of Masson's job to help him resist. Occasionally Masson fell down on being a nursemaid, and Sampson would get gloriously potted, with the consequence that our meals were likely to be a bit delayed, if not altogether missed.

If we could keep him from looking too long on the wine when it was red, we had splendid chow, for when he was himself Sampson could do anything with food. He could dope up a can of monkey meat with some kind of sauce, cut it out in little fancy figures, and one would swear it was breast of chicken. Issue horse meat arrived on the table so disguised that we'd have bet francs it was milk-fed veal.

Thanks to generous contributions from outside sources, we could and did put on a swanky mess for ourselves and our visitors, with plenty of so-called luxuries.

The pay of noncommissioned officers in the French army was pretty small, and while several of the boys were quite wealthy, many of the others had no private sources of income.

At the instigation of Dr Gros, Mr and Mrs W. K. Vanderbilt, Sr, generously contributed a large sum of money, which Dr Gros administered, that was sufficient to give every volunteer American pilot a hundred francs a month personal spending money for binges in Paris and what not, and a hundred francs for his mess dues, in addition to buying him a swanky uniform. The fund further provided five hundred francs for each victory.

Until the end of 1917, when victories came too fast, various plane-manufacturing companies and tire and machine-gun manufacturers also offered all French pilots considerable sums when their products were used in scoring victories, so that in addition to the soul-satisfying elation which ensued from knocking down one of the enemy, the financial rewards for heroism were rather tasty.

It sounds a bit sordid, but we always seemed to need francs for one thing or another, and while I'm certain none of us ever thought about it while engaged in a desperate hand-to-hand struggle in the heavens with our black-crossed enemies, I never heard of anyone refusing to accept the fruits of his labors on any moral grounds. On the contrary, no one ever allowed any grass to grow under his feet in making his claim for rewards.

As a matter of fact, our adversaries in the air never represented personalities to us. We thought of them only

Willis Haviland by his Nieuport 17 C.1 at Cachy.
(Courtesy Paul A. Rockwell)

Dudley Hill in his Nieuport 17 C.1 at Cachy. (Courtesy C. H. Dolan II)

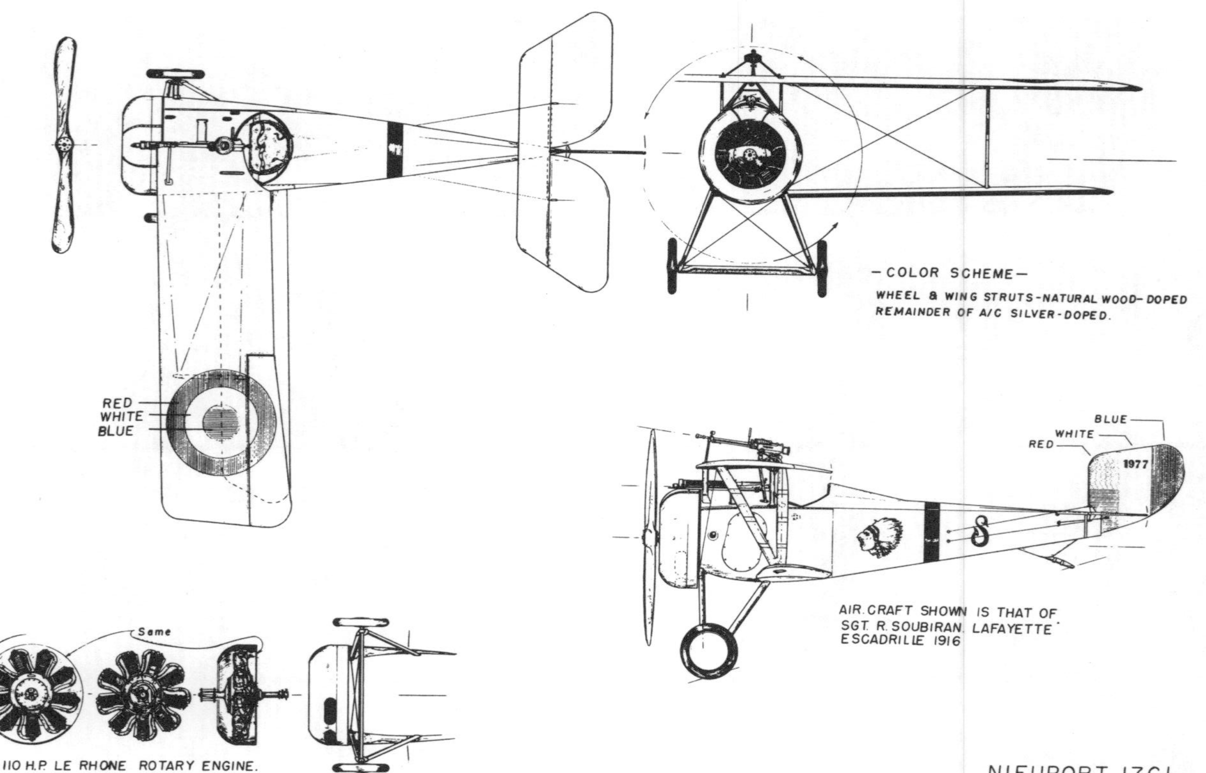
– COLOR SCHEME –
WHEEL & WING STRUTS-NATURAL WOOD-DOPED
REMAINDER OF A/C SILVER-DOPED.
RED
WHITE
BLUE
BLUE
WHITE
RED
1977
AIR.CRAFT SHOWN IS THAT OF
SGT. R. SOUBIRAN. LAFAYETTE
ESCADRILLE 1916
Same
110 H.P. LE RHONE ROTARY ENGINE.
NIEUPORT 17C.I

in terms of machines, an integral, concrete representation of the German militarism which we were combating. Our aerial battles were just like a game, with the personal element entirely lacking.

But it was a game played for high stakes, and the penalty of the loser was usually death. We couldn't shake an opponent's hand and say, "Well played, old chap. Sorry you lost. We'll come back tomorrow and give you a chance for revenge." This game was played for keeps.

Only occasionally, when perhaps we'd see a man go down in flames or jump into space, would we think of them as humans like ourselves. Then we might shudder a bit inwardly and say to ourselves, "Poor devil," thinking how lucky we were not to be in his shoes, but that would be all and quickly forgotten. We knew it was war, and war was no place for squeamishness.

The not inconsiderable sum of a hundred francs a month from each man, added to our issue rations, worked wonders in the capable hands of Masson. It meant not only excellent food, but a fine grade of table wines, plus champagne on gala occasions, which were frequent. We never suffered for anything that money could buy. We even got so swanky that we had menu cards on the table for dinner. The reputation of our mess grew by leaps and bounds.

As time went on, the Escadrille became the unofficial entertainment center for the whole front. Ours was the only mess in the army where officers and under-officers ate together. There was rarely a meal without two to a dozen guests, ranging from bemedaled, gold-corded brass hats of every Allied army down to the humblest corporal pilot. Masson had to provide for every contingency.

Some of the gang were always getting potted at some

other squadron's bar and inviting half a dozen buzzards to come back and eat. By a strange coincidence, at one time or another, nearly every pilot on the front either ran out of gas or had an unfortunate motor failure in front of our hangars just about mealtime.

We were pushovers for newspaper correspondents, American Ambulance drivers, earnest war workers of all kinds and visiting junkets of American sight-seers. Our mess was like a hotel. They were all welcomed and made to feel that we were honored by their presence, no matter how inconvenient it happened to be. Masson was never at a loss, except when Sampson was in disgrace.

Visiting brass hats were our especial delight, for in order to maintain our reputation as perfect hosts we pressed unlimited quantities of the extremely dynamic Lafayette cocktail on them. We were accustomed to it and knew when to quit, but after they had gotten over the shock of the first drink, there seemed to be no limit to their thirst until the inevitable result. We always had spare beds ready for emergencies.

We never got over being surprised and delighted as some very dignified high-ranker gradually began to unbend and become decidedly human, even to the extent of demonstrating all his little parlor tricks for our edification.

It was cold and stormy at Cachy and, owing to the filthy, inclement flying weather, little real offensive air work was done. However, Skipper Pavelka distinguished himself again by nearly ending his career through reckless bravery. He was the first man to try night pursuit in a Nieuport.

Of all the hazardous missions developed in aviation during the war, night pursuit was one of the most perilous. Landing spies, trench straffing, balloon hopping and day bombardments all had their moments, but they were hardly to be compared with flying *avions de chasse* in blackest night.

There were practically no landing lights, merely gasoline flares, to bring down a speedy little high-powered bug landing at from fifty to eighty miles an hour; no parachutes in case of trouble; not even flares to drop out in the event of motor failure and a forced landing. Everything had to be done largely by guesswork and feel, and it was just too bad for the fellow who guessed wrong—he wasn't given many second guesses. It needed the eyes of a cat and the luck of the devil himself to be a consistent night pursuit pilot and still show up regularly for meals.

Besides the hazards of take-offs and landings, there was no particular pleasure in being in the air. There were no twinkling lights or ground beacons to give a man a clue as to his location; nothing but the flaring Véry lights and the flashes of the big guns to show him the location of the front lines. Everything else on the ground was pitch black as a matter of protection against enemy bombers.

Added to that, in the great spaces of the black heavens, was the difficulty of trying to locate enemy ships whose vague outlines, except when they happened to get caught in the crossed beams of ground searchlights, could barely be seen two or three hundred yards away, even on the brightest nights, and, if found, of aiming and attacking solely by the uncertain light of the luminous tracer bullets. That was a duty to make even the insides of the hardiest souls quiver a bit in spite of themselves.

Owing to the importance of the Cachy field in the minds

of the Boche, it was subject to frequent night bombings by the Gothas. Sometimes they didn't stop at the field, but went right on to Amiens, dropping their tons of explosives on hospitals and civilian homes, killing scores of women and children. Resentment against this useless and uncalled-for slaughter ran high.

On December 9 the Boche came over and dropped eight bombs on the camp at Cachy. One of the bombs made a direct hit on the hangar of the N-3, the famous Stork escadrille of the heroic Captain Guynemer, which was located just beside that of our escadrille.

The hangar, fed by the gasoline from the wrecked ships, blazed up in a hurry, and one of the mechanics was burned to death. He was pinned under a plane knocked over by the explosion of the bomb. When the rescue squad got him out, in his charred hand was found a knife with which he had desperately tried to cut himself free.

It was a bitterly cold night, and the boys had hurriedly thrown on what warm clothes they could find at the first warning of the raiding planes. The German ships continued to circle overhead, dropping bombs all around the light of the blazing hangar. The ground was alive with running, shouting figures trying to save the planes in the other hangars, despite a merciless barrage of machine-gun fire from the low-flying bombers.

Pavelka's ship was wheeled out in the light of the dancing flames, and in the midst of the excitement, with only the flickering lights from the burning hangar to guide him, his mechanic started the motor and Skipper took off, in the hope of avenging the raid and adding to his score of victories. He had previously made two other practice night flights, and his ship had been equipped with riding lights.

Just as he left the ground, a connection broke loose, and all his lights flickered and went out. It was no moment to turn back and try to land. Geysers of earth from falling bombs were flying high in the air. Great craters appeared all over the landing field. The Skipper went on without his lights. His dash light, of course, had gone with the others, and he couldn't see any of his instruments. He was truly blind-flying, and blind-flying only by the feel of his plane.

That, however, was not considered such an extraordinary feat in those days, for that was the way we learned to fly. Our instruments were of the crudest and only the most essential. We had only a compass; a fairly reliable altimeter which showed us at least approximately our altitude from the field where we had taken off; a tachometer to show engine revolutions; an oil pulsator to show oil was flowing; a clock and a map. That was complete equipment. No air-speed or turn and bank indicator; no artificial horizons; none of the fine aids to piloting of the present day. We didn't feel the lack of them, for we had never heard of them, and nothing else but air sense and feel of the plane seemed necessary.

Skipper was in difficulties from the moment of his take-off. He was unable to signal the ground. In the roar of so many German motors, his sounded like all the others. As a consequence, he was subjected to an intense fire from our own guns.

Luckily he flew through the barrage unscathed and continued to climb out of danger from the bursting shrapnel. He knew the invaders were somewhere in the vicinity, but he was unable to see them. Searchlights played in vain against a murky sky.

He flew toward Amiens, hoping that some of them had gone on and he could cut them off, but if there were any who hadn't turned back at Cachy, he must have missed them. He never even saw the faintest of red flickers from flaming exhausts.

Although there was nothing to guide him, he had a general idea where he was until he got over Amiens. Then he was signaled as a hostile plane and all the lights went out. From that moment on, he had no definite idea of his location. It was a black night, with a trace of fog, and he was unable to distinguish any landmarks. He couldn't even see his compass, for he had no matches, and his little briquet refused to light in the strong blast of the slipstream in his open cockpit. Alone in a boundless sky, lost and unable to see, there was little chance for him to make a landing.

He had only a little more than two hours' gas, but to come down would almost certainly have resulted in disaster. Every time he neared the earth, the machine guns on the ground would start working on him. The gunners couldn't see him, but they fired at the sound of his motor. The tracer bullets whizzed by him on all sides. Some of them actually pierced his wings.

There was no opportunity for an emergency landing, for he had no idea what kind of territory lay beneath him. Perhaps it was a shell-torn meadow filled with barbed wire, perhaps a village, a forest or a mountain. There was no way to tell.

He was forced to stay in the skies as long as he had gas, a derelict ship afloat in the vast unchartered reaches of the heavens. Then the murk became thicker, and all sight of the earth was lost. His last faint chance to pick up the glowing embers of the hangar at Cachy was gone.

His heart was in his mouth every moment of the enforced flight. He cut his throttle down to the lowest possible safety point to conserve his gas and listened feverishly to every throb of the whirling motor, for a failure and forced landing in unknown territory would be almost sure to have a fatal result.

Careworn and anxious, Pavelka roared along through hours that seemed centuries. Then, just as the first faint light of the gray dawn began to penetrate the murk, he ran out of gas and his motor breathed its last.

He came down rapidly and by great good fortune in the thick, misty half-light saw the ground in time to pull out and set his ship down without blowing a tire. He found himself in the English lines at Martainville, nearly forty miles from Cachy.

Ten minutes after he landed, the fog closed in. He was royally entertained at a château where some British officers lived. He was forced to stay there four days with them before the dense fog lifted enough for him to fly back to Cachy. It was two days before he was able to get a call through and tell the Escadrille where he was. They had already given him up as killed or a prisoner.

Skipper made a score of night flights in all, sometimes accompanied by Lieutenant de Laage, the lion-hearted second in command. That they were unable to bring down any of the enemy is no reflection on their abilities, for it was an almost impossible undertaking. However, they pioneered the way for the organized squadrons of night pursuit, who, somewhat better equipped, took the air almost a year later. It was a tough racket when Pavelka first started it, and he cannot be given too much credit for his daring attempts.

Late in December volunteers were called for to go to the Salonika front, and Pavelka responded. He wanted to see service on as many fronts as possible and, feeling so keenly the death of his old comrade, Rockwell, he was becoming morose. He felt that a change of scene might do him good. He arrived in Salonika early in February 1917.

He found the picturesque life on the Near Eastern front much to his taste. The enemy were much easier to attack and much poorer gunners. Skipper did such sterling work on this new front that eventually he was bound to receive the recognition he had so richly deserved for such a long time.

In July he was cited to the order of the entire Allied armies fighting on the Macedonian front and decorated by the commander in chief with the Croix de Guerre. Naturally he was tremendously pleased that his bravery had been officially recognized. He wrote us a glowing letter:

> It is considered a great thing to have a citation of this nature. All day long I have done nothing but shake hands, and my right hand is almost worn off. Still I would rather have it so than shot off by a damned Hun. I have two machines now, a Nieuport 120 and an A.R. 170 h.p., with a Greek officer as passenger with whom I expect to make a few long-distance raids. He speaks perfect English and is a charming sort of a chap. However, he does not know much about handling a machine gun. This I will soon teach him. I expect to make my first raid in a few days.

But poor Pavelka was not fated to make many raids. A great tragedy occurred shortly afterwards. Skipper, like all aviators, was intensely superstitious. He believed strongly in signs and portents. He had once heard that if a dog howled outside your door, it was a sure sign of death. For three nights before he left the Escadrille to go to Salonika, a strange dog howled outside his windows in the barracks. He had a premonition of death and left very much depressed.

His death was a striking instance of the irony of Fate. He met by chance an English cavalry officer whom he had known in the Legion and visited him at the British camp. Paul was an excellent horseman and asked to be allowed to ride one of a freshly arrived consignment. The animal was vicious. It tried its best to buck him off, and when he found the Skipper could not be thrown, lay down and rolled over on him. Pavelka was picked up with a broken neck and died a few hours later.

He had a magnificent funeral, with an armed guard from the French infantry and one of Serbian soldiers; two services, one by an English chaplain and one by a French priest. Every aviator on the Salonika front was present.

Pavelka had traveled in many lands and escaped almost every conceivable form of death on land, on sea and in the air. He finally met his end in a slight and unusual accident which might have overtaken him in boyhood on his father's farm. It was a dirty trick for Fate to play, but he died as he had lived, a brave hero, a credit to the Escadrille and to America.

CHAPTER XVIII

Edmond Genet

In the meantime, fresh from six months of intensive training, more replacements joined the Escadrille at Cachy: myself, from the American Ambulance; the brilliant, super-gentlemanly Ronald Hoskier, whose father was chief of a Morgan-Harjes Ambulance Corps and whose mother was an auxiliary nurse in a French hospital; and little rosy-cheeked, beardless Edmond Genet, the baby of the Lafayette, who had bravely served with his regiment in the Foreign Legion through many bloody battles.

We three had been all through the schools together and were the closest of comrades, but Fate decreed that I was soon to lose them both. We found ourselves thrown at once into the thick of the fighting, for the Escadrille was again badly in need of fresh blood.

Dud Hill and Doc Rockwell had both obtained leaves to return to America, which, owing to transportation difficulties, was an arduous and somewhat uncertain voyage. Jim McConnell was flying only spasmodically between visits to the hospital, and the cold and damp had finally gotten to poor Lufbery. He became doubled up with rheumatism and had to go down to the south of France to try to bake it out in the warm sunshine.

I have no hesitation in confessing that I had gotten into this scrap through a pure desire for adventure and without any clear idea of what I was letting myself in for. I had taken a whirl for a year in a sort of moving-picture war down in Mexico, and it produced enough thrills so that I was anxious for more.

Against the expressed wishes of my father, who naturally refused to finance my trip, I sailed for France as an assistant veterinary on the *Carpathia*, carrying twenty-two hundred horses. I was willing enough, but probably a bit overoptimistic concerning my abilities as a veterinarian, and the unfortunate horses must have suffered to some extent, but the voyage produced enough revenue to get me to Paris.

I tried to enlist immediately in aviation, but was informed that first I'd have to go to the trenches in the Legion and then put in my demand for a transfer. Momentarily, under those conditions, the war sort of lost its appeal. I knew there must be a way to duck that, but I didn't know just how to go about it.

I was in a strange land, broke, and didn't speak the language so well. In the nick of time, I got a job driving an ambulance while I cast about and found the proper wires to pull. Four months later I was in, and there were many times I should have been delighted to bow out gracefully, if I could have found the proper combination. I was scared all the time, but I stuck. I guess it was because I was more afraid of being called yellow than I was of just being plain scared. Measured by any yardstick, I was far from being a hero.

Hoskier and Genet were both idealists, but the latter far outshone the sweet-natured, gentle-spoken Hoskier in his conception of his duty to France; for, to get there and fight, he had sacrified nearly everything he held dear. Genet's arrival at the Escadrille was a classic.

While several of us were impatiently awaiting at the Pool at Plessis-Belleville our orders to go to the front, keeping our hands in flying all sort of old crates and spending all our spare time in Paris, the boys at Cachy were cursing the uncomfortable living conditions and the foul weather that kept them earth-bound so much of the time.

Lieutenant de Laage and Bill Thaw were huddled close to the little potbellied stove one particularly freezing, greasy day, trying to get warm. Weather conditions were vile, and the ceiling was so low that even the crows were walking. Patrols had all been canceled.

Suddenly they were startled by the sound of a plane overhead, down so close to the barracks that the very walls vibrated.

"Who the hell do you suppose that dumb cluck is?" Bill demanded. "Flying in weather like this! He better come down while he's still got his health."

"The thought has probably occurred to him," De Laage answered dryly. "I don't see who it can be. There are no patrols out, and it's a certainty the Boches aren't flying in this muck."

They were relieved a minute later to hear short, intermittent motor bursts across the hangar and the sound of a landing plane, followed by the steady roar of the rotary as it taxied in.

A few minutes later the door of the mess room burst

open, and on the wings of a great gust of snow-laden wind a short, muffled, fur-clad figure drifted into the room. Only the tip of a reddish, frostbitten nose and a pair of wide appealing blue eyes showed through the woolen wrappings. Hastily the stranger unwrapped layer after layer of woolen and silk, then jerked off his helmet. De Laage gasped in surprise.

The chunky little figure was topped by a thatch of short-cropped blond hair above the round, innocent, pink-cheeked face of an infant. He didn't look a day over fourteen. His peach-bloom complexion showed no traces of ever having met a razor socially. He had a little snubby nose, and there was a constant expression of pleased surprise at the wonders of the world in the wide-set blue eyes. He saluted snappily and in a high-pitched, almost girlish voice announced that he had ferried up a new Nieuport from Plessis-Belleville for the Escadrille.

"Fine work, Corporal," De Laage congratulated him, "but it seems to me you were taking a long chance in this weather."

"Oh, I just got so bored, Lieutenant, waiting at Plessis for my orders that when it looked as if the ceiling might lift I just came on."

That was one of Genet's most admirable characteristics, and he had many. He never let difficulties stand in his way. He just plowed through them to the best of his ability.

He and Thaw shook hands with the cordiality of old friends, and De Laage suggested, since replacements were so badly needed and since his orders to join the Escadrille were probably somewhere in the works, that Genet simply stay instead of going back to Plessis-Belleville. The suggestion was eagerly adopted, but it resulted in unforeseen complications.

When he didn't report back, his name was posted first as A.W.O.L. and eventually as a deserter. De Laage had quite a time straightening out his status. When Genet learned that he was officially termed a "deserter" in French army orders, he nearly went to pieces. What to us was merely a tremendous joke was something on the verge of tragedy for him.

The word had a particularly opprobrious meaning to his sensitive nature. Although none of the rest of us knew it till long afterwards, he was and had been living under what he considered a black cloud of shame. It warped his nature to some extent and made him at times terribly morose and sullen.

We all knew he was carrying some sort of a burden, but it was none of our business, and we weren't in the habit of butting in on another man's past unless he chose to confide in us. I think it would have done him a great deal of good to unburden his soul, for we could have shown him how foolish he was to worry, but he preferred to keep his own secret. Regardless of consequences, he always did what he thought was the right thing.

When Genet left the lieutenant and Bill to go to his new quarters, De Laage was terribly pessimistic about the possibilities of the Escadrille's newest recruit.

"I admire the spirit of you Americans tremendously," he mourned, "but how can they expect us to fight men with babies like that, Thaw? Why, he's hardly old enough to be out of the nursery."

Bill grinned.

"You don't have to worry, André," he answered cheer-

Paul Rockwell and Edmond Genet in French Foreign Legion uniform, before Genet's transfer to aviation. (Courtesy Paul A. Rockwell)

Left to right: Lt. de Laage de Mœux, Norman Prince and Kiffin Rockwell. (Courtesy Paul A. Rockwell)

Left to right: Walter Lovell, Edmond Genet, Raoul Lufbery and James McConnell. (Official U. S. Air Force Photo)

fully. "That kid's got more experience and more guts than three quarters of the hairy-chested apes who handle a stick every day over the lines. Before he went in training, he put in over a year in the trenches with the Legion and covered himself with plenty of glory."

De Laage was first incredulous and then overwhelmed. Although he had just turned twenty at the time he joined the Escadrille at the front, Genet failed by several years to look his age, and De Laage was far from the only one to be so terribly amazed.

Edmond Charles Clinton Genet was a direct descendant of Citizen Genêt, whom the French revolutionary government sent as ambassador to the United States in 1792 and who married the daughter of Governor Clinton of New York.

Edmond was not yet eighteen in the fall of 1914 and was serving an apprenticeship in the United States navy. He had been aboard the battleship Georgia in the spring when the navy occupied Vera Cruz.

With his ancestry and ideals, it was only natural, when the war broke out, that he should want to join with the other American volunteers who had already enlisted in the Foreign Legion. But there was one big obstacle. He tried to buy his way out of the navy, but found it impossible in those first chaotic months.

After weeks of brooding and much anxious thought, he determined on a bold move. While he was on leave in New York, he applied to the French consul for a passport, giving as an excuse the necessity of going to France to look after a family estate. He was obliged to go to Washington, where, after swearing that he was twenty-one, he finally obtained his permission to land on French soil.

Only then did he inform his widowed mother of his intention. She did everything in her power to dissuade him but, inspired by an almost fanatical fervor, he was not to be denied. Requesting her to do what she could in his behalf with the naval authorities, he sailed on the Rochambeau in January of 1915 with the avowed purpose of enlisting in the French army.

Technically, perhaps, his act may be called desertion, but it was desertion, with a noble purpose, from a safe and easy berth at home to a post of danger in the trenches on the Western Front.

It was a fateful passage. By an odd coincidence, Norman Prince was a passenger on the same boat. Genet learned of his plans for the organization of a squadron of volunteer flyers, but since it was evident that it would be a long time before Prince's dream became a reality, he couldn't wait. In February, less than a week after his arrival in France, he enlisted as a second-class soldier in the Foreign Legion.

Throughout his career as an infantryman he gained the praise of his officers and his fellow Legionnaires by his boyish enthusiasm for the most dangerous tasks and his complete disregard for his own safety.

One thing bothered him a lot and was the cause of many bawlings out by his immediate superiors. Army regulations stated that the wearing of a beard or mustache was absolutely essential for a soldier of the Legion. Genet couldn't even sprout enough hair for a mustache. Among the bearded poilus (whose very name means "Hairy one"), he looked like a little boy playing soldier and required a great many highly diplomatic explanations to square himself. However, his lack of hirsute adornment didn't interfere with his courage.

As soon as it could be arranged, he fulfilled his promise to Prince and obtained a transfer to aviation. From the moment of his arrival at the Escadrille, no pilot in the air did more or better work than little Genet. Despite the foul weather and the consequent scarcity of Boches, he seemed to have a nose for smelling them out. He was having tough combats when others were bemoaning the fact they couldn't even see a Hun.

The remainder of his time he indulged in writing letters or artistic endeavors. Genet was quite talented with pen and brush. We covered the bare walls of the mess hall, when in barracks, with corrugated cardboard strips, smooth side out. Genet drew and painted vivid imaginative scenes of aerial combats between French and German planes all over the place. The entire back wall was a highly decorated Indian head. It certainly relieved the monotony of bare walls, but it was too constant a reminder of our daily stunts. We got plenty of that stuff on patrols without having to look at pictures of it while we were *en repos.*

He never indulged in our favorite sport of sneaking off to Paris without leave or coming back forty-eight hours late from a twenty-four-hour "permission." All his leaves were taken in regular order, spent quietly with his mother in Paris or with one or two of the serious-minded *haute monde,* and he reported back for duty exactly on the hour he was due. He was the startling exception.

That winter of 1916–17 was a tough one: snow on the ground, with wet, chilly winds and, up aloft, cold enough to freeze the insignia right off a pawnbroker's sign. But it didn't discourage Genet at all. It was rather soft, according to his way of thinking, after the winter he had put in in the trenches. He never hesitated to fly or fight in any kind of weather or against any odds. During his short career, he was one of the Escadrille's greatest assets.

CHAPTER XIX

Arm Bending and Superstitions

FLYING AT CACHY was sporadic, but conversely, the bar became exceedingly popular. Word in the form of highly colored rumor drifted through to Mrs Vanderbilt that the boys were indulging in considerable high and lofty arm bending to the great detriment of their health and morals. As to the latter, I'm no judge, but as to health, few people realized how necessary alcoholic relaxation was for nerve-strained aviators.

It isn't in the cards that human beings can stand up under the strain of modern warfare without some sort of artificial bracing. Every fighting man knows fear—moments of cold, paralyzing fear that chills his spine and renders his nerve centers incapable of action. Some men knew fear all the time; they were afraid of losing their lives, afraid of being afraid. Ofttimes it was a terrible foreboding before going into a tough spot where Death rode rampant. Some knew fear when faced with a menacing crisis. Others didn't feel it till after the danger had passed; then the reaction was terrific. But no matter when it came, it was imperative that they have something to lift them out of themselves.

The ground troops had alcoholic stimulus, particularly

just before an attack, for the high command knew they needed it. Aviators needed it worse and consequently had a lot more of it. There's no question in peacetime that alcohol shouldn't be mixed with gasoline, but war presented an entirely different aspect.

War fliers occupied a strata completely disassociated from the rest of the army, not only figuratively, but literally. They were young men, very young for the most part, and inclined to be reckless and wild. Death was always just around the corner. They knew that if the war lasted, they wouldn't. So they lived at a dizzy speed. If it was to be a short life, then let it be a merry one!

These youngsters resorted to many devices to make the nerve-racking business more endurable—embracing them unconsciously, for the most part, without recognizing them as the actual salvation they really were. Chief among their solaces was strong drink and plenty of it.

By that I don't mean to convey the impression that fliers were a pack of drunkards, always reeling under the influence. Quite the contrary. Some of us were frequently a bit mellow, but practically never tight.

There was any quantity of liquor available—in the mess, in squadron bars, at the village *bistro*—of the finest quality, moderate in price. No restrictions were placed on an airman at the front. He was limited only by his ability to pay and his capacity to hold it.

Hence, with very few exceptions, it was used only in moderation—a soporific for the agony of tortured nerves. I don't recall in all my time at the front ever seeing any pilot so under the influence that he couldn't perform his assigned patrol duties, or any question raised as to his alcoholic temperature being so high as to make him unfit to take up a ship. Nor is there any record of fatalities or crashes attributable to overindulgence. And without it we'd have been a sorry lot.

Squadron binges took place only on very exceptional occasions.

The washout of a comrade who had left a sum of money in trust with definite instructions that it was to be used for just that sort of an event, to wish him godspeed to whatever Elysian fields or otherwise he was due. There was always an unspoken feeling that the defunct eagle was present in spirit, since he couldn't be in the flesh, to see that his last wishes were properly carried out.

Perhaps it was some exceptional performance in rubbing out Jerries by a member of the squadron, who felt that it was only fitting and proper as a mark of respect to gallant foes, apart from his own natural jubilation, that their memories be hallowed in a fluid flood of concentrated essence of grape.

Infrequently, it was a request party in honor of some captured German airman. Rather like giving a condemned man anything his heart desires for his last meal. The brass hats always hoped the spiritus frumenti might loosen his tongue to the extent of disgorging information of real value. We always hoped they wouldn't, and they never did.

Or perhaps it was simply from the desire to play perfect hosts to visiting firemen who had been forced down by motor trouble or, having commandeered a lorry, arrived in full squadron strength with a view to perpetuating friendship and good feeling. We found that it always paid to be hospitable, particularly to the English, for their hospitality was royal and lavish. There was no British airdrome on the Western Front where a buzzard couldn't land and be offered a cheering cup almost before he had time to switch off his motor. Everything else was relegated to the background until that delightful little gesture had been accomplished.

But, no matter what the occasion for the binge, it was the invariable custom for a few of the boys, after a certain length of time, to withdraw quietly and head for the hay. Their departure, while regretted, was never resented. It was perfectly understood. They were the birds who had the early patrol. They had to leave their more fortunate brethren to carry on, for dawn comes *so* soon, and a whirling-headed hangover was not the best thing to pack on a two-hour patrol against a pack of mordant-minded Huns, presumably with clear heads and untarnished vision.

Overindulgence was frowned on by the pilots themselves; that is to say, if it interfered with work. Commanding officers were always most liberal-minded. They did as much or more elbow bending as the boys under their command. They never attempted to place restrictions, hence the men themselves maintained their own balance. A chap who let liquor interfere with his flying more than once became a pariah. He didn't last long. He either straightened out or was kicked out by popular decision. He was as much a menace as a pair of German Spandaus.

The boys whose records showed the most battles and the most official Huns were the same whose records revealed a lot of hours at the bar. The deeds of those, if there were such, who chose to "shun the fatal curse of drink" were far from impressive. They had too much time to think, to let their imaginations run riot. When they attempted to analyze the situation with a clear, cool head and mentally figure their exceedingly slim chances of coming through with a whole hide, limbs turned to water and nerve evaporated in thin air. So they worried and fretted and hung back, gradually becoming so much deadwood. They had no way to keep themselves from unraveling.

Of all the gallant, lion-hearted aces that I fought beside or knew in three armies, not one was an abstainer. Some drank more, some less, but no one shunned it. The English boys stuck pretty closely to scotch and port, the French and Americans to wine, brandy and liqueurs. Naturally, in the French army, since wine was issued as part of the regular rations, it was always on the table. Hard liquor was not so much in general use, but that was simply because it was more difficult to obtain.

No matter whether a man is visibly scared or not by a shower of flying lead, each time it happens to him it leaves an invisible scar. He begins flinching before he knows it. And in the end, the strain cuts into his nerves. If he hasn't a sedative for those strained nerves, and sometimes despite it, a bird is likely to get so screwy that he goes wild and begs for danger like dope or gets the wind up and comes completely unstuck.

Underneath, he may have all the courage and fortitude in the world, but when his imagination gets the better of him or the constant strain is too severe and his nerves go back on him, he's no more good. It's somewhat the same as shell shock. It always leaves a scar on the nervous system, and some men have killed themselves long after the war on account of it. That's where the liquor came in—to ward off those searing scars and prevent a nerve-racked buzzard from blowing up altogether. There's no way to sum up the great good it accomplished or the lives and sanity that it saved.

When a man heard bullets whistle by his head the first time, he was either scared pink or else he had no idea what that peculiar sound could be. Speaking for myself, there isn't any question. I was petrified, although I didn't realize to what extent till I set my wheels down on the home tarmac after the scrap and attempted to hop nonchalantly out of the ship. My knees absolutely refused to support me. They gave way like two pieces of string, and I had to wrap a shaking arm around a strut and hang on for dear life for over a minute. My sympathetic head mechanic, Felix Henriot, thought I had been shot through the body at least a dozen times. My face was a greenish yellow, and my wildly staring eyes strained through two smudged circles which resembled burned holes in a blanket. There was a complete vacuum where my stomach should have been, and my mouth was full of heart or Adam's apple or something.

Hoskier, Genet and I had been out together for our first offensive patrol—three greenhorns. It was bitter winter weather, there was little activity, but we were told not to go beyond the lines. It was really in the nature of a practice patrol, for no one thought there 'd be any Boches out anyway.

That meant nothing to ambitious young punks, anxious to knock down all the Imperial Flying Corps on our first patrol without an older flight leader. We got fed up with doing nothing over the lines, so we went into Germany. Ten minutes later, we ran smack into a couple of *Walfische* —fast two-seaters. I was cold all over, partly from the atmosphere, but mostly from excitement.

We swooped down on them from out of the sun. Long months of training vanished into thin air. We started firing on them from at least five hundred meters. With that warning they were ready for us when we came within actual effective attacking distance. We ran into a stream of hot lead that made me colder than ever.

Bullets buzzing past your head have a most depressing effect. There is nothing so distressing to peace of mind as their peculiar, faint whine, or the dull thud as leaden slugs rip through taut fabric and bury themselves in laminated wood, or the crackling smash of a glass-covered dial and splintered shards flying back to sting your face with needlelike points.

My motor roared with the speed of my dive, and the Nieuport shook all over from vibration and wind pressure. My single gun crackled like mad as I fired into empty space. My hand was clamped in a semiparalyzed grip over the trigger trip. I slid on down past the tail of my quarry. The enemy ship was painted a bizarre mixture of green and yellow. I had a quick flash of the observer's gun muzzles, with red flames curling from their black mouths following my dive, and behind them his grim white face and fur-clad body.

As I slid underneath him, I tried desperately to recall what page four said to do in such a situation and what advice it gave as to the next maneuver. I believe I should have pulled up underneath him in a steep zoom and tried to find his blind spot from underneath. But some of the pages must have stuck together, for while I was racking my brain the affair was taken completely out of my hands. Maybe the German hadn't read the book, but he knew the answers. I heard more bullets singing their morbid song in my ears. I stole an anxious look over my shoulder. I was no longer the attacker. I was now the quarry. The *Walfisch* was diving on me, and I was full in the pilot's gun. He wasn't a bad shot, either.

He filled my tail and wings as full of holes as a Swiss cheese. And the bullets that missed my ship whined in my ears and added their quota to my panic. He chased me down over a thousand meters into our lines, with Hoskier, perched on his tail five hundred meters behind, making a brave but futile attempt to rescue me from the jam I was in.

The Boche quit chasing me just when I thought the only way for me to get off with a whole hide was to make an inglorious forced landing in back of our trenches. Our Archie began to talk up pretty loud, and the Hun sheered off for his own lines—laughingly, I presume. I can't see why he shouldn't have laughed.

The most scared white man in all of France streaked it for home. That was me. When I shook so after getting out of the ship, I knew there was only one remedy. I swallowed half a glass of brandy neat, in one gulp, without even a shudder. It warmed a little of the arctic chill, but otherwise it had no effect. I continued to shake for an hour, and it took nearly the rest of the bottle before I could lift a glass without holding it in both hands and resting my elbows on the table.

By that time, I was rarin' to go back out and get the *Walfisch*, feeling that I had been grossly insulted; but native caution, plus a few words of advice from the captain, restrained me.

The bar was the general rendezvous for most pilots just before a patrol. I can speak authoritatively only for myself, but I was not a whit different than 99 per cent of all other pilots, at least those who had been in it for some time. During the last year and a half of the war, I rarely went up without a couple under my belt. True, it was generally only port or a very stimulative aperitif known as Dubonnet, but it had the desired effect. I had to have it or, lacking it, perhaps something far worse.

I wasn't sleeping nights. Flocks of planes chased themselves around in my tired brain all the time I should have been thoroughly relaxed. Motors roared and machine guns snarled. I pictured on a vivid background the combats I had fought during the previous day, the mistakes I had made, and visualized what I should try to do in the next fight to get more Huns. Consequently I got up for patrols with the wambling twitters, and I was quite likely to burst into tears if anyone spoke harshly to me or do a backflip if anyone dropped a shoe. A couple of shots of light stimulus and the wibble-wabbles quieted, and they didn't make a Hun too tough for me.

In addition, I carried the pride of my heart, a half-pint aluminum flask which originally cost me twenty-five centimes, filled with brandy, in the breast pocket of my flying suit. (And I'd like to have now what it cost to keep that twenty-five-centime flask filled.) This was an absolute necessity and, with judicial nipping, would just about hold out for a two-hour patrol. When I say necessity, I mean necessity without any qualifications.

When the weather on the ground was so freezing cold that motor oil had to be heated over an open fire, poured hurriedly into the reservoir and the motor started immediately to keep it from freezing up again, then it was cold.

On top of that, take a ship up to fifteen thousand feet,

sit there for two hours immovable, and mere words are difficult to describe the pure agony of mind and body. The subzero temperature penetrated the very marrow of your bones. Despite three or four pairs of gloves, fingers coiled around the stick would be paralyzed in five minutes. Then they would have to be forced open and pushed away from the stick with the other hand and the paralyzed hand beaten against the side of the fuselage to restore circulation. A few minutes later the process would have to be reversed.

Feet were twin lumps of ice, rigid and unfeeling; shooting pains throughout the entire body, eyeballs and teeth smarting and burning, icy scalp contracting till it felt as if the skull must burst through and explode in a shower of bones, heart pumping half-congealed ice water instead of warm blood—thus it can be easily understood why liquor was a necessity. Without it, a man might easily come to earth a frozen corpse.

It couldn't make us as comfortable as the people in front of nice warm fires, reading in the newspapers about our brave heroes in France and what a soft life the aviators led, but it certainly helped a lot, despite the horrified protests of self-appointed reformers and nonimbibing noncombatants. There would have undoubtedly been a considerable change in their attitudes and a broader tolerance had they personally been forced to undergo some of the suffering.

However, since the Escadrille was so much in the public eye, in order to aid us in keeping our stainless reputations and bear out the myth of heroes "without fear or reproach," Mrs Vanderbilt put the heat on. So the bar was hastily moved into the next barracks and the title vested in another escadrille. That seemed to cover the proprieties, and although the ban necessitated a long walk of nearly fifty feet, the financial situation was saved.

The constantly growing publicity concerning the Escadrille and mention of its accomplishments in official communiqués had another far-reaching effect. Shortly after the arrival at Cachy, the Escadrille was officially informed that hereafter it would no longer be known by the name of American Escadrille, but simply by its official number, N-124.

We soon found out the reason. Herr Bernstorff, the German Ambassador at Washington, was all of a dither. It appeared that he had bristled with proper Teutonic rage and finally boiled over. He had dashed over to the State Department and filed a strenuous and bombastic protest. He wished to call the attention of the American government to the fact that so-called neutral Americans were fighting with the French and that the French communiqués often contained mention of an American Escadrille. In the name of the Fatherland, this simply couldn't go on.

I presume the Department of State had to admit that it did look a little peculiar, and they were on the spot. So, despite the fact that we weren't really Americans any longer, since by some ancient law we had ceased to be citizens when we swore allegiance to the French government (as some of us found out later, much to our embarrassment) the State Department sent word by diplomatic channels to the French Ministry of War that Mr Bernstorff was making himself very obnoxious on account of the situation and asked if something couldn't be done about it.

In order to keep America's good will, the French were perfectly willing to concede small points, so the very agreeable French minister stopped the war long enough to dictate a little note which filtered out from the French General Headquarters along in the latter part of November 1916:

From the Commander in Chief to the General Commanding the Armies of the North, Villers-Bretonneux:

By decision No. 9,763 D, the Ministry of War has decided that for diplomatic reasons the Escadrille N-124 should be called the Escadrille des Voluntaires and that the name Escadrille Américaine, in use at present, must be given up. Will you be kind enough to communicate this decision to the Commanding Officer of the 13th Combat Group and to give orders that only the name Escadrille des Voluntaires be used.

[Signed] POINDRON.

Our first reaction was to tell Von Bernstorff and the French Headquarters alike to go jump in the lake, and go on using the name of American Escadrille, but saner thought made us decide that as long as we kept on fighting and knocking them down, what the hell difference did it make whether we called ourselves Americans or Zulus? The name of our outfit wouldn't change our relations with the German laddies in the slightest, and the Herr Ambassador would merely be made to look ridiculous.

However, "Escadrille des Voluntaires" had kind of a flat sound. It didn't seem to have any "zing" to it and was too much of a mouthful, anyway, particularly after the second or third glass of schnapps, without which no proper aviator considered himself to be in the spirit of the war.

So little Genet, who along with his other qualities was a bit of a sentimentalist, suddenly conceived the brilliant idea that, since Lafayette had come to America when we needed help and we were returning the favor to France more than a hundred years later, what could be more appropriate as a sort of token of respect to the old chap than to call our poor nameless outfit the Escadrille Lafayette?

It was acceptable as a compromise to the French, and so the name was born. It became so popularized that of late years the original name of Escadrille Américaine has been almost totally forgotten.

At first, it didn't find any too much favor. We found it difficult to discontinue the name which had been in use ever since the founding of the Escadrille and which meant so much to us, but once the press started using the title of Lafayette Escadrille, we bowed as gracefully as possible to the inevitable.

Coincidentally, the name of the Franco-American Flying Corps, the unofficial name of the loosely knit organization of all the 209 American volunteer pilots who trained and served with the French, was changed to the Lafayette Flying Corps. This name caused considerable confusion in later years, as it was naturally assumed that all members of the Flying Corps were members of the Lafayette Escadrille.

The title "Escadrille" is merely the French word for "squadron." At first, every American volunteer aviator was sent to the American Escadrille at the conclusion of his training, but soon, despite heavy casualties, the boys were coming through so fast from the schools that there was no place for them in the Escadrille. Our flying personnel, like every other French squadron, was kept at between fifteen and eighteen pilots. As a consequence, the young aviators at the Pool were distributed to all French squadrons in need of replacements, not only pursuit, but bombing and observation, so that nearly every French squadron eventually numbered at least one American in its ranks. But of the 209, only thirty-eight ever saw service with the American or Lafayette Escadrille. It was the only organization on the front composed exclusively of American volunteer aviators in French uniform, and it was the Escadrille which became so famous for its daring exploits.

Heaven forbid that anyone should think that any disparagement is intended of the glorious records of the men in the Lafayette Flying Corps, simply because circumstances beyond their control kept them from being members of the Escadrille itself. Each one of them proved himself a gallant hero. They were well satisfied to be where they were, and some of them, given their choice, would have doubtless chosen some other escadrille rather than the Lafayette, for life in the N-124 was not always milk and honey. There was considerable disharmony at various times, which is not to be wondered at, with the varying characteristics and the terrific strain.

Some of the most intrepid, colorful and dauntless aces, among them Austen Crehore, Frank Baylies, Dave Putnam, Charles Biddle, Tommy Hitchcock, the polo player, Billy Wellman, ace motion-picture director, and scores of others flew entirely with French escadrilles. It was our loss and a source of real regret, on our parts at least, that we couldn't all have served together in the same outfit, but unfortunately war won't permit personal desires and preferences to be taken into consideration.

War aviators individually and collectively were the most superstitious beings in the world. We're accustomed

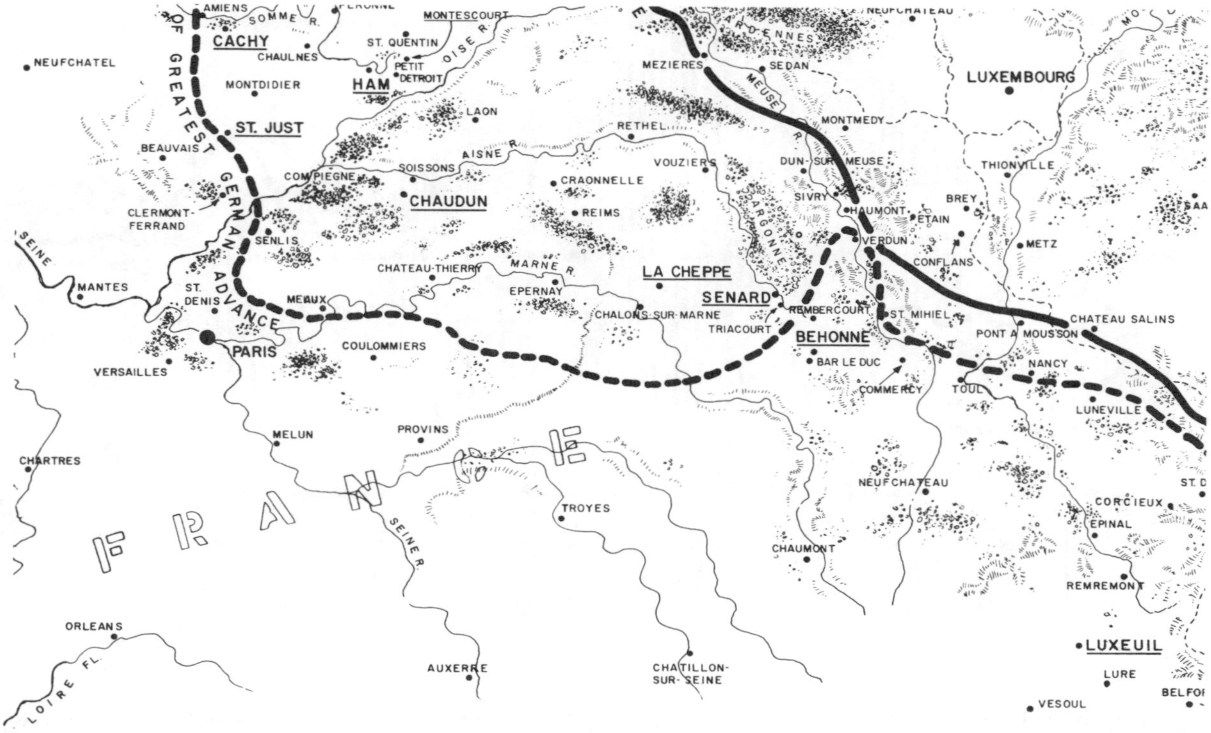

The Western Front: major operations areas of the Lafayette Escadrille. (Courtesy H. Hugh Wynne)

The Lafayette Escadrille at Chaudun, July 1917. Standing, left to right: Robert Soubiran, James R. Doolittle, Courtney Campbell, Edwin C. Parsons, Ray Bridgman, William Dugan, Douglas MacMonagle, Walter Lovell, Harold Willis, Henry Jones, David Peterson and Lt. Arnoux de Maison-Rouge. Seated, left to right: Dudley Hill, Didier Masson with Soda, William Thaw, Capt. Georges Thenault, Raoul Lufbery with Whiskey, Chouteau Johnson, Stephen Bigelow and Robert Rockwell. (Courtesy Paul A. Rockwell)

to think of superstition as a characteristic only of the ignorant, merely because some of the more uncivilized peoples are inherently that way. Such an assumption is grossly exaggerated. Just as many highly intelligent men and women have their own pet personal superstitions; the only difference being that oftentimes they won't acknowledge them or don't recognize them as such. There isn't a shadow of a doubt that people whose livings depend on the whims of chance are superstitious—baseball players, jockeys, theatrical folk and, above all, gamblers.

Frequently the great success of some persons is the result of extreme daring; a mental credence in their own capabilities that refuses to be denied. Naturally, they are willing to use any and all means to foster that belief. But the most superstitious among them is a mere novice compared to war fliers. Sometimes, when we look back on it, we want to laugh at the silly things we said and did, the idiotic articles that were so carefully treasured, and the firm beliefs that no harm could come to us simply as a result of their possession; yet the laugh dies stillborn when one remembers that we, too, were gamblers; gambling for the biggest stakes of all—our lives.

I should probably have hotly resented being called superstitious at that time. I didn't consider it in that light at all. I was just being careful, not missing anything that might help me to come through the scrap with a whole hide. Even before I went to France, I had never been guilty of lighting three cigarettes on one match or whistling in the dressing room. Not that I believed any harm could come from it. I was being considerate of the feelings of others!

However, once I began to fly those delightful little coffins known as the Blériot and wear the Chinese-pagoda-like crash helmet, I went in for protection in a big way, to overcome that most dreaded of all phantoms, the jinx. In order to drive away any jinx that might perch on me as a result of having to wear this monstrosity, I had a large white skull and crossbones painted right on the front of mine. It was most successful in driving away hard luck, and I kept it all through my schooling. Of course, the minute I got to the front, away from all school restrictions and discipline, the crash helmet was thrown in the discard, and I adopted the close-fitting leather helmet worn by all pursuit pilots. Wearing a crash helmet in a pursuit plane would not only have called forth considerable ribald comment, but would be the equivalent of social suicide. No one but Voison or Farman pilots would ever be caught wearing them, and they were so far down in the social scale and deemed so unworthy of notice that it didn't make a bit of difference what they wore.

I didn't have the death's-head painted on my leather helmet. It was unnecessary, for the helmet itself I considered to be the last word in good luck. I never wore any other during my service and would as soon have thought of going up without it as without my black cat (of which, more later). The helmet was presented to me Christmas Day 1916 in Paris by Captain Gerry Grosvenor, one of the outstanding aces of the Royal Flying Corps. We were celebrating Christmas at Ciro's in the good old-fashioned way when, during a lull, Grosvenor decided he had to have a milk bath. That idea appealed to me, too, for some obscure reason, possibly because I'd never had one, and we left the party to go to the Ritz. The idea blew up when we found that it was impossible to get that much milk, and to make up for the disappointment Grosvenor gave me his helmet which he had worn on the front continuously for a year and a half. He had been the victor in many close combats with the Huns and wished me as much luck as it had brought him.

There must have been something in it, for, wearing it, I had all kinds of good fortune, but poor old Grosvenor was bumped off two days later near Albert. The day after Christmas, he had bought himself a new helmet and, on his first flight with it, tangled with a fast-moving two-seater Albatross in his own lines. He brought the Albatross down with a dead pilot, but at the last moment before plunging to destruction the German observer fired a burst that filled Grosvenor's ship full of lead, and one of the bullets got him squarely through the new helmet. Although I was deeply grateful to him, I felt that he should never have given me his old one. He lost all his luck when he did.

About a month after I entered the Blériot school at Buc, I began my collection of medals—little pieces of lead, aluminum or gold, ranging from the size of a quarter down, stamped with the figure or bust of some saint. Most of them were presumed to have been blessed, and all possessed peculiar qualities to keep the wearer out of harm.

Every girl I met, and some that I didn't, had her favorite *médaille*, and I promised faithfully to wear it. I had about twenty at the end of the war, and no two were alike. Six or eight I wore on a gold chain around my neck which was presented with the first one. The rest I attached to the links of the chain of my identification tag, worn around the right wrist.

The favorite seemed to be various postures and facial characteristics of St Elijah, considered as the patron saint of aviators. It was explained that since Elijah went to heaven in a chariot of fire, what could be more appropriate for a patron saint of aviators? I didn't particularly care for the implication. I had no desire to go to heaven or anywhere else in a chariot of fire, but I entered right into the spirit of the thing and put a lot of faith in my medals.

Another favorite but unexplainable medal was that of various virgin saints. I can't conceive of anything more foreign to the characters of war aviators. However, all aviators wore them and generally sounded like nautch dancers every time they moved an arm.

Usually a man's length of service could be approximated by the number of medals he had jangling on his wrist. Some of the old-timers had to wear chains on each wrist to hold them. A visit to Paris without the acquisition of a new *médaille* was considered a failure. Possibly it wasn't length of service, but number of trips to Paris, which really counted and helped him to stay out of harm sufficiently to survive the dangers of the front. I wasn't such a hot number when it came to knocking down the Boches, but I consider my duties in the Battle of Paris to have been performed with masterly efficiency. Twenty medals represent a lot of service and all of it under most delightful conditions. That's what I call a war!

Little replicas of Ninette and Rintintin, the loverlike French dolls, were also considered as absolute necessities. In ivory or porcelain they could be hung on the wrist, and larger sizes in colored wools were sewed onto flying suits and helmets. No one wearing them was ever known to have any bad luck with either sweethearts or Boches.

But the most prized of all talismans for me was my black cat. Black cats are popularly supposed to be anathema, but mine must have been a different breed of cat.

For five months, I fought Huns all over the sky. I poured hundreds of rounds of flaming, snub-nosed bullets into their presumably quivering vitals. Apparently they were all armor-plated or using sky hooks. No wings ever came off; none of them ever burst into flames and went whirling out of the skies like fiery meteors.

I used every attack and combat tactic I had ever been taught and invented a lot of new ones on the spur of the moment. Tracer bullets made a white pathway right into their fuselages, but I never could get one to fall—at least where I could come back with his ears. They filled me full of lead, jeered at me, flipped their wings in disdain and flew serenely home, apparently untouched.

Then I had the good fortune to meet a beautiful Parisienne named Renée de Ranville. I poured out my woes into her sympathetic ears. She diagnosed the situation instantly. What I needed was some very potent fetish. Her first suggestion was a live monkey, but the next morning, when we tottered over to the zoo, we found that they had just run out of salable monkeys. Then, with what I thought at first was a perverted sense of humor, Renée bought me one of those big, life-sized velvet cats with arched back, tail standing straight up and a look of almost human intelligence on the whiskered face.

I lugged it back to the front and had Henriot wire it to the center strut of my right wing. From then on, that black cat rode with me from the Channel to the Vosges. Whiskers streaming back in the slipstream, he or she (I never could decide) kept an eagle eye on everything. It always gave me a lot of courage in a tight place to see the very placid, untroubled expression on her or his face. If the cat wasn't worried, why should I be?

Whether the cat was really responsible or not, I won't attempt to say, but within four days I got my first officially confirmed Boche. I was out on a lone-eagle patrol, staying just inside our lines, for at an equal distance in theirs and at the same altitude were three Hun single-seaters. Black cat or no black cat, I wasn't foolish enough to go over there and tangle with them, and I hadn't had it long enough to know what marvelous powers it had.

Suddenly they darted over and swooped down to attack a French observation plane whom I had noted a few seconds before quite a distance below me. Even though the Jerries must have been watching me, they probably decided they could dive over, sink the Frenchman and get back before I could do anything about it.

That put an entirely different complexion on the affair. They outnumbered me, but the advantage was about even, since I had altitude and they were in our lines. I plunged on down to attack them and give what help I could to the observation ship, who was putting up a stout defense.

Slicing my Spad down full motor, I started firing at about two hundred meters, first on one and then on another. They all separated, darting out at various angles. I had been diving at tremendous speed, and momentum carried me down right on past the tail of the French ship. That had me in a spot, for it was going to give the three little German boys all the advantage.

Just as quickly as I dared, I pulled out in a loop. Imagine my surprise and momentary embarrassment when, just at the top of the loop, fifty yards away, looming up as big as a house, was a sizable green camouflaged Boche observation ship of which I had seen absolutely no sign before. I have no idea where he came from. There was no sign of the three Hun pursuit ships or the French plane.

All I could see was a camouflaged monster with big black crosses. I was so astounded that it was almost an involuntary reflex that made me squeeze my gun trip. There was no mistake about where that solid stream of fire was going: straight into that oil-stained, greenish-brown belly. I couldn't have missed him with a brick.

All of a sudden, he just seemed to disintegrate in the air, and pieces of him were strewn all over the Bois-de-Chepy where he fell. He was reported and confirmed before I got back to the field.

There was no question in my mind but that it was the black cat's influence. I had been trying for months, shooting into Hun after Hun with no results; then came my feline fetish, and all of a sudden some poor blighter flies right into my guns and goes boom!

It nearly broke my heart and all but put me out of business when, late in September of 1917, the Jerries paid us a night visit carrying a lot of nasty-sounding and destructive eggs. One of these eggs lit squarely on top of the hangar in which my ship was bedded down, blew some of the planes to glory and set fire to all the rest. I searched vainly in the little pile of ashes and oxidized metal that had been my ship, but there wasn't even a whisker of my cherished and cocky little black cat to be found.

I absolutely refused to fly until I had been to Paris again. I'm convinced it would have been a fatal error. Fortunately the captain saw eye to eye with me, so once again I was able to sob out my woes on the soft, scented shoulder of the beautiful Renée. Renée was a sweet, accommodating soul in many ways, so she immediately replaced the poor incinerated hero with another one, larger and cockier than the first. It flew with me as long as I was with the Lafayette Escadrille, then I took it to the Storks, where it continued to exercise a benign influence until the end of the war.

Sometimes, if my ship needed repairs, I took up another plane and quite frequently would have a forced landing. Not once did I ever have a forced landing with any ship on which my cat rode.

And I firmly believe that my little fetish once saved my life. I got tangled up in the summer of 1918 with three very nasty Fokkers several kilometers in their lines. Two other Frenchmen who had gone over with me had been forced out of the fight, one with a punctured tank and the other with jammed guns, leaving me in a rather tough spot. I wasn't in the jam because I wanted to be. In fact, there were at least a hundred different places I could think of on the spur of the moment where I should have preferred being. I was in the middle of the three Fokkers because they had me surrounded and no apparent intention of letting me get away. With one-track minds they were working on the theory of "never give a sucker an even break." I was playing the unenviable role of the sucker.

There was only one thing I could do: fight my way out of the hole and trust to luck to get back alive. Every way I turned, those three Huns seemed to multiply, and there would be a gray, snub-nosed ship with flaming guns to head me off. Lead was singing in my ears from all angles. It looked like sure curtains, and I was fully prepared to get it at any minute, but was determined to take at least one of the blighters with me.

Figuring that I might just as well get bumped where I had half a chance of falling in our lines, I made a sharp wingover to turn in that direction. As I leveled off, there was one of the Jerries, waiting for just such a move, slicing down on me with both guns blazing. I wouldn't have given a can of tinned willy for my chances. He was coming at a bit of an angle, and suddenly I caught him full in the center of my Aldyce telescopic sight and squeezed on the trigger trips. My Spad shook with the recoil as both my Vickers snarled away without a miss. I had changed direction slightly, so that we were squarely head on. It looked like a sure collision as we approached at express-train speed. Then, when he was less than fifty meters away, he suddenly dropped off and went into a spin. I thought a wing came off, but I wasn't sure—much too busy trying to duck out through the hole I had made. I poured coal into the old Hispano and lit out like a scared jack rabbit.

The other two were right behind me, coming just as fast as I was, all four Spandaus spitting hot lead in my general direction. I could hear the whine of the bullets as they sped by me, and I hunched all up in a little ball, trying to make as small a target as possible, but it seemed to me that I was spread out all over the sky. The chase couldn't have continued over three minutes, but it seemed like as many years to me. Then from nowhere came a Spad patrol of seven ships, whining out of the clouds. The two Fokkers banked and ran, just as I had been running a minute before. It was the low patrol of my own squadron, and they certainly arrived in the nick of time. They ran those two Huns ragged, miles back into their lines, but never could catch them.

I was plenty scared with my narrow escape and, since my patrol time was nearly up, hurried back to the field. Again just in time! My whole tail assembly was torn to pieces, and two of the wires controlling my elevator and rudder were hanging by one strand. With shaking knees I examined the rest of the ship before heading for the solace of the bar. Here and there was a hole in the wings or fuselage, but I discovered no other damage until I happened to look at the cat. Sawdust was dripping out of a ragged hole in her off side. Somewhere deep in the black cat's vitals was a German slug with my name engraved on it! Since it didn't go through, the bullet must have been nearly spent when it hit, but in lining it up from the direction it entered I found that, if the cat hadn't been there, it would have in all probability neatly punctured my eardrum. We performed a neat surgical operation with needle and thread, while I blessed the black cat and its donor.

I have gone into considerable detail regarding my own pet superstitions, for, quite naturally, those are the ones I know best, but every pilot had just as many. If their talismans didn't work, then someone had hexed them, and if they were lucky, full credit was given each particular object.

While I was in training school at Pau, I made the acquaintance of a young French medical officer who had somehow gotten himself transferred to aviation. His particular pet charm that he carried with him all the time was the dried-up head of a small monkey, with parchmentlike skin clinging to the shape of the skull, which bore an extraordinary resemblance to the shape of his own head.

The doctor used to say that he was quite certain from the general bone structure that the monkey was one of his own forebears, pointing out the similarities. The head made quite a bulge in his uniform, but he firmly believed in it and wouldn't go out without it.

One morning another student rolled in with a Blériot that the doctor was waiting to take up and killed the motor. There didn't happen to be a mechanic handy, so the medico, with a reassuring pat on his fetish, stepped over to twist the tail. He caught hold of one of the blades and started to pull it, when the overheated rotary gave a backflip of a half-turn and the sharp blade of the light Eclair propeller hit him right across the skull. The blade shattered in fifty pieces, and the doctor dropped like a rock. In ninety-nine cases out of a hundred, the force of the blow would have split his head wide open, and I was pretty sick as I ran to pick him up. Before I could get there, he staggered to his feet, felt ruefully of a large lump on top of his head and demanded to know who was the cowardly so-and-so that hit him when he wasn't looking.

With the exception of a slight concussion that kept him in the hospital for two days, he was unhurt. He was thoroughly convinced that the influence exerted by the dried skull of his simian ancestor was the only thing which kept him from being killed, and he demonstrated on his talisman with a piece of match just how the blade could strike in such a way that it wouldn't crush the bone and split his skull.

One of the best known of the English pilots had a doll which he carried with him every minute. His name was Teddy Gerard, exactly the same as a very famous musical comedy actress who was extremely popular in London during and immediately after the war.

Teddy the flier met Teddy the girl on his first leave, and she had the doll made for him, with hair from her own head. That was all the talisman the pilot needed. Accompanied by his doll, he brought down over thirty of the enemy, coming through without a scratch. Romantically enough, three months after the war, the two Teddy Gerards became one.

In days of old, knights going into battle carried a lady's glove to bring them good fortune. What more fitting than, being knights of the air, we should carry some token of a lady's esteem? That the something was a bit more intimate only made its powers all the stronger. Under our helmets, nearly all of us wore a silk stocking. The top fitted over the skull, while the leg and foot went under the chin and was tucked up on the other side. It was useful in keeping our heads warm as well as being a strong charm. Not any silk stocking would do. It had to be a stocking from some girl you loved or vice versa and had to be well worn. If anything happened to you while wearing it, it was a sure sign the girl didn't love you any more or never had. The personality that the stocking assumed through having been worn was held sufficient to keep you out of trouble.

The ordinary jinxes, like the number thirteen and lighting three cigarettes on a match, most of us avoided like a pestilence. Calamity invariably followed a violation of these taboos.

Christmas night, 1916, when the Escadrille sat down to dinner with a guest or two at the table, they numbered twelve. Then, unexpectedly, Jim McConnell blew in and joined the group.

They were halfway through dinner when Jim happened to count noses and suddenly turned white as a sheet. Fine, strapping sort of a chap, McConnell was, with loads of intelligence, the last man in the world one would suspect of being superstitious.

"My God!" he exclaimed in agonized accents. "Thirteen of us here. That's sure death. Wonder who'll be the next to get it?"

It was a cold shock and made everyone rather uncomfortable, but they tried to laugh it off. But Jim McConnell, the man who made the thirteenth at dinner and called attention to it, was the next man to die.

Perhaps all these incidents can be laid to pure coincidence, and perhaps there really aren't any jinxes or hexes that exist, except in our own minds. Probably we were wrong in being superstitious. But we believed in our talismans and charms and, since they brought us through, who can say that we weren't right?

If we hadn't had them, we might not be alive to laugh about them. I maintain I'm not superstitious, but right now I wouldn't light three cigarettes on one match for all the wine in France.

CHAPTER XX

Death of Jim McConnell

In late January, we moved in the snow to a field nearer Paris, called St Just-en-Chaussée. Barracks weren't ready for us on our arrival, and for a week we lived underground like moles, sleeping on the dirt floors of the bomb shelters.

Then it was no war de luxe, and we suffered agonies in the arctic temperature. It was so cold that when Genet tried to wet his hair with his lukewarm wash water to slick it back, it froze straight up in little individual icicles before he could put a comb to it. Despite three pairs of socks and fur-lined flying boots, I froze a toe and was unable to walk for a week, while Ed Hinkle, a new arrival, froze both ears. Hinkle was more than forty years old, an ancient for war flying, but he bravely fulfilled all his duties until illness forced his retirement two months after his arrival.

It was about my third patrol on this new sector when, through overanxiety and cocksureness, I very nearly concluded my part of the entertainment. I sincerely believe I owe my life to Lufbery, who always seemed to be on hand to rescue some young squirt with a mania for getting into jams.

Fresh from that long intensive course of training in the schools, I felt there wasn't much I didn't know about pursuit and combat work. I had been told I was pretty hot stuff by my instructors, who made it legal by signing their names to high recommendations in my flight book. I found out shortly that, outside of the fact that I could fly formation, do acrobatics and shoot a machine gun fairly straight, I didn't know a thing.

I once heard a young pilot in his first three days at the front remark:

"What's the matter with you birds up here? Why don't you get more Boches? My gosh, there's plenty of 'em. Must be you aren't attacking right, or else you're not going over after 'em. I'm going out and show you goldbrickers something."

We only sighed at his abysmal ignorance and decided that there was no use trying to explain; he'd have to find out for himself. History records that this brash young man lasted exactly seven more days, and the final ceremony was quite impressive.

Although I knew enough to keep my mouth shut, I had that same superior sort of a feeling. I pitied rather than condemned the old veterans of six months or more. There were beautiful ships all our own, unlimited gasoline and ammunition. Evidently there were scads of Boches. What more simple than to go out and knock down three or four each day?

I failed to take into account that every German was similarly equipped and presumably had the same idea. I had never been under machine-gun fire and privately scoffed at the idea they could touch me.

I learned through bitter experience that first it was necessary to find your Boche and that finding him didn't necessarily mean you could get a combat. The wily Hun wanted the best of it just as much as we did. The chances were that in your first combats you might just have well stayed in the barracks.

No green pilot was worth his salt till he'd been on the front at least a month. If he survived that time, he had about a fifty-fifty chance of coming through. There was so much else to look out for that the neophyte rarely saw any Huns for the first couple of weeks, although they might be under his very nose.

There came one of those rare days of good weather, and we turned out en masse to hunt the Hun. There were about six of us on the patrol, and our sector was between Roye and Lassigny. We flew the lines for about an hour, and it became evident that we were just out for the ride. No sign of Boches at all. It got most monotonous, particularly for a man so full of desire to clean up the front single-handed.

Suddenly I spotted five black specks against a snowy background, flying quite low, far in the enemy lines. They were unquestionably Boche planes. The enemy was at hand, and I thrilled with pardonable pride. I and I alone had been the bright-eyed potential hero to discover them. At least, that's what I thought. I found out later that everyone had spotted them long before me—and, in addition, several others that I never did see.

Bill Thaw was leading the patrol, and I socked on full motor to dive past him, wildly wagging my wings. Bill looked to where I was pointing, saw the Huns and shook his head. I was itching all over, and I couldn't understand why Bill refused to get excited.

Our orders had been to keep the lines clear between two and four thousand meters, and the enemy ships were far in their own lines. They couldn't have been doing any active work, and naturally Bill decided against going in after them.

Orders were strict to stay with patrols, but at a time like that orders meant nothing to me. This was my chance to show the boys up and get me some Huns.

Hoping against hope that the rest would follow, I sliced away from the flight. As I got over into Germany, the Archies turned loose. It gave me a momentary thrill, but I wasn't to be denied. I warmed up my gun as I roared down.

The German ships grew larger and larger. They were flying close formation about a thousand meters high. White crosses stood out boldly on a gray background. They were large ships, and I saw they were two-seaters. It looked like a cinch.

I was overanxious and started to open fire from at least a half-mile away, giving them plenty of warning in case they failed to see me coming. They scattered like a covey of quail. Then I dived right into the middle of the formation. In my ignorance, I thought I could pick off a couple and get away before the others could recover and get me in range.

I didn't even come close to getting one. But they came within a whisker of finishing my career right then. Five ships turned into twenty-five. They had me surrounded on every side. Machine guns sounded like hail on a tin roof. I heard angry bees buzzing around my head. I didn't need any textbook to tell me what that was. The attack was coming from every side. Blue ravelings from tracer bullets crisscrossed the sky. I was absolutely bewildered.

I suddenly changed from a bold marauder of the skies

into a very scared youth. I began to see why more Huns weren't brought down. I had only one desire left: to get away from there as fast as I could and with a whole hide.

I made a steep bank, yanked my throttle open to the last notch and pulled up. It seemed hours before I ceased to hear the rattle of guns and realized that I had climbed out of a veritable death trap. I looked back and saw that the five ships had resumed formation and were calmly winging on their way.

I was pretty shaky and headed for the lines as fast as I could go. My first attempt at being a hero had been a dismal failure. To my anguished eyes, the trenches appeared to be miles away. With Archie banging away at me to mark my location, I kept looking back over my shoulder anticipating hordes of pursuers, but I wasn't watching very closely in front.

All at once, when I had almost reached the lines, several dark shadows passed my eyes in quick succession—solid objects between me and the sun. I knew it could only mean one thing—hostile ships. I looked up, and a cold chill ran down my spine!

While I had been watching for attack from the rear, with the blindness of green pilots I hadn't seen three Huns coming from the lines. There they were, right over my head, in a sweet position to attack. I had narrowly escaped once, but I felt that this was the finish. They had me cold. I could see the whirling propeller blades, the dirty gray bellies and the sun shining through their gossamerlike wings. The crosses stood out in bold relief.

Cold sweat broke out on my forehead. I hunched myself together in the cockpit to make as small a target as possible, but that well-known feeling of bulging all over the sky was impossible to shake off. Any second, I expected to feel lead slugs tearing into my flesh. I lived a thousand years while I waited for the blow to fall. The suspense was terrific, but it couldn't last long.

Seconds passed, and there was no chatter of guns, no thud of ripping slugs. Curious as to the delay, I stole a look upward. The anticlimax was ludicrous.

Instead of pursuing lethal intentions toward me, the three Boches were scurrying to save their own hides. Darting in and out, a constant tongue of flame belching from his gun, was a French plane with the familiar Indian head on the fuselage. The pilot was evidently a master hand. He was making a concentrated attack on all three ships at once. They were two-seaters, and with his powerful little plane he ran circles around them. Their observers seemed to be either dead or paralyzed. I failed to see but one ship make any attempt at defense.

Like a trained boxer, my rescuer danced in, jabbed and danced away. It was beautiful to watch his work. I was low in gas, but lower in spirit, so I didn't join in the pursuit. He seemed to have complete mastery of the situation. I kept on toward the lines, watching him over my shoulder, wondering which one of our patrol had been bighearted enough to follow me to get me out of a jam.

Suddenly a bright orange streak sprang up from the motor of one of the Germans, which quickly blossomed into a great crimson flower. Writhing and twisting in its death agony, the big ship, all aflame, fluttered toward earth. A long finger of greasy black smoke traced a smudgy line across the clear air.

My rescuer turned and, ringed with a bouquet of black Archie puffs, caught up with me just as I passed the lines.

We landed almost together on the field at St Just. I slid out of my cockpit and, my knees still shaking, ran over to express my gratitude to the other pilot. He raised his goggles and looked me over as he would a strange bug. It was Lufbery.

No one had been forewarned that he was coming back. He had arrived by auto, found there was a patrol out and hopped in his ship. He had arrived at the lines just in time to rescue me from a desperate situation and incidentally score another tally on his debt of vengeance.

He looked me up and down while I shriveled. Then in his queer accent he demanded:

"Vot de teufel vas you doink ofer dere all alone? Don't you know you could have got in plenty trouble if I hadn't came?"

And he was telling me!

I felt like a kid caught stealing jam. He proceeded to give me a good raking over for being foolish enough to think I could fight the whole German aviation single-handed. That he had just successfully demonstrated his ability to do practically the same thing was evidently no criterion. Then he shook hands with me and said I showed a good spirit.

I felt quite bucked up till Thaw, in a few well-chosen words, put me right back in my place. Boiled down to essentials, eliminating all profanity and references to the origin of my ancestors, I gathered from his lurid words that quitting a patrol to go over on your own, no matter what the provocation, just wasn't done. Bill needn't have been quite so emphatic. I had just found all of that out for myself.

It was my first view of Lufbery in action, and he lived up to everything I had heard about him. I realized he had saved my life and at the same time given me a practical demonstration of what a real pilot could do in pursuit work. He was my hero. From that time on, I went out with Luf every time it was possible. I stuck on his tail, watched his combat tactics and learned something in every fight.

During the next two months our regular patrols were carried on under the most harrowing of weather conditions. All the oil had to be heated before each patrol so that it wouldn't congeal before the motors were started. With such temperatures on the ground, flying above ten thousand feet was pure agony.

With four others on a patrol over the lines, we got caught in a snowstorm. My compass plate cracked, and the liquid in which it floated froze. For over an hour, with a failing motor I flew absolutely blind, never being sure whether or not I was right side up or in what direction I was headed.

When I was almost out of gas, I suddenly ran into a funnellike hole in the storm, plunged down it and landed just before the storm closed over my head again. I hadn't the vaguest idea where I was, and as indistinct figures hurried toward me I prepared to sell my life as dearly as possible, in case they proved to speak with a Weber and Fields accent. I believe one of the greatest thrills I ever had was while watching closely out one side of my cockpit, trying to identify the uniforms of the hurrying figures, hearing a soft voice on the other side at my elbow say:

"Hi there, old chap. I s'y, wot's the matter?"

Upon inquiry, I found that I had landed just south of Arras in the English lines, eighty kilometers from the field and a mile from the front lines where they made a decided outward bulge. I had been flying blind the whole time directly north along the lines, part of it inside the enemy trenches. Had the hole in the storm occurred five minutes sooner, I should have been well inside the German lines, dead or a prisoner.

After I had been marvelously entertained with true British hospitality and repairs made on my engine, I flew back that night, one of two of the patrol to return. Most of the others straggled in the next day, all having been forced down by the storm, but the captain, who had been leading the patrol, didn't show up for three days. He had landed near a château.

Then the German retreat to the Hindenburg line began in March, and we were kept busier than ever, observing the movements of the enemy and keeping the skies clear.

On March 19, a lowering, gray day with storm-driven scud, Jim McConnell, Genet and myself were named for the regular ten-o'clock patrol. I had hardly left the field when my oil line plugged up with sluggish castor oil, burning my motor completely out. I had to make a forced landing two kilometers away.

Genet and Mac continued on and, just over the lines, ran into a trio of straight-shooting enemy planes. Back and forth in the low-hanging clouds they roared in a deadly struggle for supremacy, blazing round after round of flaming lead.

Genet and his adversary circled each other in tight spirals, each waiting for the break—the fractional second when he could get the other in his sights. Genet turned

James R. McConnell. (Courtesy Paul A. Rockwell)

James McConnell at left, with his mechanics. (Courtesy Paul A. Rockwell)

his head for a brief instant to look for McConnell, and in that instant the German struck.

A bullet hit flush in one of the main center supports of the upper wing and severed it cleanly. Flying splinters and fragments of the slug gashed Genet's face. He caught a glimpse of Mac in a mad chase after the other two Germans before the gray mist blotted him out of sight forever.

With blood streaming into his eyes and his plane threatening every minute to collapse under him, Genet was forced to quit the fight, but he spent the next fifteen minutes under heavy shell fire hunting for his vanished comrade, ready and eager to go to his aid. Finally growing weakness and the fear that the whole top wing would come off his plane forced him to return to the field.

Mac didn't come back and, three days later, in the midst of the French advance on the Somme, a cavalry patrol found his body lying beside his badly smashed plane at Flavy-le-Martel.

There were several bullets in his body, any one of which would have caused his death. The retreating German vandals had stripped his dead body to his underwear, even taking his shoes. Jimmy McConnell, that genial soul and gallant soldier, was the last American to die for France before the United States entered the war.

Genet took the news of Mac's death hard. He seemed to blame himself, although Mac was a much older and more experienced pilot. He absolutely refused to go to the hospital for treatment and kept incessantly in the air, burning with a savage desire to avenge his fallen comrade. It was nerve-racking work, and he wore himself to a shadow. His wound had been more of a shock to his system than he realized. He was half sick, thoroughly fatigued, and his mental outlook was very gloomy, for he was one of the very few men who brooded and allowed himself to be cast into the depths of despondency over the inevitable empty chairs at the mess.

Most of us came to regard death very lightly. Not from a spirit of bravado, but because it was so imminent and so prevalent. We adopted the credo of fatalism, an eminently practical doctrine. If it was written, nothing we could do would stop it.

We were scared, yes, for we loved life, and the sky paths were a horrible nightmare of lurking death, but we felt that we would come through unless it was foreordained for us to die. I know I didn't have, and I don't believe any of us ever had, that feeling that the patrol we were going out on might be our last. We were always prepared for it, but unless there was a feeling of depression from a hangover, we always thought of it as happening to somebody else, not us individually.

Despite all the hokum of fiction stories and motion pictures, there was practically never any outward show of emotion of any kind over the sudden passing of a comrade. It was war, and life was moving too fast.

Inwardly we might feel that with the bumping off of a comrade or close friend a part of our bodies had been cut away by a ruthless hand, and we might mourn in secret for a day or week, but outwardly the reaction generally consisted of the terse phrase:

"Gosh, that's tough. Well, he was a good egg. Let's have a drink to him."

The nearest approach to sentimentalism was in one of our favorite drinking songs:

We meet 'neath the sounding rafters,
The walls all around us are bare;
They echo the peals of laughter;
It seems that the dead are there.

So, stand by your glasses steady,
This world is a world of lies.
Here's a toast to the dead already;
Hurrah for the next man who dies.

Cut off from the land that bore us,
Betrayed by the land that we find,
The good men have gone before us,
And only the dull left behind.

So, stand to your glasses steady,
The world is a web of lies,
Then here's to the dead already;
And hurrah for the next man who dies.

But most of the aviator's songs and poems were either extremely facetious or of such a deep purple hue as to preclude repetition. However, merely as an indication of our attitude toward extinction, here is one of our favorites entitled:

THE DYING AVIATOR

The young aviator lay dying,
And as 'neath the wreckage he lay,
To the mechanics assembled around him,
These last parting words he did say:

"Two valve springs you'll find in my stomach,
Three spark plugs are safe in my lung,
The prop is in splinters inside me,
To my fingers the joy stick has clung.

"Take the cylinders out of my kidneys,
The connecting rods out of my brain;
From the small of my back get the crankshaft,
And assemble the engine again."

Just a patriotic laddie, as anybody can see. He knew how hard up we were for motors.

However, while none of us anticipated getting rubbed out, we generally made certain preparations, just in case. The preparations in most instances were very simple: merely a letter addressed to the world at large containing directions in case of death or imprisonment. I was guilty of writing one, and I have a sneaking hunch everybody did, for one always seemed to turn up.

Usually they were classics. Rarely did anyone fail to appropriate a certain sum of money to be used for a squadron binge—this in place of the usual idea of a bunch of hypocritical mourners and flowers, which do no good to anyone. The idea was simply to leave enough to buy liquor to toast the dear departed in his new location, whichever it happened to be, depending on his previous life, and drown our theoretical sorrow over his untimely end.

Of course, there was always a serious part to the missing aviator's last will and testament—that part about whom we should notify—but that was more or less impersonal. The aviator generally finished the letter with a few sentences leaving his personal effects to be divided among squadron mates and ended with a cussing out of our enemies and admonitions for the living to go after 'em, sometimes in a serious vein, but more often in the spirit of sportsmanship with which we fought the war in the air.

For there certainly existed a certain amount of sportsmanship and chivalry among the knights of the air, particularly in the early days—not to the extent, as some lurid fiction writers would have us believe, that, if we had an enemy cold-cocked and saw that he was out of ammunition or in distress, we'd bow gracefully out and politely give him another chance when he was better prepared. No, we'd take every possible advantage of him, just as he would of us, when it came to lethal duels. But there were exchanges of little courtesies, such as a salute or wave of the hand to some adversary when the duel had been called a draw; or letters passed back and forth, dropped over the lines, inquiring about the fate of a comrade or expressing regret for the death of some gallant enemy pilot, which rarely failed to bring an answer; or a wreath dropped during the funeral ceremonies of some well-known ace.

For a long time, the Germans dropped notes with the news of all our missing airmen, whether they were killed, wounded or merely prisoners, and we rendered them a like courtesy. Occasionally the notes were facetious, as in the case of a French captain who took a whole squadron of Caudrons over into Germany, got lost and ran out of gas. He landed his whole command on a German airdrome. The French got a note of sincere thanks from the Germans, acknowledging the delivery intact of so many nice Caudrons and pilots, but asking what they would do with the captain! I don't recollect hearing what the answer was, but I'll wager it was a classic.

Early in the war, a German plane, flying over a drome on which Bert Hall was stationed, dropped an expensive fur glove. Hall picked it up, and the following day the German came back and dropped the other glove with a note in which he begged the finder to accept it with his compliments, as he had no use for one glove. At that time, furred gloves were an unheard-of luxury, and Hall was delighted to accept his gift, dropping a note of sincere thanks to the donor.

There were many instances of this kind, and while they were frowned on by all the brass hats outside of aviation, who couldn't seem to reconcile chivalry with the general policy of conducting a war in which bitterness and hatred seemed as necessary as guns and ammunition, nothing they could say or do could quell the feeling.

Perhaps it won't be that way in the next war. Who knows? Maybe, with the strangeness of an unfamiliar element all worn off and the great hordes of winged death that will fill the sky with their monstrous roar, it will be all cut and dried; individuality will be completely submerged and knight won't be able to meet knight in the struggle for supremacy. But we are more than grateful that chivalry did exist and that great adventures were conducted by sportsmen against sportsmen in a sportsmanlike spirit.

Of course, because of the very nature of the work, the bond of comradeship in the aviation was far closer than in any other branch of the service. To a certain extent, every pilot was dependent on every other pilot for his life. With the pilots constantly facing death together, really genuine affections were developed, despite petty bickering and squabbles.

I am certainly grateful to good old Jimmy McConnell. I didn't have money enough to buy a sleeping bag, didn't have nearly enough blankets, and Jim knew I hadn't been able to sleep warm the whole winter, despite the sterling aid rendered by Whiskey. So, in his last letter, he willed me his own luxurious sleeping bag, in which I slept comfortably warm the rest of the war. He didn't know he was going, but if it was written in the stars, he was unselfish enough to think ahead. He realized he wouldn't need any sleeping bag where he was going.

The finish of his letter was classic. The last two paragraphs read:

> My burial is of no import. Make it as easy as possible for yourselves. I have no religion and do not care for any service. If the omission would embarrass you I presume I could stand the performance.
>
> Good luck to the rest of you. God damn Germany and vive la France.

That was just like Mac. He feared neither man, god, devil nor death. In accordance with his wishes, he was buried without service at the spot where he fell.

CHAPTER XXI

Deaths of Genet, Hoskier and De Laage

AT ST JUST, several additions were made to the personnel of the Escadrille: Steve Bigelow, the pleasure-loving, near-graduate playboy of several colleges and a piano-playing fool whenever we could beg, borrow or steal a piano; tiny Billy Dugan, former assistant manager of a United Fruit banana plantation, who had served heroically with the Legion through every battle since the beginning with his regiment, the Swallows of Death; Walter Lovell, former ambulance section chief, and husky Harold Willis, who had served as an ambulance driver, both Harvard graduates.

A little later came the old Alaskan sourdough, Kenneth Marr, who was never called anything else but "Si," a contraction of "Siwash," with which tribe he was reputed to have been extremely intimate; another wild Indian named Courtney Campbell, who had been a former professional dancer and turned out to be the wild man of French aviation, having three of the narrowest escapes from accidental death possible for one man to survive; John Armstrong Drexel, a very superior personage, who spent only a cou-

Capt. Thenault and Lt. de Laage de Mœux.
(Courtesy Paul A. Rockwell)

Ronald W. Hoskier (Courtesy Paul A. Rockwell)

Walter Lovell by Spad 7. (Courtesy Paul A. Rockwell)

Stephen Bigelow in Spad 7. (Courtesy C. H. Dolan II)

ple of weeks with us and left for the drawing rooms of London to become liaison officer between the Americans and English, and a rather nondescript blister, nicknamed "Useless," who had spent some time as an ambulance driver and showed a marked preference for making all his patrols either in the bar or, in the rare cases when he was in the air, behind our balloon lines.

While the French were making great advances into German-held territory, America declared war. We were all naturally jubilant. Almost daily we waited word from Paris, expecting that, with our experience, we would be called on to help the United States form a real aviation corps. Then we could fight for our own country in our own uniforms. We who had gone through the mill and survived would be enabled to give our countrymen the benefit of our hard-won knowledge. Alas for our great hopes and expectations! They were but idle dreams—but they were such nice dreams till we were rudely awakened! Reports came that our countrymen neither wanted nor needed us. They had other plans in which we played no part.

Meanwhile, during the advance, despite frightful flying weather, we worked like fiends. Bill Thaw, who was cited for the work he did, was worth a whole squadron. Flying low over the retreating German troops, he'd get a complete check on where they were and what they were doing, fly back and wait for the French cavalry to arrive, make a report, then fly back for another check. He was in the air ten hours a day and, thanks largely to his intrepid flying, the French knew to a dot just what was going on in front of them.

Half the Boche aviation was out trying to stop Bill, but he couldn't be annoyed. He simply ignored them, but if they got too quarrelsome he'd stop long enough to bring one down and then go on with his work.

He landed in one village, just as the Boche evacuated. It was the first time in three years that the place had been free of the invaders. He was welcomed with open arms and hailed as a savior. He immediately made friends with a very lovely young French girl who gave him a lot of valuable information. She had been there all the time. She told him that the German army was really hungry, that even the officers didn't have enough to eat, and that she had been offered as much as fifteen francs for a pot of coffee.

All the people in the village had been without meat since the previous November and said they would have died if it hadn't been for American charity.

Although the little French girl had had a Boche sweetheart, she was all for having Bill take her back with him. Much as it distressed him, Bill couldn't see his way clear. That was the only time he ever held out on us. Although we generously offered to substitute for him, in relays if necessary, he wouldn't tell us where the place was.

The French advanced so quickly and so far that on the 8th of April, in order to be anywhere near the front, we moved our field nearly forty kilometers further toward Germany, at the edge of the ravaged village of Ham, which had been for nearly three years in German hands.

It was a scene of wanton destruction and utter desolation: ruined villages, torn-up railroad tracks, blasted bridges and roads, whole rows of beautiful trees lining the national highways ruthlessly laid low. Everything movable had been taken and all else had been torn to pieces or rendered useless.

Here, in our desperate air duels against the frenzied

enemy, we suffered more severe and irreparable losses, but all the fatalities weren't by any means at the hands of the enemy.

Bearing out our belief in hexes, Monday became a real Jonah day. For seven successive Mondays, there were from one to three crashes and deaths from various escadrilles on the field. It got so that whenever there was a crash, we knew it was Monday without bothering to check up on a calendar. It couldn't be laid to week-end hangovers, for Monday hangovers were no whit different from any others. We didn't have Sundays or week ends off. Every day was a working day, for this wasn't a union war.

The hex started the Monday we arrived, when, early on a foggy morning, somebody happened to look through the frameless window in the house on the edge of the field where we were quartered. With an oath he shouted to us to come and look.

We rushed to the window, awe-stricken and sick at heart, to see a Farman, flaming like a torch, appear like a ghost ship out of the mist and crash onto the field, burning its occupants to a crisp. We never knew who was in it, whence it came or why it was in flames. What difference did it make then?

Another jinx started to operate at the same time. Ham must have been cursed. Lieutenant de Laage owned a loose-moraled little bitch which he called "Meess." At St Just, she whelped the fruits of her wanton misconduct, a miscellaneous lot, among which was little Archie.

He was black, the runt of the litter, and somewhat resembled in color and general characteristics an exploded Heinie anti-aircraft shell, being about as much use—hence the name.

Poor little Archie had distemper, then got run over by a motorcycle and was partially paralyzed, but Genet, out of the kindness of his heart, nursed Archie back to semi-health and adopted the little cripple for his own. It was a fatal mistake. Archie promptly put the curse on him.

Monday week, after our arrival at Ham, half sick from his wound and fatigued with constant flying, Genet went up for his second patrol of the day in the company of Lufbery. He had already done a two-hour early-morning show, and he seemed so tired that the boys tried to get him to lay off, but he stubbornly refused to listen to reason.

Haviland, whose plane was disabled, tried to borrow his ship and do his patrol, but Genet insisted he was all right and flew—to his death.

Luf and he flew low on account of the clouds. German anti-aircraft pounded at them continuously. Suddenly Luf noticed that Genet made a half-turn as if he were going back. Luf tried to follow, but lost him in the clouds.

There seems to be no doubt that Genet either fainted from exhaustion or else was hit by a shell splinter, with the possibility that his Nieuport was badly damaged. He fell with motor going full speed and hit in the middle of a hard-packed dirt road, probably unconscious long before he struck.

It was five kilometers inside our lines and only a few hundred meters from where McConnell had been brought down a month before. I have never seen a more complete wreck. He had dug a hole five feet deep in the hard-packed road. The tank was a flat piece of metal, the wheels were ribbons, and there wasn't a piece of wing or framework bigger than a match. Every bone in his body was broken, and his features were completely gone.

Poor little dreamer! He was the first American to be killed after the United States entered the war, and the Escadrille lost one of its most sincere and conscientious pilots. He gave his life for his ideals.

Genet, the "Benjamin of the Escadrille Lafayette" as Captain Thénault called him, was buried with fitting honors in the military cemetery at Ham, in the midst of a driving snowstorm. At the moment when Captain Thénault, who had read the office, said "Amen," the sun pierced the clouds for an instant and illuminated the bier like a benediction from heaven.

Happily, soon after the war, through the kindly intervention of the Secretary of the Navy, Genet's name was cleared of the technical charge of desertion placed against it on the records of the United States navy.

Secretary Daniels wrote Genet's mother a letter which began:

MY DEAR MRS GENET:

There has but recently been brought to my attention a story full of interest to me, a story glorified by the unselfish patriotism and final sacrifice of an American lad.

The letter went on to say that in fighting under the flag of France, Genet was "giving to his own country his valuable services in so serving France" and concluded:

Edmond Charles Clinton Genet, having honorably terminated an enlistment with an ally, since he died on the field of battle . . . the offense is nullified by his conduct in the common cause under the flag of our ally. I myself am honored in having the privilege of deciding that the record of Edmond Charles Clinton Genet, ordinary seaman, United States Navy, shall be considered in every respect an honorable one.

So ended the career of this brave-spirited boy who risked everything to serve his own country and France with a purity of purpose that can never be forgotten.

At first, after Genet died, nobody moved to take Archie, but eventually, Hoskier, who had been very fond of Genet and whose heart was as big as all outdoors, felt sorry for the masterless waif and adopted him. That, too, proved to be a fatal error.

Just at this time we were being equipped as rapidly as possible with the new flat-winged Spads, with the 140-horsepower Hispano-Suiza motor. They were the finest and strongest pursuit ships of the war, and we disposed as quickly as possible of the slower, rotary-motored Nieuports and other heterogeneous ships which had somehow been dumped on the squadron.

Among these latter was a Morane Parasol two-seater which had been used for gunnery and training purposes. It was a honey to fly, and occasionally we liked to take it over the front, sometimes with another pilot as machine gunner or frequently Lieutenant de Laage's orderly, Jean Dressy, who had gone through a training school for aerial machine gunners.

Orders came to fly the Parasol to the rear, but the following Monday, the day before it was to leave, Hoskier asked to fly the ship for the last time, and Dressy begged to be allowed to go.

Over the lines they engaged in a savage duel with three black-crossed Albatrosses. For over fifteen minutes Hoskier and Dressy put up a spectacular and valiant struggle against the heavy odds. Dressy fired off every cartridge in his twin Lewis guns and drove one of the attackers whirl-

The wreckage of the plane in which Hoskier and Dressy were killed. (Courtesy Soubiran Collection)

The funeral of Ronald Hoskier and Jean Dressy.
(Courtesy Paul A. Rockwell)

The funeral of Edmond Genet. (Courtesy Soubiran Collection)

ing and twisting out of the fight. But the fatal conclusion was almost inevitable.

Hoskier was horribly wounded and either fainted or hadn't the strength to bring it out when the delicately balanced Morane fell into a spin from which it never emerged and crashed in the first-line French trenches.

With Dud Hill and Doc Rockwell, who had just returned from their leaves in America, I went up to the lines at midnight in an ambulance and recovered the battered bodies. We brought them back to a little mortuary in Ham, where they were put in plain pine coffins.

Hoskier's parents were notified, and two days later the heartbroken De Laage and myself went by car to Compiègne, the nearest railroad station, to meet them. It was the first time I had ever seen the gentle, cultivated officer break and give full play to his emotions. He cried on my shoulder like a little child all the way there.

De Laage not only loved the brilliant and gallant Hoskier, as we all did, but he felt as bad over Dressy's death as if it had been his own son's. Dressy's family had been in the service of the De Laage de Mœux family for generations. All during the war, Jean had been his orderly, and in one of the early cavalry charges, before their transfer to aviation, Dressy had saved his life when the lieutenant's horse was killed and De Laage himself sorely wounded.

Upon our return to Ham and before the double funeral services, Mr Hoskier asked me to take him to the chapel to see Ron. We were quite alone. I stood back as the bereaved father gazed with infinite sadness on all that was mortal of his beloved son. As he rejoined me and we turned to go away, a weird and inexplicable thing occurred.

For almost three days, Ron's cold, stiffened, battered

body had lain untouched in the pine coffin supported on trestles. As we started to go out, I heard a faint sound and, turning back, saw a steady stream of blood dripping slowly from one corner of the plain box, each drop echoing with a hollow noise as it struck the uncarpeted cement floor. It gave me a cold shock, for it seemed as if it were a sign from the dead to the living loved ones.

We all began to look askance at Archie, but De Laage pooh-poohed any thoughts of a jinx, and because the pup had been Genet's and Hoskier's, of both of whom he had been very fond, the lieutenant adopted him.

Three Mondays later our gallant, courageous and well-beloved officer met his own death in one of those stupid accidents which take the bravest and most skillful of pilots, together with the timid and unskillful.

Trying out a new Spad, gathering terrific speed as he left the ground, he pulled up in a climbing turn, ordinarily a reasonably safe maneuver. But at fifty meters from the ground his motor momentarily cut out, and before he could straighten out, the plane slipped on a wing and crashed, killing him instantly.

With him went the soul of the Escadrille, for no truer, finer gentleman ever existed, and his friendship was more precious than almost any other gift that life had to offer.

Three deaths on three Mondays and all of them the successive owners of the little jinx dog, Archie. For a time, Archie was a pariah, living on scraps which bighearted Sampson, who didn't worry much about a jinx because he didn't have to fly, fed him. However, just at this time, Sampson was caught swapping off some of our food to get more wine for himself and given fourteen days in clink.

Then came Lieutenant Maison Rouge from another

French escadrille to replace De Laage. Maison Rouge was a nervous, sensitive sort of Frenchman, and he was in a tough spot. All the gang were heartbroken at the loss of De Laage and couldn't reconcile themselves to the thought of having anyone attempt to take his place.

So the new officer was far from popular, and no one bothered to warn him when he took over Archie because it had been De Laage's. Archie didn't get in any dirty work until some time later, when Maison Rouge was involved in a mid-air collision with the wild man, Campbell, escaping annihilation by the narrowest of margins.

After that, Maison Rouge became too nervous to fly any more with what he called *les sauvages* and soon left the Escadrille for more congenial surroundings. With his departure, Archie was shunned by everyone, including Sampson and, apparently feeling he was losing his grip because he hadn't gotten Maison Rouge killed, simply laid down and died of some unidentifiable disease. It was a great relief to everyone when the last clods fell on the unhallowed ground of his final resting place.

CHAPTER XXII

Archies Over the Chemin-des-Dames

WHILE THE Spad was a honey of a pursuit ship and we all came to swear by it, at first some of us weren't too well pleased with having to give up the sweet-flying, easily maneuverable, rotary-motored Nieuport for the heavier, water-cooled, stationary Hispano-Suiza. It packed a lot more gadgets to watch in the air.

So when the Nieuport turned out the new streamlined "type 28" with the 150-horsepower Gnome *monosoupape* or single-valve motor and the French government ordered quantities of them for delivery on the front, we disgruntled ones fell on them with cries of joy and war whoops of satisfaction.

We flew the pants off them for about two weeks, then suddenly, without warning, orders came to withdraw them and, willy-nilly, we went back to Spads. Upon inquiry, we were informed that they had developed a structural weakness, and we were much too busy with other things to delve further into the cause.

It wasn't until well over a year later, when the United States, desperate for any type of pursuit ships, purchased the whole lot of discarded planes, that we learned what had been the original cause of their hasty withdrawal. Much to the embarrassment of a great many American pilots, it had been discovered that, under the terrific pressure of a power dive, the fabric on the leading edges of the wings couldn't stand the strain. It would split and peel back, leaving only the bare skeleton of the wing, which detracted considerably from its usefulness. Fortunately it didn't happen to any pilot of the Escadrille while we were gleefully stunting them about over the lines. While we were perfectly contented with the ill-famed "28" ships and groused largely when we were forced to give them up, it was only another case of where ignorance was bliss.

As long as I live, the music of "Katinka" and "Allah's Holiday" will bring back a flood of memories of our lighter moments in the Escadrille at the front. Until Dud Hill came back from America, we had only a few ancient French records, military marches and uninspired French ditties, all badly scratched, to play on our wheezy old phonograph that we had picked up, God knows where. Dud, like an angel of grace, brought back half a dozen new records, and they were played from early morning till late at night. If only the folks at home could have known how much we craved music, I'm sure we'd have been deluged with records, for no one can conceive of the pleasure those few gave us.

Then, owing to the carelessness of overexuberant pilots and the hazards of transportation in our constant moves, every record except those two were broken. But they were played constantly and became part of our very existence.

Daylight hours were naturally either devoted to flying, sleeping or reading, and writing letters. Unless there was a big binge on, evenings were devoted to music, on a piano if we were fortunate enough to have one (both Steve Bigelow and Harold Willis could make a piano do cart-wheels and backflips) or, in lieu, our meager collection of phonograph records was played over and over.

Occasionally the captain, bolstered up by a few quaffs of the cheering cup and laboring under the fond delusion that he was a second Paderewski in the flesh, would maul a protesting piano with heavy hands. But even his police dog, Fram, who worshiped him, would slink out with reproachful eyes whenever the recital commenced, and with due regard for his ravaged canine emotions, we were generally successful in dissuading the captain from further efforts.

Meanwhile, there 'd be a bridge, poker or roulette game, at which vast sums were won and lost, mostly on the cuff, interspersed with a little mild quaffing. I O U's were freely given, for ready cash was always conspicuous by its absence, and we knew that if we lasted long enough we'd come out fairly even, or if we went west we'd no longer have any worries about who owed us or vice versa. Rarely did we indulge in African dominoes, for it was too difficult to keep score.

Generally we turned in very early, for our work was most exhausting and the enervating thin air of high altitudes seemed to induce a constant desire for sleep.

Taking it all in all, our squadron life was very quiet, and we existed only for the times we could wangle a leave to go to Paris. Then we tried to crowd all the excitement and general hell-raising we could into a few short hours. I'm far from being the only man who has mournfully remarked after a hectic forty-eight hours among the houris and bright lights of the Big Sinful City, "Gosh, I gotta go back to the front for a rest." Despite its hazards, it was a haven of rest for the weary.

At Ham, the Escadrille was strengthened by the arrival of the youthful and scholarly Ray Bridgman, who had already seen active service with another French pursuit squadron while awaiting the need for a replacement with us, and Charles (Harp) Dolan and Henry (Hank) Jones, both fresh from the training schools.

In the beginning of June, the Escadrille was ordered from the unlucky field at Ham to a newly created drome at Chaudun, behind Soissons, to fly over a sector which included the historic Chemin-des-Dames.

Chaudun proved to be as lucky as Ham was unlucky, for while there were the usual number of mishaps, freak accidents and narrow escapes, we suffered no fatalities. Fate seemed to be trying to give us a break, and we needed it.

The field at Chaudun was large and smooth, with plenty of landing space for all the six escadrilles, except at the far boundary, where there was a deep irrigation ditch ten feet wide that had been red-flagged and otherwise well marked by the Engineers. Warning of it was posted in orders, and from the air it stuck out like a sore thumb. Apparently, even the blindest and dumbest truck driver would have had to go out of his way to come anywhere near it.

On the day we moved from Ham, after nearly sixty ships from our whole group of escadrilles had landed without accident, our worthy colleague "Useless," nearly the last man to arrive, after carefully dragging the field and making sure where the ditch was, headed straight for it and piled up a new Spad in a beautiful smash. The captain was justifiably furious and, although he should have known better, after giving "Useless" a well-deserved bawling out, told him that, since he had cracked up his own ship and couldn't go on patrol, he could go back to Ham by auto and ferry over Bobby Soubiran's Spad, Bobby being on leave. The rest of us were all tickled to duck the job, for it was a long, arduous trip by car over shell-torn roads back to Ham, but the captain's order to "Useless" proved to be a serious error of judgment. The following day "Useless" returned with Bobby's Spad and, in a well-executed maneuver, piled the second one up in the ditch not ten feet from the spot where he had crashed his own the previous day.

As far as the Escadrille was concerned, that practically concluded his participation in the war. He was more of a menace to the French than he was to the Germans. He was transferred to being a truck driver in a bombing outfit, where his habits found little favor, and a short time later he was painlessly separated altogether from French aviation.

We hadn't been long at Chaudun when Campbell, the wild man whose whole life seemed devoted to giving other people thrills and to whom trouble gravitated as naturally as iron filings to a magnet, pulled off the first of his famous escapes from shaking hands with the ubiquitous old gentleman who carries a scythe.

Indulging in some of his usual fancy acrobatics with his Nieuport at about fifteen hundred meters over the field, while he was test-hopping a new motor, Campbell pulled into a snapping loop at the end of a short power dive. Just in the middle of his loop, he heard wires twang-

The field at Ham. (Courtesy Soubiran Collection)

Robert Soubiran's Spad on the field of Ham.
(Courtesy Soubiran Collection)

Two views of the field at Chaudun. Kenneth Marr can be seen in top photo. (Courtesy Soubiran Collection)

Courtney Campbell stands by his Nieuport 17 C.1 which lost a wing at three thousand feet.

The Lafayette Escadrille at Chaudun, 1917. Front row, left to right: Didier Masson, Stephen Bigelow, Chouteau Johnson, William Thaw, Capt. Georges Thenault, Edwin C. Parsons, Thomas Hewitt, Harold Willis and Willis Haviland. Back row, left to right: Ray Bridgman, Robert Rockwell, Henry Jones, David Peterson, William Dugan, Douglas MacMonagle, Walter Lovell and Lt. Arnoux de Maison-Rouge. (Courtesy Paul A. Rockwell)

ing and wood cracking. Goggle-eyed, upside down, he saw his left lower wing separate completely from the fuselage and go floating off into the great unknown.

With somewhat over a million chances to one against his keeping out of a spin and losing the rest of his wings—a most disconcerting procedure for any pilot—he miraculously found and held a perfect counterbalance on coming out of the loop. Setting his three-winged ship in a slow glide, without attempting to spiral down to the field immediately below, which would have been instantly fatal, he held the delicate balance and volplaned all the way down to a safe landing in a beet field ten kilometers from Chaudun. On the way, he passed his slowly settling missing wing, which came to earth ten minutes later.

Not in the least shaky or upset by his incredible escape, he rode triumphantly back on the seat of the meat wagon which had been hastily dispatched to pick up his mangled remains and, after several detours to the bar, was in the air in another ship thirty minutes later.

We had a tremendously long sector to cover, from Soissons almost to the famed cathedral city of Rheims. It was obviously impossible for one patrol to keep that whole area adequately covered. While we were at one end of the sector, a hundred Boches might sneak over at the other, do their monkey business and get back safely without our knowing anything about it. So we privately worked out a very effective scheme with our Archies, in which they proved extremely helpful, justifying their existence, in our estimation, for the first time.

As far as we were concerned, Archies and Archie batteries on both sides were just a waste of good material. They threw thousands of shells into the air, making themselves very obnoxious by their noise and occasionally coming close enough to force us to change altitude and direction in a hurry, but their record of hits and general efficiency was pretty low.

Sometimes when things were pretty slow on the lines and we got fed up with just riding around, we'd go over in the particular spot in the Heinie lines where we knew there was a very touchy Archie outfit and tease them into throwing a few score shells up at us, just for the fun of playing hide-and-go-seek with them. It was all in the line of duty, for we were making them waste shells without any particular danger to ourselves. After a while, they'd apparently get wise that we were just doing it in the spirit of good clean fun, and they'd refuse to play any longer.

Archie shells were of two varieties, shrapnel and high explosive, both with time fuses. Of the two, shrapnel was the most dangerous, for it would spread, while H.E. had to be almost a direct hit. Shrapnel, however, was generally used only in the lower altitudes, up to ten thousand feet, while I have been at sixteen thousand and had an H.E. break five hundred meters over my head.

I should estimate that I had been the target for probably five thousand shells, but I was hit only once and that once at an altitude where I thought I was perfectly safe, somewhat over four thousand meters, approximately thirteen thousand feet.

I had had a brush above the clouds with a big two-seater, and after I had fired about twenty rounds from a short distance, he plunged through the clouds, smoking, with me hot after him, anxious to finish the job or be sure where he fell.

As I came out of the brilliant sunshine into the dark

shadows after a sharp dive of three or four hundred meters through a thick mist, I couldn't see a thing for a moment. Then, in the middle of a large green forest, I spotted a flaming pylon which I took to be my quarry.

Not knowing exactly where I was, I started to go on down further to check on him, when suddenly, bursting all about me with the roaring growls of an angry bulldog, was a complete ring of Austrian 77s. They had my range to a gnat's eyebrow, and I knew that I was over the St Gobain Forest.

I always had a lot of admiration for the chappies who ran that battery. I had received little messages of hate from them before. They were always on the job, mealtimes as well as other times, and they shot closer than all the rest of the Hun batteries put together.

I started to duck out in a hurry and for some reason was looking at my right wing, when I saw a strut sliced clean through and vanish as though it had never existed. I hope it was my heart that came up into my mouth, but I've always doubted it.

I scurried out of there and headed toward the field, praying the wing would stay on till I could get down. In unison with me, it shivered and shook, but my prayers were answered and it held. That was another occasion when, as soon as I had gotten my underwear changed after I landed, I sat right close to a bottle till the shakes had quieted. My compliments to the St Gobain battery.

However, as a shining example of the overzealous inefficiency of most Archie batteries, I recall a very sad incident that occurred at Cachy. A very young and very pompous shavetail had been assigned, quite evidently without proper education concerning the appearance of aeroplanes in flight, to the command of a battery. Under his direction, the battery was likely to whale away at the faintest sound of a motor.

One day, after filling the air full of shells, a miracle occurred. He made a direct hit, and the crippled plane was seen to fall. Highly elated, he telephoned to headquarters very boastfully, anxious that no other battery should try to horn in and claim the credit. He was most insistent that, under his able direction, his battery, and his alone, had scored the hit.

Some hours later he received a rude jolt. They had found the "enemy machine" which he had brought down. As a result, he was very quickly separated from any active service on the front, for the wrecked plane proved to be a Nieuport, clearly marked with the French *cocardes* or tricolor circles, and the very dead, unfortunate pilot was a splendid young Frenchman named Savage.

I presume equally stupid errors must have occurred on the German side as well, but such unfortunate mistakes didn't tend to help endear Archie batteries as a whole to our hearts.

However, the system we worked out on the long Chemin-des-Dames sector was a honey. We divided all the batteries up into four sections, numbering the sections, in order from Soissons to Rheims, one, two, three and four.

Suppose, for example, that we were away at the end of our sector, in Section Four. The Archie battery of that section had us under constant observation. Away down in Section One, some of the enemy were sneaking across without active interference from French pursuit.

The battery or batteries in Section One would telephone Section Four immediately. A battery in Section Four nearest us would send up one shell, far-enough away so that it wouldn't be dangerous, yet close enough for us to see it immediately. From that signal, we'd know that there were Boches in Section One and high-tail it for there at full speed. Then the battery in Section One would throw up shells to show us where the enemy were in case we failed to spot them immediately.

There was little chance for error in this system, for the French Archie shells always exploded with white smoke, while the Boche was black. We were enabled, by working this scheme all the time we were in that sector, to give our Jerry pals quite a number of surprise parties, probably to their vast amazement, as they must have wondered how we could always be on the job so quickly. Anyhow, it made our Archies in this case, despite our doubts concerning their general usefulness, of real assistance.

CHAPTER XXIII

Jimmy Hall's Miraculous Escape

THE ESCADRILLE received two splendid replacements about the middle of June. The first was the dashing young former ambulance driver, Douglas MacMonagle, and the second was that famous warrior and writer, James Norman Hall, the hero of three armies.

Jim was and is one of the most lovable men in the world and a bubbling well of energy. Writing was a habit with him, even during the war. Every time he got hurt and was forced out of active service, he used his convalescent period to write a book. When he was well enough, he'd push his way back to the front and gather material for another one.

He didn't need to write about the experiences of others. His own adventures or misadventures furnished plenty of material. He could get in and out of trouble with equal facility. During his short periods of service with the Escadrille, between visits to the hospital, he was by far and away the most popular and best liked man in the squadron.

Jim was rather an idealist, and though he seldom voiced his opinions, we knew he was possessed of a real love for France and a deep, abiding hate for the Huns—

not for them as individuals but in abhorrence of the barbarism for which they stood.

Quiet and retiring, almost to the point of shyness, with an even disposition and a sunny smile, brave as a lion, Jimmy made his presence felt in every army and on every front.

Almost at the beginning of the war he enlisted in the British infantry as a private. He went through all the hardships and privations in the trenches as one of the "Contemptibles" until he stopped a shell early one morning and got a "Blighty" that sent him back to England to be invalided out.

While he was getting well, he wrote the book called *Kitchener's Mob.* With Ian Hay's *The First Hundred Thousand,* it was one of the earliest and finest sagas of the trenches and enjoyed an equal popularity, for they were both written by men who had been through the hell.

Most men would have considered at that point that they had done their duty and would have made arrangements to get as far away from the war as possible, using their wound stripe as an alibi; but not Hall. He considered he had just begun to fight.

With the first book off his chest, he hopped over to France, enlisted in the French army as a second-class soldier in the Legion, got a transfer to aviation and, from then on, adventure piled on him thick and fast.

There must be a special Providence that watches over chaps like Jim, for even the most vivid imagination can hardly picture the strange story that lies behind his first crash at the front, after the five months of intensive training which included the usual trials and tribulations of the student pilot.

When Jimmy showed up at the squadron, we were all tickled to death, but unfortunately his first period of service was only a little over a week in duration.

The day after his arrival, he was assigned to a ship, but it wasn't a new one by any means. Newcomers to the outfit very rarely got a new ship. The veterans got the choice planes and the youngsters the hand-me-downs.

Jim's ship had seen yeoman service and was about ready to be retired, but since new planes were becoming exceedingly scarce, the last ounce of service had to be extracted from the old ones. Hall made no protest. He pushed the old crate up to the lines two or three times and seemed happy to have anything to fly.

A week or so later, he was assigned to a sunset patrol, with Bill Thaw leading, Lufbery, Dugan, Bridgman and myself. Just before we took off, Bill told us that the rendezvous was at four thousand meters over the reservoir. This meant that everyone would wait at thirteen thousand feet over an old reservoir which was almost at the lines, make formation there, then climb together to the lines at sixteen thousand, which was our assigned altitude. Jim was cautioned to stick right with the patrol, for it was a nasty sector, and it was only his third time over the lines.

The Huns had an unpleasant habit of hanging around some convenient cloud in large gangs waiting for a stray who might have wandered away from the herd and who, poor blighter, would have small chance for a getaway.

We took off almost together, with the exception of Hall, who was having trouble getting his fatigued motor started. Naturally we couldn't wait for him, but since he knew the rendezvous there was no occasion to worry. We expected he would meet us there.

James Norman Hall (Courtesy Paul A. Rockwell)

William E. Dugan (Courtesy Paul A. Rockwell)

Edwin C. Parsons (Courtesy Paul A. Rockwell)

It was fully ten minutes before he could get his old mill grinding, and once he got in the air he climbed so slowly that by the time he'd gotten to four thousand meters at the reservoir, we'd all gotten into formation and gone on. Much annoyed at having missed the rendezvous, Jimmy gave her the gun and drove ahead to catch up. He had been told that if for any reason he missed, he was to stay back around the balloons till he saw us come down the sector. Then he could come out and join us, but he was not to go playing up and down the lines all by himself.

Jim didn't feel like waiting around the comparative safety of any balloons. He was a bit impatient to get into action, so he sailed right on up. He turned at the lines to follow them toward Rheims, searching for five Spads with yelping Indian heads on the fuselages.

Far down below him were a couple of artillery ships crossing and recrossing the lines for the evening shoot. To his right were the French sausages, and at an equal distance to his left were the German *Drachen* swaying gently in the evening breeze like pond lilies on the surface of a millpond. But there was no sign of any patrol of Spads.

He knew we were somewhere on the sector at the altitude he was flying. And, since he was keeping a close watch for enemy ships, he felt very secure.

Suddenly, five or six kilometers inside the German lines, he saw a number of black specks flying in close formation. The patrol at last! Five of the ships were together, and up above was another one, doing loops and barrel rolls in Bridgie's best manner. Jimmy was tired of flying alone, so he pointed his nose straight into Germany to meet the gang.

He had a momentary qualm of uneasiness as he recalled

that only six ships were assigned to the patrol. His should have been the sixth. There were already six planes flying in the formation for which he was headed, but it was quite probable that some lone eagle had joined up with the patrol. So he never gave it a second thought.

The planes of the patrol grew steadily larger, and in a minute Jimmy flew right into the middle of the formation, waggling his wings up and down by way of greeting. He wanted to tell us that, though he might have been a little late in arriving, now that he was here the party could start any time. It did.

He looked around a little to see where each one of the gang was flying. A sudden chill galloped up and down his spine. Something was most decidedly wrong.

In the slanting rays of the setting sun, all the trim little Spads were curiously misshapen. Upper wings were longer than lower, and there were V struts where no V struts ever existed. In place of red-white-and-blue *cocardes* and striking Indian heads, there were sets of menacing black crosses. Square-cut goggles set above wolfish grins leered at him from every side.

Jimmy had most confidently and enthusiastically winged his way into a sunset patrol of Fokkers, the stinging hornets of Germany!

Hall decided instantly that he had come to the wrong place. He was perfectly willing to call the whole thing off, proffer proper apologies and politely withdraw, but it seemed that the Boches had other plans which didn't permit of his absence during the festivities.

For a half-second nothing happened. No doubt they were dumfounded at the temerity of an enemy pilot flying right into the jaws of death. It was something they'd all dreamed about happening, but never believed possible. However, they weren't long in getting out their stingers. They played around Jimmy as a cat does around a mouse.

Hall tried every acrobatic maneuver he knew to slip away from that ring of barking Spandaus, but there wasn't a chance in the world. Every way he turned, there was a black-crossed ship ready and anxious to get him.

Immelmanns, loops, zooms and dives—nothing made any difference. Machine guns tapped at him from every angle. Tracer bullets left a tangled cobweb of phosphorescent blue smoke in the clear air, holding the little Spad in the center like a fly in a spider's web.

The result was inevitable, and the end came quickly. Half a hundred slugs poured into his wings and fuselage, then three hit him almost simultaneously. One creased his forehead, another his groin, while the third struck him full in the shoulder and paralyzed his entire left side.

Knocked unconscious by the shock and losing blood rapidly, Jimmy fell forward on his stick. By the greatest of good fortune, the nose of the ship was pointed toward the distant French trenches as his light went out.

Almost vertically, motor roaring full, the little ship, with his unconscious body jammed against the stick, plunged fourteen thousand feet toward earth.

His speed was so great that the Germans couldn't hope to follow. Firing a few tentative bursts after the doomed ship, they resumed formation, satisfied that another of the hated French had died *pour la patrie.*

Motor moaned and wires shrieked as the death ship hurtled downwards. Apparently nothing could save Jimmy from instant annihilation. Striking the ground at that speed would have meant total disintegration of both plane and pilot.

Then a series of miracles happened. Less than a hundred and fifty meters from the ground, Jimmy had a moment of lucidity. His eyes opened, and his brain sped a message of warning as the earth rushed up to meet him. He reached across his body with his right hand and shut off his motor; then, taking a firm grip on the stick, he pulled back with all his remaining strength and quietly fainted again.

Nearly any other ship in the war would have shed its wings on that breath-taking dive, or when it was so abruptly pulled out at such tremendous speed, but the Spad was a real plane with no structural weaknesses. Though wires wailed and every spar groaned in protest against the terrific strain, the wings remained intact.

Down it swooped toward the torn-up ground, fluttered, wavering with loss of speed, then turned abruptly toward the German trenches. It slipped, made another turn toward the French lines, fluttered again and crashed amid a great cloud of brownish-gray dust. That was the greatest miracle of all.

The fuselage hit lengthwise in a first-line trench, fitting into the trench with barely a foot clearance on each side. The wings rested on the parapet on each side, so that, when they broke off from the force of the impact, the body of the plane was wafted to the bottom of the trench as gently as a falling leaf.

When Jimmy woke up again, it was to find himself lying on a stretcher and being carried down the trench to a first-aid station. His eyes were open, but blood from the wound in his forehead prevented his seeing very clearly.

His first thought was concerned with the nationality of the soldier who held the front handles of the stretcher. Wiping his eyes with his sleeve, he tried to distinguish the color of the uniform, but the soldier's broad back was covered with mud.

He raised his eyes, and his heart leaped. The shrapnel helmet was French, and the man holding the handles in the rear spoke as he saw Jimmy's movement:

"*Tiens, petit, ça va?*"

Jimmy could only nod weakly, his heart too full for words. He had fallen over fourteen thousand feet, totally unconscious, from six kilometers inside the German lines, to crash in a first-line French trench.

While they were carrying him to the dressing station, Jimmy's mind flashed back to a conversation he had had with one of his French comrades. Speaking of thrills and dangers, this chap had remarked that, if a man were willing to stake everything for it, he could accumulate in fifteen or twenty minutes an experience which would compensate him a thousand times over for the hazard. Since he'd always have something pleasant to think about, he could never be bored with life.

Until that moment, Jimmy wasn't quite sure that he knew what the Frenchman meant. Then he knew for sure. That trip down the trench gave him five minutes of perfect happiness, to find that he wasn't in German hands, that he was going to have sympathetic care among his own kind no matter how badly wounded he was. It was five minutes of pure joy without any background, no thought of yesterday or tomorrow, to spoil it.

In the dressing station, they couldn't find a scratch or a bruise on him from the crash. He had nothing but the wounds received fourteen thousand feet in the air from the concentrated guns of the Jerries.

Still they weren't sure that the shock of the crash, plus his wounds, might not prove fatal, so they carried him back late that night to the base hospital.

The Escadrille was notified, and Bill Thaw and the captain jumped into a car and tore up to the hospital. When they returned and told us that Hall had been decorated with the Médaille Militaire and the Croix de Guerre, we all felt pretty low. When they rushed medals through like that, twelve hours after a boy had been knocked down, it generally spelled disaster. It meant that they had no hopes of his ever pulling through and they wanted to pin the medals on him while the happy recipient was still able to appreciate the honor.

Jimmy had already enshrined himself in our hearts. Of all men, we didn't want to see him go west. Jimmy himself felt the same way about it quite strongly. He had no intention of cashing in his checks by any such simple means as six Germans and a fourteen-thousand-foot drop out of control. He was made of sterner stuff. He fooled them all and got back to the front in an incredibly short time.

In the meantime, however, he didn't indulge himself in idle gratification of fleshly desires. As was his custom after one of his narrow escapes from being the permanent occupant of a six-foot wooden box, he wrote a splendid book called *High Adventure*, a delightful recountal of his adventures in the air up to his most recent interruption.

CHAPTER XXIV

Interlude at Dunkirk

At CHAUDUN, we received endless visits from American sight-seers, who, with probably the best intentions in the world, found excuses to come out to the front and see how their dear compatriots were faring. It put a heavy strain on our larder, and since we rather ungraciously consented to try to be on our best behavior, it rather cramped our styles when it came to the various amusements with which we were wont to relax from the arduous cares of the day.

Stray mademoiselles were bewilderedly hustled away with scant ceremony from the sacred precincts where they had previously found such a warm welcome; gambling was at a low ebb, and even arm bending was indulged in very surreptitiously on account of a nervous premonition that some kind-faced, bespectacled lady of mature years might leap out from behind the bar waving a handful of religious tracts. But we had our reward.

With great ceremonies, we were presented with a large American flag, and poor Bill Thaw had to dress up, stagger out and accept it with a delightful speech which no one could hear or understand. We posed for hundreds of pictures in bizarre costumes ranging from pajamas to civilian slacks and sweaters, with only a sprinkling of uniforms. We refused to dress up for the amateur photographers and break out in our good uniforms. They might get soiled, and they had to be kept bright and shining for adventures in Paris, which, after all, we considered the most important part of the war.

It was too much trouble to dress up and put on the dog every time some personally conducted tour tally-hoed up to the barracks and then have to undress to go on patrol. But if those pictures were reproduced in America, we must have looked like a ragamuffin army of hoboes, instead of the brave, gallant young pioneers who were carrying the torch for Democracy and Freedom, as we heard ourselves extolled ad nauseam.

But we still heard nothing definite about a transfer to the American forces. In fact, the rumors were extremely disquieting, and we were all much downcast.

Unfortunate and untimely propaganda claimed that the United States had hundreds of aviators ready for the front and thousands of planes nearly completed (which, incidentally, we knew to be already outmoded). They would blacken the front with these American planes and blast the German aviation from the skies. Bitter experience made us a little skeptical of the last statement. It was possible, but hardly probable.

However, it seemed that, with such magnificent preparations, they had no need for us who had long been carrying the burden. It cut us all pretty deeply, for we began to feel that we were practically outcasts; men without a country.

Chaudun, of course, had it advantages as well as its disadvantages. It was near enough for the sight-seers to make daily trips from Paris; consequently it was near enough to Paris for us to slip away frequently for a few short hours within the alluring boundaries of that metropolis. We didn't always await official permissions, and sometimes it took quite a bit of scurrying around and double duty to cover up for some missing comrade, but everyone proved his loyalty many times over. He never knew when it might be his turn to need protection.

It was most fortunate that we commuted as much as we did, for it was to be a long time and rough going before we were again to be in such an advantageous location.

In the middle of July we were ordered to Dunkirk, on the far northern end of the lines, to assist the combined French, English and Belgian armies in a great drive in Flanders.

Just before we left, two other young Americans joined the squadron. First came tall, skinny, phlegmatic Dave Peterson, the only man who seemed never to get a thrill from his great adventure as a war bird. Nothing seemed to stir the tranquil depths of his nature. He simply couldn't be elated or depressed, frightened or overjoyed. The second replacement was hard-luck Jimmy Doolittle. He had been badly cut up about the head when, while waiting to be assigned to the front, he had spun in with a Nieuport at the Pool at Plessis-Belleville. He was just recovering from his wounds when he got to the Escadrille.

On the move to Dunkirk, which we made in horrible, greasy weather, Doolittle became lost in the clouds. He flew blind for a bit, then decided to come down and see where he was. Most unfortunately, he had gotten a bit off his course, and when he emerged from the thick pea soup, he found himself directly over a German aviation field!

He didn't know it was a German field and, seeing hangars, was on the point of landing to ask directions, when several vicious machine guns opened up and he spotted a black-crossed ship being hastily wheeled out to take off after him.

Jimmy hastily sought refuge in the clouds and turned back in the direction of the lines. He came out again and breathed a sigh of relief as he saw a British observation balloon. Then more complications arose.

A pair of daring Huns were using the cover of the clouds to make an attack on the sausage, and a lone English plane was having his hands full trying to beat them off. Doolittle hurled himself into the struggle and, in the hectic battle which followed, got a flesh wound in the calf of his leg.

At the same time, his motor was badly hit, so he had to come down to a forced landing, which most unfortunately proved to be a plowed field. He struck crosswise in the furrows and turned over. In the crash, an old face wound, the result of his former accident, reopened.

After a long stay in the hospital, he was invalided out of the French army and came back to America. He made several vain attempts to get into the American army and finally was enlisted as a civilian instructor at Gerstner Field in Louisiana. There, a short time later, a panic-stricken student froze onto the controls, and both he and poor Doolittle were killed in the crash that followed. By a strange coincidence, another Jimmy Doolittle, in later years, became one of the most daring, courageous and intrepid fliers in the American army, and is still going strong.

On that same cross-country hop to Dunkirk that spelled

disaster to Doolittle, Harold Willis and I laid the foundation for a lot of white hair on our own account.

Willy, in his thorough, methodical way, had prepared a map, but not anticipating such nasty thick weather, I hadn't bothered.

Since the ceiling was so low that the hop had to be made at an altitude which effectually prevented picking out any landmarks, Harold told me to stick along with him, and I gladly consented. He was my guiding star all the way up, for until we came in sight of the ocean, I hadn't the foggiest idea where we were, and I'm not so sure he did, either, despite his map, but he got us there safely. I was so fearful of losing him that I was never more than twenty feet from his tail.

We had just passed Albert, which I recognized by the recumbent statue atop the town hall, which the Germans had knocked over, but which had miraculously never fallen, when suddenly I saw Harold flip his Spad over on one wing and sheer off in a tight bank. Without taking any time to wonder why, I instinctively followed his maneuver. From the corner of my eye, I had a fleeting glimpse of a great gray bulk and two white faces in a wicker basket. Then the thick mist swallowed everything.

It was a British observation balloon nearly hidden in the low clouds. We missed the cable by inches, which, had we tangled with it, would have spelled disaster not only for us but for the men in the balloon as well. Willy had seen it at the last split second. It was certainly fortunate that he had keen eyes, for I was watching him so closely that I never would have seen it or known what happened to me. As I went up alongside of him, he waved and made the gesture of wiping perspiration from his forehead. Possibly, it was more than a gesture, for his face was white, but I'll wager that mine was pea green.

Our field at Dunkirk was named St Pol and was right on the ocean. It was smooth, long and narrow, but had certain disadvantages, besides those of having to go in swimming through barbed-wire entanglements on the beach and shallow water. It had been in the process of construction for a landlocked harbor and consequently had a rather high sea wall. The prevailing wind being from the ocean meant that we generally had to take off across the narrow part of the field and hop the sea wall.

Shortly after our arrival, some lame brain in the security of a comfortable office in Paris thought up a brilliant new idea to give pursuit pilots a headache. His marvelous conception was to equip pursuit ships with bomb racks in the cockpit and send the bombs over low on the morning of attacks—to harass German aviation fields and keep enemy ships out of the air.

Having weighed this fertile brain child carefully and given it the full measure of his approval, this Einstein of the nonflying personnel at headquarters smacked his lips over the idea. He rushed madly about, giving the necessary orders. Then he washed his hands of the whole matter and promptly forgot it.

Our reaction to the theory of this mental giant was anything but flattering to either him or his immediate ancestors. He had started something that gave a few of us many moments of sorrowful anticipation and deep distress of mind while we were endeavoring to put his theories into practical execution.

To begin with, a Spad was a flat-winged ship of great

speed but small lift and the same gliding angle as a brick. It was tough enough with a full load of gas and such a short run to get them off the ground without hitting the sea wall. Adding a couple of heavy liquid bombs seemed like suicide.

The captain picked Doc Rockwell and myself to pioneer the bombing attempts. Doc had a cracked cylinder, and there was no time for the installation of a new motor before the big attack for which we had been sent up there was scheduled to take place. We both concluded the war was over for us and resigned ourselves to our fate, making elaborate preparations for the disposal of our personal possessions.

I stalled the fatal moment off as long as I could, but finally, under repeated urgings from the captain, who was becoming a trifle annoyed about the delay, I made a practice flight with a couple of bombs aboard and, having missed the sea wall by inches, on the takeoff, tried to hit a barrel moored out in the ocean.

If my first attempt was any criterion and the stunt had come off as scheduled, I should probably have spread bombs and Spad all over Germany.

Sighting the bombs had been figured out by our armament officer, a gentleman of Polish extraction named Ciecomski, in which he had used as aids a broken slide rule and a dream book. That seems to be the only feasible explanation, for his instructions were to go to a thousand meters, fly straight till the objective disappeared beneath your lower wing, pique at a forty-five degree angle for five hundred meters, straighten out, count ten and let fly.

With this somewhat complicated but cleverly worked out system, I was completely satisfied when the bombs hit the ocean, but needless to say, the barrel remained very much intact.

The three mornings that Doc and I were supposed to go out before dawn and clean up the German aviation fields, it rained cats and dogs. Each morning when the heavens opened and the storm howled was like getting a reprieve. In the meantime, the infantry went ahead and made a very successful attack without us, on the theory that, if we couldn't fly, neither could the Germans, and so Rockwell and I took a new lease on life.

However, in this sector, I had a couple of rather narrow squeaks from concluding my part of the entertainment, and in one, through carelessness, I nearly got Lufbery brought down, which was a rather ironic way of repaying him for saving my life earlier in the spring.

The Flanders front was a pretty dead sector as far as the air was concerned. Day after day, with monotonous regularity, our flights went out and came back to report that they hadn't seen an enemy ship. Yet Luf had a most amazing faculty for finding Boches where there just weren't any. I made four two-man patrols with him and nine in five- to seven-ship formation, and there wasn't one of those flights on which he didn't find at least one. He had seven combats and downed two of the enemy.

We would start a patrol on the lines, move further and further in and never see a sign of a black-crossed ship. Archies would fly thick around us, but no inquiring Huns would come nosing along to see what all the shooting was about. On other sectors the air would be thick with them at the first few bursts.

All of a sudden Luf, flying wide wing, would be missing from the formation, and in a second or two we'd locate him somewhere behind or below, chasing some Boche observation ship which his bright eyes had located.

Or possibly it might be some lone pursuit ship that had taken the chance of trying to pick off a straggler from our patrol. The Boche would find he had his hands full, for the straggler would be Luf.

Two black specks against a clear horizon, chasing each other around like flies on a windowpane, and we'd know that Luf had located his quarry. A steep bank, and we'd wing our way to help him out. He generally didn't need help. The battle would be over before we could get there. Either he'd gotten his man or driven him down, which was nearly as satisfactory. It kept the lines clear.

The dark, mottled camouflage of the Germans was most difficult to see against the dark background of the earth, yet Luf could pick out the slightest movement, and he knew that movement meant planes.

But if Luf couldn't find trouble on the lines, he'd go over after it. He led a four-ship patrol over one summer day, right into the heart of the German's own lines. Besides myself, Harold Willis and Walter Lovell were the other two pilots. It was a great combination, for there wasn't one of the three on whom you couldn't stake your life.

We had tried the lines for half an hour with the usual lack of activity. Luf got disgusted and turned straight into Germany. We got only a few lackadaisical Archies, and he forged steadily onwards.

I was acting as sky man that day, supposed to prevent surprise attacks from top and rear, so that the others could give their full attention to finding and attacking anything in front of or below us. I confess that I was considerably worried when we kept right on going, wondering if Luf had Berlin as an objective, but he evidently knew just what he was about. We traveled about twenty-five kilometers straight in, while I twisted and turned above the three planes, keeping a sharp lookout behind and above.

All at once, I looked down and saw that we were directly above a German aviation field. Luf was getting set to attack a formation of six or seven German planes that were evidently practicing formation flying. He jockeyed around into the best spot, with what little sun there was between him and the enemy. Then the three planes plunged in, and for about ten minutes there was a tremendously thrilling dog fight. The whole sky above the terrain seemed to be full of twisting, tumbling planes with shrieking motors. Machine guns beat a devil's tattoo. The Germans, of course, were taken by surprise, and it took them some time to get their guns warmed up, but once started they put up a valiant defense.

However, Luf and the other two boys always kept the advantage of altitude on them, diving in and pecking away, then surging up for a new attack. Two ships tumbled out of the fight. One went down with his propeller stalled, the other in a spin.

Meanwhile, I circled over the arena getting a wonderful view of the whole affair. I was thrilled to death, anxious to take part, but realized that the safety of the others depended on their having protection from overhead. I had a gallery seat in a tournament of aerial knights jousting to the death. But I got so interested in the show they were putting on that I neglected my first duty—that of keeping a close watch. The first intimation I had of impending trouble was the chatter of machine guns on each side of me and *above!* I heard the nasty whine of bullets passing my head. Then I quickly awoke to the fact that I had been asleep. The Germans had gotten a quick patrol off the ground while the dog fight was in progress. The patrol had taken altitude and sneaked around behind us.

We were caught in a trap between two layers. I don't know how many ships there were—possibly only two or three. I only know that one very savagely inclined Teuton was sitting less than fifty meters away, right on my tail, and unless something was done about it pretty quickly, the war was all over as far as I personally was concerned.

I had to warn the others and try to save my own hide. There was only one thing to do to take care of both emergencies. I yanked the throttle wide open and pointed my nose straight down. Willis said I passed him like a bat out of hell. He thought the Hun had me. So did I.

Seeing me go down with the Boche on my tail was sufficient warning for the boys. Led by Luf, they fought their way clear in a few seconds and beat it for the lines.

I went down two thousand meters full motor, making plenty of knots before I dared pull out. At the start of the dive, the Boche was hammering me with everything he had, but I gradually sliced away from the snarling gun. I could dive faster than he, and I knew it. I staked everything on that. My wings would stay on, and there was a strong probability his wouldn't if he tried the same thing.

When I was convinced that I had outdistanced him, I yanked my stick back, uttered a fervent prayer and pulled out. Every spar and wire quivered and shook. They screamed loud in agony from the strain, but they performed their duties nobly. The Hun was fully three hundred meters behind me when he saw me pull out. He tried his best to follow, but he had to come out more gradually and dropped another couple of hundred meters before he leveled off. By that time I was on an even keel and headed for the lines. The enemy took up the chase but, being so far behind and below, he never had a chance to fire.

When I was once more on the edge of friendly territory, I got brave again and turned to meet him. We circled each other cautiously a couple of times, then simultaneously decided to call it a day. I waved a derisive farewell and nearly fell out of my cockpit when he responded in kind. It was my only experience of exchanging personal courtesies in the air with the enemy.

Landing just at dusk with my main tank empty and less than two minutes' gas in my reserve, I found that I had already been reported brought down. Luf was unrestrainedly glad to see me back safely and, feeling that he was partly responsible as long as he had taken us over there, neglected to give me much hell for not being on the job. He felt rather bad, though, for he was quite convinced that between them they could have gotten the whole smear if they hadn't been so rudely interrupted.

Naturally, being so close to England, it was a great temptation to fly over to London between patrols, either for a meal or to spend the night. Strict orders were posted that we shouldn't make any unauthorized visits to our sister country.

Therefore, after having finished a patrol one bright morning, I came in, serviced up and decided that I could do with a bit of good old rare roast beef. I didn't confide in anyone where I was going, for I presumed that attempts might be made to dissuade me. No questions were asked and, smacking my lips in anticipation, I gleefully flew down the coast a bit, taking altitude, and then turned across the bright blue waters of the Channel.

But I didn't know that there was a military order that every plane crossing the Channel must be registered out and the English authorities advised of its departure, so they could wireless ahead its description and probable time of arrival. This was only a simple method of precaution, for there were too many chances that some bold German in a captured Allied plane might come across and wreak havoc.

As a consequence, when I got over Dover, I got one of the jolliest receptions ever accorded a visiting airman from several straight-shooting English Archie batteries. I quickly decided that perhaps I wasn't welcome and, quaking in my boots, beat it back in a hurry to Dunkirk.

The incident raised quite a smell, and there were several official inquiries. Fortunately I had been too high for anyone to get the number or recognize the insignia of my ship, so when in the regular routine course of inquiry it was discovered that my plane had been one of those in the air when this gross breach of discipline had been committed and I was called on the carpet, I simply put on my blandest expression and denied any knowledge of the affair.

The commandant had a fishy gleam in his eye, but he couldn't doubt my protestations of innocence, and the matter was finally dropped, greatly to my relief.

Our stay at Dunkirk provided a very pleasant interlude for the tough months to follow. It was a continuous round of sea bathing, poker and drinking parties with the pilots of several English squadrons near whom we were billeted. They were royal hosts, but terribly overoptimistic about their abilities as poker players.

On August 17, the Escadrille as a whole was honored by its first citation:

The General Commandant in Chief cites to the Order of the Army, the Escadrille N-124 (Escadrille Lafayette):

An escadrille composed of volunteer Americans who have come to fight for France in the spirit of purest sacrifice. Under the command of Captain Thénault, who formed it, it has maintained without ceasing an ardent struggle against our enemies. In exceedingly difficult combats and at the price of severe losses, which, far from discouraging it, have exalted its morale, has brought down twenty-eight officially confirmed planes of the enemy. It has excited the profound admiration of the officers who have it under their command and of the French escadrilles who, fighting by its side, have striven to vie with it in valorous deeds.

[Signed] PÉTAIN.

CHAPTER XXV

Verdun—The Tragic Death of Doug MacMonagle

IN THE MIDDLE OF AUGUST, just when we were really enjoying the war, we were ordered back to Verdun. There, based at the flying field of Senard, we went in for some really intensive air work, the most exhausting of all our campaigns. After our arrival, we had twenty-four successive days of brilliant sunshine, a great rarity in France, and the total flying hours piled up in that one month alone was staggering.

During that time nearly every one of us put on at least three shows a day, which, added to the fact that our sleep was very much broken, owing to the nightly incursions of the German bombing squadrons, was tremendously fatiguing.

Only twice did the Germans stop at our field, and each time they destroyed one or two hangars with several ships (and incidentally my black cat), but they passed over us regularly, and we never knew when we were going to be the objects of their affectionate regards. It was most inconsiderate and annoying.

Then is when we really came to appreciate the generosity of our English friends. Without the aid of John

Dewar and Black and White to ease off the nerve strain, we'd have been in a pretty thin way.

Before leaving Dunkirk, through the kindly offices of some of the high-rankers with whom we had palled (and whom we relieved of their excess cash at the great national pastime, so that they really were paying for it), we got an order on the English quartermaster to purchase at wholesale price as much scotch as we wanted. We bought fifty cases at a ridiculously low figure.

Then came the question of transportation. Every lorry was loaded to the gunwales with material for the long haul, which was nearly from one end of the lines to the other.

No pilot could carry more than a couple of bottles in his ship. For a time we considered discarding such nonessentials as tools and spare motor parts to make room in some truck for the cases of liquid sunshine. Eventually, after much discussion, a solution was found.

Whiskey and Soda had a nice padded trailer, their own especial property. We merely substituted whiskey for Whiskey and Soda. Every case fitted snugly in their traveling compartment, but it left no room for them. Consequently two docile but very bewildered lions rode all the long way across France sitting on the seats of two lorries between driver and helper. Needless to say, the men in whose charge they traveled breathed a sigh of relief when they arrived.

At Verdun we got a tremendous thrill in seeing on the front our first uniformed American troops, a couple of regiments of Engineers. We began to feel that maybe, after all, America was really going to take an active part in the war. Till then, it seemed as if the nation had been wagering all its effectives in the Battle of Paris.

Douglas MacMonagle (Courtesy Paul A. Rockwell)

The author's Nieuport 17 C.1, accidentally turned over in a ditch beside a railroad embankment. At this time, the author was flying one of the Escadrille's newly issued Spad 7's. Ham, May 1917.
(Courtesy Soubiran Collection)

Harold B. Willis' Spad 7 after his capture at Dun-sur-Meuse.
(Courtesy Alex Imrie)

Shortly after our arrival, following months of near-victories which I had never been able to get confirmed, I accidentally got my first Boche, and Campbell again distinguished himself in his second flirtation with the Grim Reaper. He provided a considerable thrill for everyone but himself, apparently, by sticking his wheels through the top wing of Maison Rouge's Spad.

It was always Campbell's delight to see how close he could fly to anyone without actually hitting him. He was a pain in the neck on patrols, particularly to the man directly in front of him. Many times, when I had been leading a patrol, I came back with the leaping jitters if he had been behind me, for he'd keep his whirling propeller blades not three feet from my tail. I'd spend more time trying to keep out of his way than I would looking for Boches. It was impossible to shake him off, and no amount of pleadings, coercion or threats of physical retaliation was sufficient to make him desist from his distressing tactics in the air.

This time, while making Maison Rouge extremely unhappy by indulging in his usual monkey business, somebody misjudged, and Campbell's wheels, ripping through fabric and framework, sank deep in the unfortunate Lieutenant's wing. Locked together like Siamese twins, the staggering planes made two complete turns of the field, while we ran out the meat wagon and tried to follow them. Finally Campbell socked on full throttle, heaved manfully on his stick and, almost taking the Lieutenant's top wing off, managed to pull his wheels out and soared away.

Maison Rouge landed at once, deathly white, but Campbell put on an acrobatic exhibition which nearly took off the tops of the hangars before he landed without even a flat tire. Far from realizing what a narrow escape he'd had, he demanded approbation for the clever way he had handled the whole affair.

Very shortly, Maison Rouge was replaced by a gallant, fearless and gentlemanly French lieutenant, Louis Verdier-Fauvety, transferred from one of the other escadrilles in our group. He was extremely popular with everyone and remained as second in command until the transfer of the Escadrille to the American aviation. Then he returned to his old command in the French forces, only to have Fate play a scurvy trick on him a few months later. That's what made us fatalists. A pilot could survive all sorts of dangers from fire, collision and enemy bullets, then meet his finish in the silliest of accidents or the most unexpected occurrences on the ground.

In 1914, while a member of the 8th Hussars, Verdier had been severely wounded in action. After he recovered, he transferred to aviation and became one of the bravest and most skillful of pursuit pilots.

In August 1917, just before joining us, he had a most remarkable escape from death in the air. In the midst of a hot combat, he and Lieutenant Ciecomski, the demon armament officer, collided at eleven thousand feet above the trenches. The two locked ships whirled down together for two thousand meters, then broke apart.

Verdier's stabilizer and the right half of his elevating plane were torn completely away. He had absolutely no control of his ship. Whirling, spinning, swooping crazily, he fell for more than two miles and smacked directly into the center of a great forest. Crashing into the treetops, his plane broke all to pieces, but his only injury was a split lip and a bruised forehead from his jammed goggles.

Ciecomski, whose plane was not quite so badly damaged, having a broken prop and torn wing, came down normally in a long, motorless glide after he tore loose from Verdier's ship. He, too, could have landed quite without injury, except that he encountered some high-tension wires which turned him over in the air a couple of times before he finally hit the ground. He ended up with a fractured collarbone.

Verdier always undertook the most dangerous of missions, particularly the hazardous work of machine-gunning the trenches and roads from low altitudes. He was a remarkable pilot, with seven or eight official victories, and fought many desperate battles in which his plane was riddled time and again, but from which he emerged without injury.

After four years of war, in the thick of it all the time, and during nearly all of it exposed to the perils of the air, in which his only wound was a split lip from a two-mile fall, he was killed in August 1918 during a night bombardment of his airdrome. He was trying to see that all his men were taken care of, and he was the only man to be killed or injured in that particular raid.

Fate had willed that he was to meet his death on the ground. If he could only have stayed in the air all the time, he might have survived the war. There were so many jams that a pilot could get out of, even with our old war crates, simply by the use of a little headwork, trusting in the strength and stability of his ship and a dash of good old high-class luck.

In September, a few days after Campbell's awe-inspiring exhibition of damfoolery, Si Marr, who was later to be the first commanding officer of the famous Hat-in-the-Ring squadron, also became a prominent member of the Club of the Should-Be-Dead.

He was on a low patrol with Hank Jones and Doug MacMonagle on the Verdun-Argonne sector. They contacted four very vicious Albatrosses some distance in the German lines. For ten minutes there ensued one of the hottest dog fights of the entire war.

Jones and MacMonagle each tangled with one of the black-crossed ships, while Marr was forced to take on the other two. He succeeded in driving one of his foes out of the fight disabled, but while his whole attention was concentrated on getting the first German, the other swung on the tail of his Spad and got him in a wicked crossfire.

Marr was a skillful pilot and all but succeeded in avoiding the relentless battering, but the Jerry was no amateur, either, and he clung to his position with implacable persistence. Marr indulged in a series of wild acrobatics, but he was unable to dislodge the vicious enemy who continued to pour an unceasing stream of hot lead into his wings and fuselage.

Suddenly, in the midst of one of his maneuvers, Si pulled back on his stick and found that it offered no resistance. All the wires to his elevator had been neatly cut through by the hail of lead!

Although it seemed inevitable that he must crash out of control, Marr didn't lose his head or consider for one second that he was done for. During the course of a highly adventurous life he had been in plenty of tough situations before.

He still had the use of his rudder and one aileron. He banked suddenly, closed his throttle and dropped in a screaming dive. His enemy started to follow him, but

Jones, who had disposed of his adversary, hopped on his tail, and the Boche was forced to turn and defend himself against Hank's blazing guns, leaving Marr free to save himself without the added hazard of flying lead.

Si had turned toward the lines as soon as he discovered he was in distress, and as he went down he started to experiment. He found that by increasing the speed of his motor, the resultant air blast would blow the elevator up and his nose would gradually rise until he was flying level. As he retarded the motor speed, the elevator would drop and he would be gliding down again. Alternately speeding and slowing his whirling propeller, he gradually settled down to earth.

By the time he had come down six thousand feet, he had become so skillful in the use of his motor, figuring to a hairsbreadth just what angle of glide certain revolutions would give him, that he was able to make a normal, if somewhat speedy and bouncing, landing in the ruined Forest of Hesse without so much as blowing a tire. He borrowed an infantry staff car, rushed back to the field and got his mechanics and some wire. Late that same afternoon, after repairs had been made on the disabled plane, Si flew it out from the shell-torn forest and went back on the lines for another patrol.

His escape was the result of a great combination of intestinal fortitude, headwork, luck and a marvelously balanced ship.

A few days later, there occurred a most pathetic combination of circumstances. It hit us rather harder than the usual to-be-expected loss of a comrade, for we had the living still with us.

Doug MacMonagle's mother had come all the way from

San Francisco to Paris to see him. In the midst of our furious flying during the intensive attacks and splendid weather, Mac couldn't be spared for leave. In some miraculous way, Mrs MacMonagle wangled permission to come to the front.

On the morning of the day when Doug was to go to Ravenel, the nearest railroad station, to meet her, he made a regular scheduled morning patrol. It was fated to be his last, for in the middle of a hot combat over Hill 109, a German slug with his name on it found him squarely between the eyes.

They brought in his battered body just before Mrs MacMonagle arrived. After that long exhausting trip under arduous war conditions, she missed him by only a few hours and could only remain for his funeral. Her courageous demeanor in the face of that bitter blow was magnificent.

The Engineers had not yet organized a band, but they thoughtfully provided us with a firing squad and a bugler to play taps. Doug was the first American to be buried at the front with solemn military honors by his own uniformed countrymen. We were very happy to be able to arrange to do that much for his bereaved mother, and she was deeply appreciative.

Fortunately for our peace of mind, tragedy was not our sole companion on the front. Occasionally, something really funny would occur, some little incident that really didn't amount to much, but would suffice to brighten us for days.

One of these distinctly amusing incidents happened a few days after Mac's tragic death, when a German observation two-seater out of gas landed on the field and the theory of chivalrous conduct was put to a strain much too severe.

While his cowed, frightened little *Unteroffizier* observer crouched silent in his cockpit, the extremely snooty officer pilot refused to surrender or talk to anyone except the highest-ranking officer on the field.

When the commandant arrived, the German naïvely asked to be serviced up and allowed to go on his way; mentioned that aviation was a sporting game and we should play it like sportsmen; said he'd do the same for any Allied aviator in distress.

The German was indignant when the commandant quietly and politely explained that, owing to the fact that there was a war on, he was unable to grant the request, reasonable as it seemed.

Then the Boche made another proposition: If we would furnish him the gas so that he could get into the air, we could send any plane we chose up after him and he'd take the chance of battling his way back to his lines. But he insisted on fair play. Five minutes' start and only one plane to come in pursuit.

Of course, he got the horse cackle from everyone and was taken away, sadly shaking his head over the unsportsmanlike conduct of his enemies.

During the course of our stay at Verdun, the Escadrille was selected to form part of the escort for a gigantic daylight bombing raid on Dun-sur-Meuse, about forty kilometers in German territory. Acting as nursemaid for a flock of slow-flying Sopwith bombers was not our idea of a perfect day, but it was all part of the game.

On the way over, after a hot, intensive and extremely unpleasant Archie barrage from the German batteries in the

Argonne Forest, Harold Willis and I, top men on the left flank, were attacked by three very vicious Fokkers, attracted by the shell fire.

Harold was behind and slightly above me. He saw one of the Fokkers slice in on my tail. He picked that Jerry off me so quickly that I doubt that the buzzard knew what hit him, for he went spinning off like a gigantic top into the wide-open spaces before he had a chance to get started.

But while Willis was performing this most charitable act for me, the other two cracked down on him, and poor Harold didn't have anyone to take them off his tail. They sunk him with a perfect flood of lead.

His motor dead, tank full of holes, even his goggles shot off, Willis made a safe landing in Germany, but he was in a thin way. None of us ever anticipated being taken alive, and we felt the clothes a dead man wore didn't mean much to him. Willy, as so many of us did on hot days, had gone up in his pajamas (a very classy, green-striped pair) and an old greasy brown sweater, the pride of his heart, for wind protection, but without identification papers, money or even cigarettes.

Although sartorially elegant, he was the perfect example of what a sterling young aviator should not wear or equip himself with when going into Germany.

Harold had been one of my best pals, and although the high protection patrol above us had seen him go down, they were too high to tell what his finish had been. I was deathly afraid that I knew, but I was in a hurry to find out. The usual routine reports on his fate might take months. So, later that same day, I fixed up a message, put it in a cardboard cylinder, hung it on a little silk parachute and dropped it far in the German lines, asking for news.

Two days later an artillery outfit away up the lines telephoned that they had an answer. Willy was a prisoner, but in good health. So I wrapped his uniform, boots, cigarettes and money in a nice package and took them over, being careful to address the bundle to *Lieutenant* Harold Willis.

Willy's rank was only sergeant, but I wanted to impress his captors with the fact that he was an officer, for the life of a private or noncom in a German prison camp was said to be anything but sweet. Of course, Harold had been smart enough to claim commissioned rank, and since he had no papers and no mark of rank on him, my message and bundle only bore out his assertions.

Willis was the only Lafayette Escadrille pilot to be captured alive. After several abortive attempts, he succeeded nearly a year later in making his escape from the prison camp at Villengen in Baden.

With several other daring souls, he made elaborate preparations for months for the break. Some of the boys had made scaling ladders for getting over the electrified and barbed-wire enclosure; others made flimsy bridges built out of small pine boards from Red Cross food boxes. Willis was too heavy to trust himself on any of these weakly constructed artifices and evolved a daring scheme that had every chance of success through its very daring. He provided himself with a wooden gun carved from a broom handle and a prison-tailored uniform that resembled those of the guards. At the first alarm, when his co-conspirators short-circuited the big arc lights which flooded the camp with brilliant light, he dashed out of the barracks straight to the guardhouse.

In the darkness and confusion, waving his gun aloft,

shouting unintelligible German, he was able to pass out of the enclosure with the rest of the guards when the big gates were opened.

Of course his deception was quickly discovered when an auxiliary lighting system flashed on. There was nothing left but to make a dash for it. Heavily weighted down by spare clothes and several pounds of food, avariciously hoarded for many weeks, he dug up the slope of a hill for fifteen minutes under intense rifle fire from the excited guards.

Once over the crest, he was so exhausted that he threw himself on the ground, unable to move for fifteen minutes. Fortunately the man hunters missed finding him, and eventually he cautiously stole on to a prearranged rendezvous which he had made with Lieutenant Isaacs, an American naval officer, who had been captured when his ship was submarined.

Isaacs was not at the rendezvous, and Harold's heart sank. He was deathly afraid that Isaacs had been recaptured. It seemed as if he were fated to make the long dash for freedom alone. But a mile further on, he was hailed by a cautious voice, which proved to belong to the missing naval man. Isaacs had heard the swish of a rubber raincoat and, knowing that the Germans didn't possess such utilitarian articles, he had taken the chance of calling to Willis.

Day after day, wet, miserable and cold, they lay hidden under rocks or dripping trees, for they walked only during the deepest blackness of the night hours. One would keep watch while the other slept, for in their hiding places they were constantly surrounded by woodsmen and children. Stiffened by exposure to the elements, they would keep circulation going by sitting on the ground and rocking back and forth from the hips. Feet became torn and bleeding, and when their food supply ran out they kept alive by filching and eating what raw vegetables they could find in fields and gardens.

They had a dozen narrow escapes from recapture in their heartbreaking, pitifully slow odyssey through the land of the enemy, where every man's hand was against them.

Through all perils and hardships, they eventually won their way through to the Rhine, but here, once again, their hearts were nearly broken by the apparently impossible task of getting into it. It seemed as if all their suffering had been in vain and they were doomed to utter failure.

They found themselves on a high cliff, where they could hear and see the water lapping the gravel at the bottom, but they could also hear the footsteps of the Rhine guard, one of whom was posted about every hundred yards. It was a tight-strung cordon designed to prevent any illegal passages over the river to Switzerland.

They retraced their steps inland about a quarter of a mile and found a little brook, which they knew must empty into the river. They waded down this brook, under a railroad bridge, and passed directly through the little town of Hauenstein, under bridges which connected the streets, through two tunnels and finally half under water through a series of natural cataracts to the level of the Rhine.

Willis plunged in and was almost engulfed by the swirling current. He was carried under water and almost drowned while he struggled to shed his water-soaked clothes which threatened to carry him to the bottom.

It seemed to him centuries later that he touched bottom

on the other side, more than a mile below where he had gone in. Almost paralyzed by his long immersion in the icy waters, he dragged himself up onto the shores of Switzerland, naked as a jay bird, but a free man once again.

He tried without success to find Isaacs and was most fearful that his comrade had gone down, for, like most navy men, he hadn't spoken very confidently of his swimming ability.

Willis went inland till he came to a railroad and started at a dog trot down the track. He soon gave that up, as running in bare feet on the rock ballast was anything but comfortable. Finding a road, he followed it till he came to a tavern, where he was royally welcomed and put to bed with hot food and plenty to drink.

In the morning the Swiss frontier guards showed up with Isaacs and provided both the boys with clothes. They had found him even further down the river and given him the kindliest possible treatment.

Transportation back to France was furnished them, and Willis arrived in Paris just in time to take part in the Armistice celebration. It nearly broke his heart that he couldn't have gotten back sooner, for he felt that he had a lot of unfinished business with his ex-captors.

From his early days as an ambulance driver right through to the end, Willis's whole war record was replete with heroic feats, and his dramatic escape from the hands of the enemy was a fitting climax to the career of a stout lad, a sterling pilot and a grand comrade in arms.

On the same day that Willis was lost to us, Campbell pulled the third of his narrow squeaks. The field at Senard was long and narrow, with hangars on one side its full length. There were nearly sixty planes, both bombers and pursuit ships from the field, on the raid. Since everyone would return at the same time, all in a hurry to land at once, very strict traffic regulations were issued by the commandant. On landing, everyone must taxi clear to the end of the field before turning to go to the hangars. By not turning in midfield, much greater space was given for landing ships, and much of the hazard of collision could be avoided.

Amid ships landing on all sides, Campbell found his spot and sat down. It happened to be about opposite our hangars. At the moment the space was clear. Campbell apparently saw no reason for taking a long taxi ride. Either unconscious of the fact that he was disobeying orders or thoughtlessly taking a chance, he swung his plane and started to taxi across traffic.

A bomber had been maneuvering for the spot and was almost down. He hadn't a chance to pick up flying speed or avoid the crash. He smacked squarely into Campbell's plane, his propeller cutting through the top wing not a foot from Campbell's head. The bomber finally landed unharmed, but the pursuit ship was rolled over a dozen times and reduced to matchwood.

But Campbell, with his apparently charmed life, emerged from the tangled wreck without a scratch. He looked it over nonchalantly, lit a cigarette and calmly continued his stroll across traffic to the hangar on foot! With silver tongue and honeyed words, he even talked the commandant, a bit of a martinet, out of any punishment for his deliberate disobedience. He played his luck hard while it lasted, but even Lady Luck can be tempted too far.

CHAPTER XXVI

The Luck of Jimmy Hall

At the end of September 1917 the Escadrille was ordered back to Chaudun, our former field. Here we were joined by Chris Ford, the thirty-eighth and last American to become a member of the Lafayette Escadrille while it was still a French unit.

A week after our return, Dave Peterson had a close shave, when two men from every squadron in the group were selected, protected by their comrades, to make simultaneous attacks at a zero hour on a row of German sausages.

The attack was jimmied up and almost ruined when two of the men from another squadron got impatient and swooped down on their balloon before the given hour. Pete saw what had happened and, afraid they would haul his *Drache* down, dived six thousand feet full motor after it.

He got the balloon, but he was so close to the ground and catching such hell from Archie and the circle of machine guns that he had to yank out with both hands. Of course the strain was so terrific that something had to give.

Every one of the wire fittings, screwed deep into tough spars and cross members, was torn sideways against the grain, almost an inch. It slacked brace and flying wires to such an extent that Pete might just as well not have had any. He came back to the field with his wings flopping like a wounded gull. As was customary with him, he showed no emotion over his narrow escape, merely commenting that he was glad the Spad was a strong ship.

Just when we were on the point of despairing of ever hearing from the American brass hats, through the tireless and unremitting efforts of Dr Gros and one or two other military men who had a real conception of the war and the necessity for trained, experienced men, the American army in October finally sent out a delegation of high-rankers to the front to make an examination of the Lafayette Escadrille pilots.

After comprehensive physical examinations, which, much to the dismay of some of the boys, included urinalysis and blood tests, we were put through a long series of rather ridiculous physical demonstrations which weren't particularly helped by frequent visits to the bar to bolster up our courage.

Then the awful truth came out!

In solemn, owlish conclave, the board decided that not one of us, despite hundreds of hours in the air, most of us aces, all thoroughly trained war pilots with many victories to our credit, could ever be an aviator. Their tests definitely showed that physically, mentally and morally we were unfit to be pilots. It was truly pathetic.

Dud Hill's blind eye, Bill Thaw's bad vision and crippled arm, Lufbery's inability to walk a crack backwards, Dolan's tonsils, Hank Jones's flat feet—everything was revealed in the pitiless light of publicity. We were just a broken-down crew of crippled misfits! There was hardly a man on whom they didn't have to ask waivers.

However, while we were waiting to hear the tragic results, and while Paris was filled with American aviators and Y.M.C.A. men, with bars, theaters and night spots doing a capacity business, the Escadrille continued to carry on the war.

It was still the only American outfit in active combat service at the front, although not entitled to wear the uniform of its own country. At the same time the Escadrille was once again cited by the appreciative French, which entitled us, as members of a twice-cited organization, to wear the *fourragère* in the colors of the Croix de Guerre. It was the second escadrille in the French army to be so honored, the only one preceding being Escadrille Spad 3, the Storks, commanded by the famous and beloved ace, Captain Georges Guynemer.

In early October we were all surprised and delighted when Jimmy Hall showed up again, bright and smiling, eager to get his hand on a stick that carried the Indian-head insignia on the fuselage. He had been sent from the hospital to Escadrille N-112 as a replacement, but as the only American in the squadron he wasn't particularly happy, so his request to be allowed to return to the Lafayette was eventually granted.

His first flight after his reappearance was again nearly his last. This time Dugan, Lovell, Hall and myself were selected for the high patrol, coincidentally over nearly the same spot on the Chemin-des-Dames where Jimmy had almost gotten it the first time.

In perfect formation, we cruised over the lines for about an hour without seeing any trace of enemy ships. I was leading the patrol with Jim as sky man. We went further and further in the enemy lines, almost to their balloons, with Archie giving us a warm reception, but still no Huns.

Suddenly, some thousand meters below, I spotted three two-seaters in close formation sailing for our lines. They should have known we were there from the quantity of hate that had been thrown up around us. Even though they were looking into the sun, we shouldn't have been hard to see, but they paid us no attention. They sailed along as unconcernedly as if they were twenty miles back of their balloons.

I wagged my wings and we sliced down on them. There was no cold meat about that bunch, even for four of us. They presented an almost impregnable defense. They had guns forward and back, they were in their own lines, and Archie was still doing his best to discourage us.

Dugan, Lovell and I each picked out a ship and made our attack from the dive. It had to be quick jabs rather than a sustained attempt, for we were met by a whistling barrage of steel-jackets that warned us we weren't playing with children.

After we had tried the individual attack system two or three times without success, we got together underneath one of the ships and tried to find his blind spot from below. That didn't work so well, either, for while we were after him his pals were raking us from each side, and it began to look like a rough stand-off. We couldn't take that cross-fire with any expectation of getting back for chow.

I presume there was some sort of a combination that would have gotten at least one if not all three of those Boches. But I didn't know the answer, neither did Lovell or Dugan, and we were no beginners at the game, either.

I hated to let them go, but it seemed that all we could do was to continue harrying them and keep them from crossing the lines to perform whatever mission they were on.

Bullets were whistling around our ears from all angles, and we drew off a little way for a conference.

Just then I saw a Spad start a vertical dive on the last of the three-ship combination. He was about four hundred meters higher and coming down like a streak of chain lightning.

"Good egg!" I thought to myself. "While we've got their attention down here, you saw the opportunity to sneak down and pop one off before he knows you're there. Smart laddie!"

But the Boche observer was on the alert. He turned his Spandaus up and shot a steady stream of fire on the diving ship. I couldn't see any tracers coming from the muzzles of the Spad, and I marveled that he had the moral courage to hold his fire so long. On and on he came, sizzling through the air, and still no sign of firing.

I couldn't understand why he didn't turn if his guns had jammed and avoid the withering fire from the rear cockpit of the Jerry. It looked like sheer suicide, but it was all over in the twinkling of an eye.

I couldn't see how a collision could be avoided, and every nerve in my body shrieked a protest as I waited with drawn breath for the inevitable rending crash and the fiery explosion that was sure to follow.

The Boche observer must have thought the same thing, for, just before the moment of impact, I saw him let go his guns and collapse in his cockpit as the wheels and wing tip of the Spad brushed across the big top wing of the German ship. If he had continued to hold his position, standing straight up, the lower wing of the Spad would have neatly sliced off his head.

The Spad pulled up and over and fell into a spin; I caught a flash of Jimmy Hall's insignia. I watched it as long as I could, and it was still spinning. There wasn't a doubt in my mind that Jim had been mortally wounded by the defensive fire of the German and was spinning down out of control. He had probably meant to crash the German ship before he died, but missed even that. I didn't believe that he could ever get out of this one. Two miracles would be too much to expect.

The three of us worked on the three Huns as long as our gas lasted, but, while we kept them away from the lines, we had no luck in knocking any of them down.

When we finally drifted back to the field, it was with heavy hearts, for we were all set to report that poor old Jim had finally gotten it. As I taxied up to the hangar and got slowly out of my ship, the first man to rush up and greet me was poor old Jim!

I hugged him enthusiastically and then demanded how come. I don't think I ever saw anyone more embarrassed or abashed. He acted like a kid caught stealing jam. He stammered and stuttered and finally broke out with the truth.

When he saw a chance to peak on the Boche and make the attack, he had gotten so interested in getting the Hun in his sights correctly, so that he wouldn't miss, that he forgot to pull the triggers!

His dive was so fast that when he finally woke to the fact that the Jerry was properly set and he hadn't fired, it was too late. He had to pull out with all his strength to avoid a collision. He felt his ship strike the enemy, and when he went into the spin he was quite convinced that he had dropped a wing or shed an aileron.

He was thoroughly resigned to his fate and spun down about six thousand feet before he very gently tried to bring the ship out. Having no expectations of success, he was tremendously surprised when the plane answered instantly to the controls.

Elated beyond measure, he streaked for home and landed. The extreme tip of one wing was bent, a rib was broken, and there were a couple of stray bullet holes, but outside of that there was no damage except to our ravaged emotions.

Jimmy was still frightfully embarrassed when he had finished the story, but not a bit excited over his narrow escape. He seemed to think it was all in the day's work and the sort of thing that happened to everybody. Things like that happened so often to him that it is no wonder he got that impression. His was a sort of charmed life.

From that time on, he began to hit his stride, knocking down Boches right and left. His biggest day was in the spring of 1918 when, flying alone, he caught up with four Huns. For twenty minutes he plunged in and out of that quartette, throwing hot lead at them from every quarter.

When he withdrew from the field of battle, unscathed himself, he had brought down one in flames, driven down two of the others, which were most probably destroyed, and convinced the fourth that he should have stayed in the infantry.

Eventually Jimmy transferred to the American air force with the rank of captain and was assigned as flight commander to the 94th (Hat-in-the-Ring) Pursuit Squadron. A month later, by a freak combination of circumstances, which included another exceedingly narrow escape from death, Jim concluded his active part in the hostilities for the balance of the war.

In order to have anything to fly at all, the first American pursuit squadrons on the front were equipped with the long-discarded Nieuport 28s, celebrated for their unfortunate propensity for disrobing in mid-air.

On May 7, 1918, flying one of these delightful little air buggies, Hall went out on patrol with Eddie Rickenbacker and another pilot from the 94th. Under severe Archie fire, they penetrated quite some distance in the German lines. Suddenly a quintette of Fokkers came nosing along, attracted by the incessant anti-aircraft fire, anxious to see what all the shooting was about.

The Americans had the altitude on the Hun formation and prepared to slice down for an attack. Swinging around into the sun where they couldn't be seen, their noses went over, and with screaming wires they started to dive.

Jimmy had his Hun right in his sights and both guns beating a wild tattoo of leaden death when, from the corner of his eye, he caught sight of something flapping.

Reluctantly he released his triggers and tore his gaze away from the enemy. His heart stood still for a breathless second. The worst had happened. The leading edge of his right top wing had split, a large piece of the fabric had peeled back and was flapping grotesquely in the slipstream.

Even as he looked, other pieces began to work loose and roll back faster and faster as the rushing air worked under them, revealing the stark skeleton of the frame.

Gingerly he pulled out of his dive. He had lost all ambition to get the Hun flier. He turned toward the distant

French trenches, breathing a heartfelt hope that enough of the fabric would stay on to carry him home. It was questionable, but he did the only thing he could do. Retarding his motor, he put the ship in a slow glide, and momentarily the fabric stopped peeling.

The Nieuport was completely out of balance and exceedingly hard to handle. There could be no maneuvering, despite the fact that Archie was beginning to break closer and closer around him. It made a vicious sound, particularly when he was incapable of swift flight and unable to duck and dodge.

The fire of the German batteries became more and more accurate, and Jimmy was tossed about like a chip in a whirlpool.

Suddenly the ship stopped as if it had hit a stone wall, shuddered, gave a great lurch and fell into a wicked tail spin. The motor fell forward, wrenched completely out of its bed and held on by only two bent bolts. The most remarkable hit of the war had just been registered! An incendiary Austrian 77, one of the regulation German anti-aircraft shells, had made a direct hit squarely in the center plate of the whirling Gnome motor. There it stuck, with half its wicked end exposed, and failed to explode! The force of the impact had ruined the motor, of course, and wrenched it loose, throwing the ship more completely out of balance than before and hurling Jimmy into the spin. It was truly an amazing hit, and the most remarkable thing about it was the usual Hall luck. Of all the hundreds of shells that had exploded around Jimmy, casting their jagged fragments far and wide, the one that finally hit him proved to be a dud.

As his spin carried him down, the German whom he had

been attacking became the aggressor. Following Jimmy closely in a fast dive, he poured round after round into the helpless ship. Perhaps he thought that Hall was using a ruse to get away, or possibly he merely wanted to be sure of the credit for bringing the American down, but in any event he was going to make absolutely certain that the enemy plane would crash. It was entirely unnecessary, for Jimmy didn't stand the slightest chance of escaping.

Again he was most fortunate that the aim of the excited German was somewhat erratic, for though bullets whistled all around him, not one found a mark in his quivering flesh.

Jimmy didn't even have time to pray that the fabric would last on his wing or that the two bolts holding the wildly swaying rotary would stand the strain. He was much too busy trying to get the crippled ship out of its spin, knowing that it meant certain annihilation if he failed. Faster and faster he spun, with the carpet rushing up to meet him.

At the last split second, with all his controls in neutral, Jimmy gave a desperate tug on his stick. Miraculously the Nieuport responded. With a sickening slip, it slewed out of the spinning nose dive into a flat spin and hit, bounced and hit again, with a horrifying rending of wood and fabric. The crash wiped off the landing gear as neatly as if it had been done with a knife. Jimmy counted a hundred constellations as his nose hit the crash pad with force enough to jam it back almost flat against his face. The belly of the fuselage skidded along the ground for a few more feet, nearly breaking Jim's ankle and straining one leg badly, before its nose plowed in and the wrecked plane came to an abrupt stop.

Sick at heart, Jimmy sat helpless in his cockpit as his aerial pursuer flew ten feet over his head and waved a hand in greeting. At that moment Hall would have given anything for another ship to go up after the assassin who had tried to take advantage of his helpless condition.

He was immediately surrounded by a crowd of curious Krauts, gently lifted from his ship and carried to a near-by dugout. There was no officer present, and he fully expected to be stripped of all his possessions, but he was treated with utmost courtesy. His nose was treated and bound up, his leg put in splints, he was given a cup of *ersatz* coffee and a German cigarette. Then they let him sit outside in the sun to await the arrival of an officer.

Jimmy happened to remember that he had a copy of the squadron orders in his pocket and tried to find a place to dispose of the incriminating evidence. There were too many eyes watching him, so, using great caution, he wadded the flimsy tissue up and crammed it into his mouth. Chewing hard, he was able to swallow it without discovery. It wasn't a very satisfying meal, but Jim claims that his stomach received it in a spirit of admirable resignation.

Only a short time later officers arrived. He was gently aided into a car and whisked away to the headquarters of the squadron who had aided in bringing him down. He was shown every courtesy by the young pilots, who even forebore to ask him questions, though Jimmy knew they were burning up with curiosity. He wanted to talk to them, but didn't dare, for fear of revealing some information of value, so their conversation was limited to generalities.

They kept him for lunch, played the piano for him and acted in every way as genial hosts. There was no bitterness in their recital of the fact that Rickenbacker and the other pilot had returned safely to their lines, but had succeeded in bringing down one of their comrades in flames during the fight. Jimmy felt a lot better, since the score was evened.

After lunch he was questioned by a major of intelligence, but gave out no information, and there was no resentment. Then the pilots took him to the hospital in a squadron car.

A day or two later one of them made a trip of thirty kilometers to the scene of Jim's wreck to get his helmet and gloves that he had forgotten. That was real chivalry, but they carried it even further. Hall asked them if they would drop a note over, advising his friends of his safety. One of the chaps very graciously volunteered to take it and was himself shot down and made prisoner as a result.

Two days after his crash, the pilot who had followed him down and the officer commanding the Archie battery, who had really gotten Jim by a direct hit, almost came to blows, over Hall's bed in the prison hospital, as to who should get the credit. They were like two dogs fighting over a bone. By that time Jimmy was a little more reconciled to his fate and able to extract some small amount of humor from the situation. The Archie commander was pretty proud of his exploit, just a little apologetic and very insistent. If Jim was confirmed to him, it meant a citation and a five-hundred-mark bonus. The pilot was equally insistent, and the discussion waxed hot.

Then the Archie chap brought in uncontrovertible evidence: a photo of Hall's wrecked ship with the shell still sticking in the motor. He appealed to Jim to decide the issue. Still just a little irritated by the unfair advantage that the airman had taken over him, Hall was more or less pleased to acknowledge that the claim of the artillery officer was justified and that he had been primarily responsible for the destruction of the ship.

It is mighty hard to keep a good man down, but by persistent effort the enemy finally achieved it as far as Jimmy Hall was concerned. He made several attempts to escape, but they all ended in heartbreaking failures. It was some time after the Armistice when he finally returned to Paris to commence the gigantic task of compiling a complete history of the Lafayette Escadrille and Flying Corps.

But after crowding the adventures of a lifetime into his short years of glorious service, no matter where he is or what he does, Jimmy Hall can never be bored with life. He will be repaid a thousand times by his memories.

CHAPTER XXVII

Luf's Last Take-off

ABOUT THREE WEEKS after our return to Chaudun, the last casualty occurred in the Escadrille. Campbell's strange and unbelievable luck deserted him. He had wooed the capricious lady and wooed her well, but she finally tired of him.

Perhaps the fact that some prankish soul had absconded with the pride of his heart and chief talisman had something to do with it. The jinx preventer had been a pair of pink round garters that Campbell claimed he had obtained from a virgin in the dark of the moon. He wore them constantly as sleeve holder-uppers and thoroughly believed in their potent power, for they had been with him on all his previous flirtations with the angels. Since their disappearance, there hadn't been a dark of the moon to enable him to go after a new pair.

He was out with Hank Jones on a high patrol over the Chemin-des-Dames, when they met and got all tangled up with a vicious patrol of four Albatrosses. Completely surrounded and cut off from the lines, the two youngsters battled desperately to fight their way out of the perilous situation.

Campbell stayed close to Hank's tail, and with blazing guns the boys finally managed to blast a hole through the encircling enemy and dive desperately for the safety of the lines.

His plane badly damaged and his tank punctured, Jones was happy to escape with his life from the deadly trap. As he roared across the trenches, he glanced back over his shoulder, expecting, as he had been all through the savage dog fight, to find Campbell with his propeller almost stuck in his leader's ear.

To his great astonishment and alarm, he saw the wild man, a faint speck in the distance, hot on the tails of the four black-crossed planes, chasing them into Germany.

That was the last ever seen of him. No word ever came from the enemy of his fate, and his body was never found. He mysteriously died as he had lived, recklessly and foolishly brave to the end.

A few days later, I had my last great adventure with Luf. We had started out on a five-ship formation, but from one cause or another it had narrowed down to Luf and me. The weather was pretty greasy, with great tumbling masses of high-rolling cumulus clouds over the lines. We made a pass at a couple of low-flying enemy two-seaters, but they had been watching us and hedgehopped into their lines.

We roared on across. A white mountain of mist lay athwart our path. Luf darted around the edge on the German side. Coming around the other end, just slightly above us, was a speeding formation of black-crossed enemy pursuit ships. Before we could turn, we were in for it.

We were badly outnumbered and certainly wouldn't have given combat under ordinary circumstances, but we had no choice. It was a desperate situation, and we had to fight our way out as best we could.

Two of them swung on Luf and two came at me, with a fifth circling overhead, watching his chance to duck in and snipe whenever he had the opportunity.

As of most dog fights, there remains in my mind only a hazy recollection. Everything was as mixed up as in a nightmare. The two buzzards on my tail had me in a cross-fire. There was a constant chatter of machine guns belching red fire. My mouth and nose were full of the acrid tang of burned powder. Motors sobbed and wailed in power dives and tremendous sweeping zooms.

I caught a flash of Luf in a great loop, and then he was picking one of the Germans off my tail. We were both performing the wildest acrobatics and mad gyrations. Luf's two attackers seemed badly puzzled by his erratic movements. Instead of trying to defend himself, he was valiantly attacking their comrades. It wasn't ethical!

One of them swooped down on him and missed completely. The Boche's dive brought him down so near to me that we came within an ace of colliding. He made a wing-over directly in front of the whirling blades of my prop. I could count the stitches on his wings. For an instant we seemed to hang poised, motionless in mid-air. He loomed up as big as a barn door.

I was scared stiff, and nervous reaction as much as anything else caused my hand to close over the trips. It was just a short burst, with both guns chattering a castanet of death. Splinters flew from his spars. His head turned toward me, and I caught a glimpse of white teeth in a whiter face behind square-cut goggles. Then he threw up both hands. I must have plugged him through the body.

The Albatross turned over on its back, and the last I saw of it, it was slowly settling in wide side-to-side swings like a falling leaf.

Then a black object hurtled by me, twisting and spinning like a top. A long gray muffler trailed from one end of the grotesque figure. With a sickening sensation in the pit of my stomach I watched it for a second till it disappeared from sight. For all I knew, it might have been Luf, falling to a horrible death.

Although the air was full of raveled blue lines of tracer smoke, the nerve-racking chatter of guns had ceased. I stole a hurried glance over my shoulder and exhaled a great pent-up sigh of relief. The two murderers on my tail had disappeared. The sky above me was clear except for one ship, and it bore—the tricolored *cocardes* of France!

The steady beat of my Hispano faltered and then ceased altogether. I looked at my pressure gauge. The needle pointed to zero. I dove headlong to keep my prop turning and switched on my gravity tank.

Fifteen minutes later, when I landed at Chaudun with a dead stick, I found that my main tank had been ripped wide open by four slugs. Petrol was still squirting out, and it was miraculous that I hadn't been set afire.

Luf landed twenty minutes later, after staying as long as he dared, stalking the two remaining enemy ships which had run for cover in the depths of the cloud. When they failed to emerge, he finally concluded they had gone right on through.

He had forty bullet holes in his fuselage, all back of the cockpit; not one in his wings or around his motor. Luf was tremendously bucked up over our triple victory. It was his fourteenth and fifteenth.

The Lafayette Escadrille Memorial in Paris.
(Courtesy Paul A. Rockwell)

The Lafayette Escadrille reunion at Asheville, North Carolina, June 1960. Left to right: Harold Willis, Frederick Prince, Charles H. Dolan II, Henry Jones, Edwin C. Parsons, Paul A. Rockwell, Capt. Philip Flammer, representing the United States Air Force, and Capt. Louis Richard, representing the French Air Force and the present Lafayette Escadrille. (Courtesy Paul A. Rockwell)

He cleared up the mystery of the sudden disappearance of the two buzzards on my tail. One of them he had gotten on his first burst, and his ship had disintegrated in the air. It was the body of the pilot I had seen whirling down beside me. The other he had set afire a moment later after a short but vicious duel.

From the way they had maneuvered, Luf concluded that they were green pilots. If they had been veterans, the chances are that neither Luf nor I would have come back. Green or not, they gave us a busy and thrilling fifteen minutes. I never want to come any closer to saying, "Howdy, Saint Peter."

Having seen one man go down in flames, and having so narrowly escaped doing the same myself, I asked Luf what he would do if he got afire. As clearly as if it were yesterday, I remember his reply in that queer accent:

"Vell, first, I vould do eferyting I could to get de fire oudt. Den if I saw it vas no use, I'd jump. Get it all ofer wit qvick. Mebbe you might fall in a tree, but anyhow, you couldn't be no woise off."

That very calm, philosophical solution seemed perfectly logical at the moment, when no danger threatened, but it must take a mighty lot of courage to leap off into the void, knowing that it is the end of everything. To stay with the ship would be to endure the slow agony of roasting, but there would always be a faint hope that some miracle might happen.

When the final test came for Luf, he demonstrated once again his magnificent courage in tragic proof that he meant just what he said.

In the meantime, early in December 1917, the Escadrille was ordered to the field of La Noblette on the Champagne sector, not far from Châlons-sur-Marne.

Acting under advice from high officials, all the pilots, with the exception of myself—I was on leave in America—presented their demands to the French army for release, expecting to receive immediate commissions in the American army. Their releases were officially granted, but no commissions arrived.

So from the 1st of December 1917 until the 18th of February 1918 they flew as civilians in the uniform of the French army.

In January and early February, five other young Americans with the most brilliant records in various French pursuit groups joined the Lafayette Escadrille for transfer, although they had little opportunity to do any active work with the squadron. They were Phelps Collins, Paul Baer, Charles Biddle, George Turnure and Charles Wilcox, all of whom later made distinguished names for themselves with the Americans.

On the 1st of February, American mechanics arrived at La Noblette and were put in training by the French mechanics.

On the 18th the Lafayette Escadrille passed out of existence as a French unit and lock, stock and barrel, became the 103rd Pursuit Squadron of the American Air Service, the first American pursuit squadron on the front in the World War.

They were allowed to keep their Spads and Indian-head insignia, which the old members carried all through the war, but the unsentimental brass hats refused to let them keep Whiskey and Soda. It was with moist eyes and real regret that the boys parted from their mascots, who were ingloriously carted off to the Paris zoo dumbly protesting the curtailment of their liberty.

Meanwhile, when the commissions finally arrived, there was weeping and wailing and gnashing of teeth. Thaw and Lufbery were given majorities, there was a sprinkling of captaincies, but most of the boys received commissions as first and second lieutenants, to be placed under the commands of newly arrived ninety-day wonders, full of ambition and disciplinarian theories, but who had never heard a gun fired in anger.

What price experience and heroism!

The boys of the Escadrille were, almost without exception, disgusted and indignant. Instead of being allowed to continue flying as a unit, as they had hoped and requested, the old Escadrille was all broken up. Only a few of the original members remained with it to the end of the war. Many of them were sent to Paris and had to wait months for a chance to fly.

Lufbery was given a nice shiny desk and some freshly sharpened pencils at the Instruction Center at Issoudun, with absolutely nothing to do. Luf knew nothing about paper work and cared less. His place was at the front, leading his patrols into combat. His desire for vengeance was far from satisfied, and as a kiwi he was of absolutely no use to himself or the army. It was a heartbreaking interlude.

He fumed and fretted, pleaded and implored to such an extent that finally some sympathetic soul in the royal chambers of the mighty gave in, and he was ordered to the 94th and 95th pursuit squadrons at Villeneuve in Champagne. Hard luck still dogged his heels.

No fighting could be done, because, although the squadrons had a few of the old Nieuport 28s for equipment, they had no guns. For a whole month Luf spent his time teaching the men combat tactics and flying with them to the lines, where they looked longingly across at patrols of enemy planes which they could not attack.

The guns came at last, and in April the 94th started patrol duty in the Toul sector. There was little activity, for the Germans were conserving everything for the big pushes that were to come. Lufbery led patrols daily and followed his old practice of lone-eagle hunting, but with little success. It was practically impossible to find an enemy, much less force a combat.

However, on the 19th of May a big German photographic plane came across the lines and roared within sight of the 94th's field. Luf's own plane was out of commission, so he grabbed another Nieuport standing on the line and took off. The tragic battle and ending took place within sight of the field.

Luf reached the enemy ship about five minutes after he took off. In his usual fearless but crafty way, he darted in to close quarters and fired several long bursts from short range.

The ship was a three-place, and it is quite possible that it was one of the armor-plated type, for Luf's unerring aim had no apparent effect. A minute later he swerved away from the attack and busied himself with his guns, which seemed to have jammed.

He quickly cleared the jam and sliced in again for another savage attack under the tail of the black-crossed plane.

Machine guns hammered in long chattering *rafales* from both ships. Suddenly the Nieuport wobbled and shuddered like a stricken animal. The whole forward end burst into a great fan of red flame.

Luf made several frantic efforts to put the Nieuport into a slip and blow the flames from his body. It was impossible to hold the slip. The cockpit was a roaring inferno.

Unable to stand the searing flame, hoping against hope, Luf climbed back, far back on the slippery fuselage, clothes afire in a dozen places. Then, true to his prediction, he jumped—jumped on the millionth chance that, aiming himself like a human projectile, he might hit in a little stream which shone like a silver thread thousands of feet below him. It was a vain hope, for a fall from that altitude into water would have crushed every bone in his body just as did the earth.

He fell into the garden of a peasant woman's home, a hundred yards from the little stream, in the tiny town of Maron, just north of Nancy. A tablet on the house marks the spot.

And so, valiantly, perished one of the greatest of all fliers and a gallant American. In those last few seconds he could have no regrets. I know he didn't want to die, but if it was so written in the stars, he died as he would have wished—with his boots on, fighting to the last.

Raoul Lufbery had extracted an overwhelming payment for the death of his beloved friend and comrade, and the scales weighed heavily in his favor as he went to join Pourpe in the Great Unknown.

I have always been proud and happy that it was my great good fortune to fight side by side with all of these gallant heroes.

Perhaps, in view of later developments, it may have been a financial mistake, but since I was going on leave to

America at the time the rest of the boys were putting in their applications for American commissions and transfer, I decided to wait until my return to file mine.

I came back to the front just prior to the official change-over and found conditions in a most chaotic state. I realized that if I transferred, it would perhaps be many weeks, perhaps months, before my application would be acted upon and I should have another opportunity to fly.

So I decided to remain with the French, and during the war, at least, I never regretted my decision. They gave me every consideration, and I was most content. I was the only pilot of the Escadrille itself to remain, but there were many others in the Flying Corps who, for one reason or another, followed my example.

At my own request I was transferred to Escadrille Spad 3 of the Storks, an escadrille composed largely of aces, which had been commanded by the beloved Captain Guynemer before his death, and in which I remained until the end.

I was fortunate in getting a few more unwary Huns before they called the whole thing off. I kept out of trouble myself, more through good luck than good sense, for if I had had good sense, I probably wouldn't have been in the shindig to start with.

However, it was a great adventure, and while I did my fair share of grousing during its progression, I wouldn't swap my experiences, both at the front and in Paris, for all the money in the world.

I hope that the next inevitable conflict comes along before I have to stagger to it with a cane, tripping over my long gray beard. Fed up at times as I was with the last, believe it or not, I'll be the first one there for the next.

Of course, the real career of the Lafayette Escadrille ceased when it passed into the American army and merged its identity and personnel with all the other pursuit squadrons.

Thirty-eight daring, plucky young Americans had been on its active roster. They had a sum total of fifty-seven victories, officially confirmed, over enemy planes. Nine were killed while in the Escadrille, one so seriously wounded that he was invalided out, and one taken prisoner.

From April 20, 1916, to February 18, 1918, as a unit they served France, and incidentally America, with honorable distinction. They were the first and only group of organized volunteer active combatants flying and fighting against Germany, and their exploits made history.

Many more of these young heroes were killed while in the American Air Service, two others taken prisoner, and several have died since the war. But their glorious exploits and the magnificent accomplishments of the Lafayette Escadrille will forever remain imperishable.

THE END